Nazis score 39.6 percent in Lippe election 30 January 1933 Hitler named Chancellor with a non-Nazi government 27 February 1933 Reichstag fire 5 March 1933 Reichstag elections: Nazis score 43.9 percent 24 March 1933 Enabling Act 30 June 1934 three-day Röhm purge begins 2 August 1934 Hindenburg dies; army swears allegiance to Hitler, completing his takeover 18 June 1935 Anglo-German Naval Agreement signed 3 October 1935 Italy invades Ethiopia 7 March 1936 Hitler remilitarizes the Rhineland August 1936 Hitler's memorandum on Four Year Plan 25 October 1936 Rome-Berlin Axis 5 November 1937 Hitler's top-level contingency planning session for German expansion 13 March 1938 Anschluss 30 September 1938 Munich agreement 30 January 1939 Hitler's Reichstag speech prophesying the Final Solution 15 March 1939 Hitler's troops occupy Bohemia, Moravia 23 August 1939 Germano-Soviet Pact 1 September 1939 Poland invaded 3 September 1939 England, France declare war on Germany 9 April 1940 Denmark, Norway invaded 10 May 1940 Belgium, The Netherlands invaded 28 May 1940 Belgian king surrenders 22 June 1940 France falls August–October 1940 air war over Britain 6 April 1941 Yugoslavia, Greece attacked 22 June 1941 USSR invaded ("Barbarossa") 5–6 December 1941 Russian counterattack outside Moscow 7 December 1941 Japanese attack Pearl Harbor 11 December 1941 Hitler declares war on US 19 December 1941 Hitler takes command of German army 20 January 1942 Wannsee conference for Final Solution 1–2 November 1942 German-Italian front broken at El Alamein 7–8 November 1942 Anglo-American landing in North Africa 18 November 1942 battle for Stalingrad begins 2 February 1943 surrender in Stalingrad 13 May 1943 Germans, Italians surrender in Africa 25 July 1943 Mussolini overthrown 3 September 1943 Italy surrenders 6 June 1944 Normandy landing 20 July 1944 Stauffenberg's attempt on Hitler's life 25 August 1944 Paris liberated 16 December 1944 Battle of the Bulge begins 29 April 1945 Hitler steps down, marries Eva Braun 30 April 1945 the newlywed Hitlers commit suicide

HITLER AMONG THE GERMANS

HITLER AMONG THE GERMANS

Rudolph Binion

ELSEVIER

New York/Oxford/Amsterdam

ELSEVIER SCIENTIFIC PUBLISHING COMPANY, INC.
52 Vanderbilt Avenue, New York, NY 10017

ELSEVIER SCIENTIFIC PUBLISHING COMPANY
335 Jan Van Galenstraat, P.O. Box 211
Amsterdam, The Netherlands

The photograph used in the cover design
is the property of the Zeitgeschichtliches
Bildarchiv Heinrich Hoffmann, 8 München 40,
Germany. It is reproduced here by
permission of the owner.

Library of Congress Cataloging in Publication Data

Binion, Rudolph, 1927-
    Hitler among the Germans.

    Bibliography: p.
    Includes index.
    1. Hitler, Adolf, 1889-1945. 2. Heads of state—
Germany—Biography. 3. Psychohistory. I. Title.
DD247.H5B54   943.086′092′4[B]   76-26937
ISBN 0-444-99033-X

Manufactured in the United States of America

Designed by Loretta Li

For M.

CONTENTS

PREFACE

Adolf Hitler was somewhat an outsider among the Germans he led. A native Austrian born on 20 April 1889, he spent his first six years in the Austro-Bavarian borderland, where his father was a customs official. Then he saw no more of Germany proper until he moved there at age twenty-four. Arriving in Munich on 26 June 1913, he registered as stateless, presumably to avoid being traced from Austria for having evaded conscription. In Munich, as for some years previous in Vienna, he earned a modest living as a self-taught, *arrière-garde* artist. At the outbreak of war in August 1914, he volunteered for the Bavarian army. He was inducted that 16 August and served until 31 March 1920, nearly seventeen months after Germany surrendered. By then he was in Bavarian politics, having joined the tiny German Workers Party in September 1919 and rapidly become its moving spirit. During his incarceration for his abortive Putsch of 8–9 November 1923, the Bavarian authorities tried to deport him to Austria, but the government in Vienna ordered the border closed to him. He was released on 20 December 1924. The following 7 April he disclaimed his Austrian nationality. Yet he only assumed German nationality on 26 February 1932, when he ran for president of the Weimar Republic. He lost this race to the incumbent, old Hindenburg, chief of the general staff of the German armies at the time of the 1918 defeat. The following 30 January, Hindenburg named him to head a coalition cabinet intended to secure a parliamentary majority, ending two-and-a-half years of rule by executive decrees. He easily established his personal dictatorship instead. Then he militarized the nation and on 13 March 1938 annexed his native Austria to the Reich pending further conquest.

Conquest was the goal Hitler had set for the Germans when he built up his national following. To conquer they needed only unity of will, he argued, and for this they needed only to be rid of the Jews. But at the last, after his scheme of conquest had led to a new world war and a new defeat, he pointed to the extermination of European Jewry as his redeeming achievement. The new defeat, unlike the old one, did not take the Germans by surprise; on the contrary, it was dragged out painfully and driven home with finality. Yet Hitler was not deserted in the process, but held full sway over Germany to the last despite his growing seclusion and infirmity. All this linked up psychohistorically. That linkup is my subject.

Psychohistory deals with the motives of bygone doings, whether individual or collective. Motives can be called psychological causes, but doings have no other efficient causes. Thus to say that a given war broke out to relieve social tensions can only mean that the purpose of relieving social tensions actuated the war makers. This is no social explanation that a psychohistorical explanation would supplement; it is a psychohistorical explanation requiring evidence in kind. Further, in psychohistory as elsewhere, to multiply causes is no mark of sagacity. There is more to be learned from the determinative reasons for an act or course of action than from the totality of reasons for it. Thus my concern with Hitler's politics was to isolate the few decisive inner demands and constraints behind the vast recorded outcome. This rule of exclusion held equally for Hitler's constituency, Germany at large. That constituency was susceptible to Hitler at a key psychic sore spot: the German trauma of defeat suffered in 1918. So I could approach that trauma through Hitler's politics pitched to Germans in the mass.

To probe Hitler's politics, I immersed myself in his words and deeds until I could feel out the motive forces behind them. Each successive insight led me to validating material previously unknown or overlooked. Such documentary finds clinched the insights that led to them, but they cannot be made to entail those insights. Indeed, no amount or kind of evidence can turn a psychohistorical insight into an inference. Take this example from the work ahead. Hitler's aim of eastern conquest originated as an aim of reconquest. That is, his arguments for an eastern conquest originated as reasons for regretting that the defeat in the west had undone Ludendorff's eastern conquest of 1917–1918. Yet he disregarded this precedent of 1917–1918 when he propounded his eastern aim. It follows, but not deductively, that for him the eastern conquest he called for was at bottom Ludendorff's lost conquest. This insight actually came to me before, and led me to, the evidence for it—his speech of 31 May 1921 on that lost eastern conquest. But such an insight is not necessitated by any or all of the facts it throws up, or fits, or illuminates. Nor can it be tested: history is once only. Yet it will be as clear as a fact of perception in the present case to anyone who looks psychohistorically—who puts himself in Hitler's place and asks himself what that projected eastern conquest meant to Hitler unconsciously as the idea for it came to him. For this exercise the historic context must and will be supplied.

One kind of unconscious determination behind the Hitler story requires a general word of introduction: the traumatic kind. A traumatic experience is one too painful to be assimilated. It engages the mind at first in a full-time, futile struggle to accommodate or ignore it. Ordinarily a distressing event or circumstance can be "put out of mind"—that is, pushed into the unconscious and there construed in some harmless way. If it is too obstreperous or upsetting to be conveniently overlooked, it is denied nonetheless, and strenuously, at the unconscious level. Mental pain is diminished then at the price of mental strain. A trauma, though, is a discomfiture all too drastic and anguishing to be coped with in this way. Attempted unconscious denial avails as little as against an aching physical wound. The struggle of denial intrudes upon consciousness in failing efforts to twist the unwanted experience into tolerable shape, to vitiate its significance, to minimize one's real or felt responsibility for it. I say "failing efforts" because I am considering the normal pattern. Successful conscious denial of an obtrusive fact of experience is insanity. An exact, continual, unbearable remembering is, at the other extreme, the traumatic neurosis. This neurosis is like a first approximation to the normal mode of coming to terms with a traumatic experience, or rather of endeavoring to come to terms with it, which is to relive it—to contrive a new experience that is unconsciously taken to be the old one even while consciously the connections between them go unnoticed. Every emotionally charged component of the old experience enters into the new one vicariously—starkly overdrawn as a rule, and with key relational elements reversed, such as east and west, or before and after. The point of reliving a traumatic experience seems to be to will, to control, to master it after having been overcome by it the first time, and to inure oneself to it so that it will "pass" after all. Traumatic reliving has an imperativeness about it that becomes veritably titanic in the face of outer resistance. All one's instincts, interests, and ideals fall in with it. And all one's inhibitions will fall before it: anyone suitably traumatized can massacre innocents, especially by remote control. The afflicted ego reverts to earliest, purest self-will. A corrective tendency, prominent in traumatic reliving, is to ward off the traumatic blow, which is redelivered nonetheless. But another corrective tendency can win out if enough guilt is felt: to convert the blow into a punishment due, to make the misadventure over into a misdeed that is then expiated. When this succeeds, the whole enterprise of uncon-

xii

scious reliving defeats itself. Otherwise it is commonly just futile, and hence repetitive—a lifelong desperate, senseless routine.

This traumatic mechanism will be seen to have operated not only with Hitler individually but with Germans collectively. A collective mental process is hard to conceive of, but that is not my fault. So is the individual mind as it is known from psychoanalysis hard to conceive of, with its unconscious perceptions and memory traces and built-in archaic fancies. As a pioneer in the field, Caroline E. Playne, remarked half a century ago (in *The Neuroses of the Nations,* New York 1925, p. 54): "Collective mentality can no more be reached directly than can individual mind." In the one case as in the other, causes are known only from their effects. Yet that is knowledge.

To convey such knowledge of my subject will necessitate jumping back and forth in historic time: reader hold tight. Worse, it will require overquoting Hitler to prove my points. These are largely new. Yet I have leaned heavily on other scholars' works where they have sufficed for my purposes, as in the analysis of Hitler's hopeless foreign program and practice. Familiar matter is barely referenced, although I well realize that straight facts can look crooked when they support unaccustomed interpretations. I have used appendixes for cumbersome technical data, including some previously published in the *History of Childhood Quarterly* (see Sources). I wish to thank this journal for permission to republish, and its editor, Lloyd de Mause, for unfailing encouragement. My thanks are due as well to Brandeis University for supporting my initial research in 1970–1971 (also for a schedule adjustment in 1974–1975 that made the writing possible), and to the Marion and Jasper Whiting Foundation for a grant that covered my final research in Germany and Austria during the summer of 1975. Archivists and librarians eased my way most notably at the Universitäts-Archiv Greifswald, Munich's Institut für Zeitgeschichte, the National Archives, and Boston's Countway Library. The late Ernst Deuerlein assisted my inquiries, as did (to alphabetize) Eberhard Jäckel, John Knodel, Paul Monaco, Robert Murciano,

Agnes F. Peterson, Marc Poulain, Bradley F. Smith, George H. Stein, John Toland, and Eduard Wondrák. My working draft was read by Stephen Kern first, then by Claudia Koonz, Christoph M. Kimmich, Bradley F. Smith, Lancelot L. Farrar, Jr., and Albrecht Tyrell: their marginalia were invaluable. My deepest gratitude is reserved for my wife, who shared in my involvement with the all too human horrors of Hitlerism.

HITLER AMONG THE GERMANS

That is the miracle of our times: that you found me—that you found me among so many millions! And that I found you is Germany's fortune!

ADOLF HITLER, 13 September 1936,
at a Nuremberg Party Rally

I

THE "JEWISH POISON"

The greatest danger is and remains for
us the alien racial poison in our body.
All other dangers are transitory. This
one alone is perpetually present for us
in its resultant effect.

ADOLF HITLER, 27 February 1925.[1]

Adolf Hitler changed markedly with the close of World War I.
Before then his occasional speechifying met with smiling sufferance at best.[2] Once on an anniversary of the revolution of 1918,
which symbolized for him the collapse of the Reich, he remarked: "I don't think I could have spoken to twenty people
before that time without being at a loss for words."[3] Yet early in
the postwar period he was already a spellbinding orator, drawing deep and powerful shared emotion from his audiences. In
the spring of 1919 a member of the party he was to join, the
German Workers Party, heard him address a soldiers' council in
Munich and noted "his almost occult power of suggestion over
the assemblage."[4] Then on 5 June 1919 a professor who gave the
first class of a training course for Reichswehr political lecturers
in Munich, among them the thirty-year-old Hitler, observed a
small group that formed afterward. "It seemed to be held en-
thralled around a man in its midst who was addressing it uninter-
ruptedly and with mounting passion in a strangely guttural

voice. I had the peculiar feeling that its excitement was his doing and yet was prompting his words at the same time."[5] The hate and pain that sounded in Hitler's oratory of 1919 and after, its shrill pitch and brutal inflections, were foreign to the prewar artist and wartime dispatch bearer. New too after 1918 was his compelling sense of purpose manifest on the rostrum and off. Earlier he was inward and awkward, bookish and prankish, unassuming and undemanding. "Hitler was then . . . just about the opposite of what he was later," declared his regimental adjutant of World War I, Fritz Wiedemann, in 1948.[6] Wiedemann well remembered the perennial private first class as "a particularly quiet, modest, dutiful subordinate" with no capacity whatever for leadership.[7] Encountering Hitler at a regimental reunion in the early 1920s, Wiedemann "could tell at a glance that he had become another man."[8] Of all his features not in evidence before the postwar period, the most arresting was his hypnotic gaze.[9]

The change in Hitler had an ideological aspect that seemed to govern the rest. Apparently he was not an anti-Semite until the end of World War I despite his subsequent claim to have become one earlier in Vienna.[10] His boyhood friend from Linz, August Kubizek, later described him converting to anti-Semitism when they roomed together in Vienna in the spring of 1908. But Kubizek's account, loosely aligned on Hitler's own in *Mein Kampf*,[11] is at odds with the best evidence on the decade that followed. Fritz Wiedemann and Hitler's fellow dispatch bearers Ernst Schmidt and Ignaz Westenkirchner flatly denied his anti-Semitism for 1914–1918.[12] Anti-Semitism is conspicuously unmentioned in the four relevant memoirs on him in the Nazi Archive (one by a cotenant of a men's hostel in Vienna and three by regimental comrades)[13] and is absent from all his known correspondence predating the 1918 defeat. He had positive relations with a whole run of Jews, from the doctor who treated his mother in Linz until her death in December 1907 to his battalion and, briefly, regimental adjutant who obtained the Iron Cross First Class for him in August 1918.[14] The pretended firsthand accounts besides Kubizek's that accord with Hitler's own dating of his anti-Semitism back to 1908 or 1909 are no evidence. One

2

is by a thrice-convicted swindler;[15] another is a rewrite by a Nazi;[16] the third is the handiwork of a professional inventor and con man.[17]

In contrast, Hitler's politics after World War I were actuated by all-out anti-Semitism from the start. His earliest extant political document is a reply dated 16 September 1919, requested of him by the head of the propaganda section of the Reichswehr in Bavaria, to an outside inquiry about the Jewish peril. Depicting Jewry as a race both parasitic and subversive, he urged a "rational" anti-Semitism whereby Jews would be methodically divested of their legal rights with the "final aim" of their "total removal"—this, incidentally, under new, ruthless, national-minded leaders "with an inner sense of responsibility."[18] A month earlier one of his lectures to troops awaiting demobilization had prompted his company commander to order less plain-spokenness from the podium lest the Reichswehr be charged with Jew-baiting.[19] Anti-Semitism reportedly shaped his speech to the soldiers' council the previous spring.[20] And his best war-time buddy, Ernst Schmidt, who served with him further in and around Munich for a few months beginning in December 1918, recollected that by this time Hitler was already advancing in private that perception of Germany's defeat which he said in *Mein Kampf* he gained when the news of the revolution reached him in a military infirmary at Pasewalk. This was that the Jews had defeated Germany from within on the basis of the Kaiser's fatal truce with their party, the Socialists, at the start of the war. "There is no dealing with the Jews," he concluded, "but only a hard showdown."[21] Since he dated his political calling from that moment of truth in Pasewalk, his stay there would seem to have been pivotal for the change he underwent. So a close look at that stay is in order.

Hitler was entrained from Flanders for Pasewalk, north of Berlin, after being hit by British mustard gas fired at 4:35 A.M. on 15 October 1918.[22] His gassing followed four years of service in Flanders with the front-line, battle-scarred List Regiment. He had been hospitalized once before—on 9 October 1916 in Berlin-

3

Beelitz for a shrapnel wound in the left thigh.[23] Reassigned in Munich that 3 December pending full recovery, he sent nostalgic messages back to his regiment,[24] then in January an urgent appeal to Wiedemann to reclaim him before he was shipped elsewhere. He had muttered to Wiedemann on being found wounded: "It's not so bad, Lieutenant Sir, right? I can stay with you, with the regiment!" Wiedemann later remarked: "For Private First Class Hitler the List Regiment was home."[25] Westenkirchner and Schmidt concurred: the regimental circle "had become his home" even as he had stopped receiving mail from Munich after his first year or so of service.[26] He was "home" again on 5 March 1917. Coaxed into taking a first seventeen-day furlough the following October, he spent it with a comrade's parents in Berlin.[27] In late August 1918, newly decorated with his Iron Cross First Class, he was sent to Nuremberg for a week with the papers for a depleted regiment that was fusing with his.[28] That 10 September he was off on a second seventeen-day furlough, this time with Ernst Schmidt to Schmidt's sisters in Dresden by way of Brussels, Cologne, and Leipzig.[29] The war-weariness tempered with cynicism that he encountered inside Germany in 1916–1917 infuriated him.[30] "For us the World War cannot be lost," he always insisted.[31] He insisted all the more as the mood of discouragement spread to the front in the face of the Allies' late-summer offensive of 1918 and turned into defeatism with the government's bid for an armistice in early October. Ernst Schmidt remembered that their new comrades from the depleted Nuremberg regiment "were quite radical and grumbled more than we had ever heard. Hitler could go absolutely wild at such grumbling, and raged and yelled really dreadfully at the pacifists and shirkers who would lose the war yet."[32] And Ignaz Westenkirchner recollected: "Toward the end of the war, when to the rest of us the game seemed to be up, he would go wild if anyone expressed doubts about victory. He would stick his hands in his pockets, pace up and down with huge strides, and rage against pessimism. He still believed in victory at the time he was gassed. For him the heavy attack in Flanders by the English in October 1918 was a proof that our submarine campaign was succeeding."[33]

4

The English mustard gas fired at La Montagne early that 15 October struck Hitler together with several of his comrades. The one of them not totally blinded, Hermann Heer, led the others to safety behind the lines.[34] Hitler, after a night in a field station in Oudenaarde, was shipped to Ghent and from there to Pomerania.[35] He was checked into the hospital at Pasewalk on 21 October. He was checked out on 19 November as fully cured, but claimed afterward that he could still read only newspaper headlines by then.[36] Either way, he had seemingly run the normal course of convalescence from mustard gas poisoning: a gradual recovery beginning after a few days and lasting three or four weeks.[37] The official particulars of his recuperation cannot be supplied because the Gestapo seized and destroyed all known copies of his hospital records. A copy of the paper issued for his service file was for years in the hands of a Bavarian anti-Nazi, Wilhelm Hoegner, who recollected: "According to the medical report he was reclassified on 13 November 1918 as fit for active duty; at that time his only remaining complaint was a burning in the mucous membrane."[38] This burning too fits the normal syndrome along with an initial swelling that subsides somewhat earlier. Had that "report" contained any visibly embarrassing indications, Hoegner would have spotted them. Why, then, did the Gestapo go after it?

The likeliest answer is that it was signed by Edmund Forster, then the ranking psychiatrist at Pasewalk. A formal case record by Forster—a second hospital paper—evidently also existed once, with copies kept under cover into the early 1940s by Wilhelm Canaris, chief of the Wehrmacht's secret service, and Heinrich Himmler.[39] There or elsewhere Forster officially put Hitler's blindness down to psychopathic hysteria.[40] He could misdiagnose it as hysterical the more readily since in October 1918 the effects of mustard gas were still unfamiliar behind German lines. But his finding of psychopathy suggests that, on the mental side, Hitler's case did not quite run to type after all. So does the fact that he handled the case in the first place. Mustard gas victims are not ordinarily unhinged, but only sink into "a deep apathy. . . . They feel woebegone, miserable; they are despondent and disconsolate. . . . All they want is to lie groaning softly in

5

utter despair. . . . They are not to be dissuaded from imagining that they are permanently blind" until, after a week or two, their eyelids unswell enough to reopen. "And then their spirits also start reviving."[41] *Mein Kampf* tells of a radical departure by Hitler from the subsequent straight course of convalescence: a hysterical relapse at the Pasewalk chaplain's announcement of the revolution and armistice. "It went black around my eyes again," Hitler related. He added that he groped and stumbled back to his ward just as, two pages earlier, he claimed—falsely—to have groped and stumbled back to his field post after being gassed.[42] But his special pathology is most clear-cut in the hallucination through which he emerged from the two-day[43] fit of mortal distress that ensued. The several versions of this hallucination were all derived from him in the early 1920s. In all of them his eyesight is restored as, in an ecstatic trance, he is summoned from on high to deliver Germany from defeat.[44] Forster's handling of the patient as hysterical must have been material to that relapse and revival. That handling can be reconstructed in some measure from Forster's side.

The 1914 mobilization found Edmund Forster an associate professor of psychiatry at the University of Berlin, practicing in its affiliated Charité clinic. A reserve officer in the navy, Forster donned his uniform at once and served in Kiel until the end of 1914, then in the battle zone of Flanders until he turned forty. On this date—3 September 1918—the head doctor at Forster's command post of Cöpenick attested concerning Forster's hospital work in Bruges: "Himself of an energetic and spirited disposition, he made the treatment and cure of so-called war neurotics his special concern and, in many cases, went about it somewhat roughly in that he applied the standard of his own strength of will to others."[45] By his own account of 1917, Forster would impress upon war neurotics that they were really only shirking and knew it; that this was an indignity and, if they persisted, a punishable offense; and that their trouble was not a sickness requiring a cure, but a weak will that needed strengthening.[46] Nine days after leaving the combat zone Forster married a secretary of Matthias Erzberger, the Centrist leader who was to negotiate and sign for Germany the Armistice of 11 November. On

6

duty at Pasewalk at the time of the Armistice, Forster left for
Berlin on 14 November to resume his civilian occupations while
affiliating with a local military hospital until his discharge on 30
June 1919. One of his postwar assistants recently recollected of
him at the Charité: "He took hysteria to be mostly humbug and
treated hysterics accordingly: he would shout at them that they
ought to be ashamed toward real sufferers. I still well remember
such scenes and our annoyance that he should score successes
with such a method and that those he 'cured' should even remain devoted to him!"[47] His elder son remembers that, while
never brutal, he "had no use for the hysteric," whom he saw as
"a faker out for attention" and "a scoundrel to be treated by
Draconian methods."[48] The director of the Charité in Forster's
time declared: "Pure Forster speaks out of his studies of affectiv-
ity and of hysteria."[49] Forster conceived of hysteria as simulation
with an emotional charge. He identified a symptom as hysterical
if it advantaged the patient and was played up.[50] In a publication
of 1922 he wrote: "War hysterics would produce every imagin-
able symptom from fear of the front, get sent by inexpert doctors
to hospitals in the rear or even back home, and use their special
technique there to lay first claim to supplies meant for the war
wounded. At the same time they would speak with indignation
about slackers and tell whoever would listen how they could not
understand that cowards should exist at such a moment: except
that they, alas, were sick they would be reporting for any run of
duty up front, however dangerous."[51] The junior faculty of the
University of Greifswald, in nominating Forster late in 1924 for
a chair there, conceded: "His impulsive formulations, such as his
conception of hysteria, have drawn criticism."[52] The medical
faculty, on endorsing the nomination early in 1925, noted
darkly: "It is not unknown to the faculty that certain difficulties
attach to Mr. Forster's personality."[53] About those difficulties a
psychiatrist under him and one above him at the Charité remembered: "Forster was inclined to temper tantrums that we would
joke about" and "His quick temper often gave him trouble."[54]
His professional files are singed from the heat of his frequent
quarrels with colleagues.[55]

Forster was appointed to Greifswald in April 1925. There he

pioneered brain surgery and, in January 1929, conducted a daring self-experiment with mescalin to confirm his view of hallucinations as due to failure of the power to distinguish imaginary from real.[56] The following year brought him an ominous setback when he sponsored his chief assistant, Julius Zádor, for faculty status. Zádor passed muster academically, yet of the nineteen full professors eleven voted no in writing and another four orally. One of the eleven put the issue plainly as "my people and country being increasingly foreignized from the east."[57] Zádor was a Hungarian Jew. This was eight months before Hitler's first big national showing at the polls.

On 19 May 1933, in the fourth month of Hitler's rule, a Munich medical weekly carried an article by Forster about prognosticating and preventing suicide, which stated at the outset that suicide "need not necessarily be pathological; . . . *completely healthy persons* can choose suicide after mature and free reflection as the only practical way out of a difficult situation."[58] Forster left Greifswald by car that 5 July—with Zádor, recently dismissed as a Jew—and returned about 7 August. While away he visited Paris, where he stayed with his brother, an Embassy official; he also stopped over in Basel at some point, and on 16 July was at the family estate in Nonnenhorn on Lake Constance to celebrate his mother's eightieth birthday. In the émigré German weekly *Das neue Tage-Buch* of 16 September 1933, editor-in-chief Leopold Schwarzschild related: "About two months ago Professor Forster came to Paris for a brief stay. In conversation with a collaborator of *Das neue Tage-Buch* he remarked resignedly that 'his turn' could be expected soon"—and this with express reference to two recent victims of Hitlerism who "also . . . knew too much."[59] That collaborator was Walter Mehring. In 1964 Mehring recollected "that creepy Parisian exile episode when, in the Café Royal," Forster "treasonably revealed the ominous Pasewalk hospital documents to the collaborators of *Das neue Tage-Buch*: Leopold Schwarzschild, Joseph Roth, Ernst Weiss, and myself."[60] In 1975 Mehring added that Forster spent three days in this circle and gave Schwarzschild two copies of the Pasewalk "case record" for safekeeping.[61] In *Das neue Tage-*

8

Buch Schwarzschild did not reveal Forster's link with Hitler, but did connect him with another two "of today's potentates," affirming that in his Berlin days he had treated Hermann Göring for cocain addiction and certified Bernhard Rust at a sex crime trial as legally irresponsible.[62] Göring's morphine addiction—with documentation from after Forster's Berlin days—and Rust's mental derangement both came into the Comintern's otherwise fanciful *Braunbuch über Reichstagsbrand und Hitler-Terror,* completed in Paris in July and published in Basel early in August 1933.[63] Conceivably this, then, was what prompted Prussia's Prime Minister Göring or Minister of Education Rust to initiate the order telephoned from Rust's Ministry to the Curator (administrative head) of the University of Greifswald on 28 August 1933 to suspend Forster and investigate him as "politically unreliable" under the terms of a law of the previous 7 April "for the restoration of the Civil Service." To its follow-up letter urging expeditive action the Ministry appended extracts from a thickly Nazi denunciation of Forster, authorship undisclosed. The presumption against Forster was sustained by a sister superior, another sister, and an attendant from his clinic—the first questioned by the Ministry, the others in turn by the Curator as instructed. Forster was alleged to have tossed off remarks about the Reichstag fire as a put-up job, a speech by Hitler as low-level, and a war wound of Rust's as self-inflicted.[64] The allegation is credible, for a friend he had seen that summer in Basel recollected: "He had obviously got it into his head to make as many disparaging comments as he could about the regime, which he hated."[65] Irrelevant charges loomed larger, particularly of fast living in the clinic and of experimentation with patients standing on a wobbly table. The Curator consulted six professors who saw him on other business. They urged him to induce Forster to resign with a three-quarter pension as provided by the new law. All viewed Forster as "a psychopath easily excited at times and strongly inclined to depression at others."[66] But Forster's elder son, then thirteen-and-a-half, remembers him as poised and deliberate until this crisis.[67] And to his widow the Curator wrote afterward of "the grave difficulties that befell your husband and . . . the deep

9

depression and state of excitation they brought about him."[68]

At the first word of the proceedings against him Forster traveled to the Ministry in Berlin. On his return he put his affairs in order, then tried to kill himself—once with nicotine extract, once by hanging. His wife thwarted both attempts, then engaged one of his younger colleagues to help her watch after him.[69] On 5 September he saw the Curator, who found him subdued. While denying the political necessity to dismiss him, Forster accepted the proposed way out, "asking only if at all possible not to announce that he was dismissed under Paragraph Four" (as politically unreliable). His brother, visiting him for his fifty-fifth birthday, framed the resignation with the Curator; it was cleared with the Ministry by telephone and signed. But then the Ministry called back, instructing the Curator to question the three doctors on hand from the clinic. Two were pro-Nazi and the third anti-Forster, yet the three of them rejected or trivialized every stated charge. Still the Curator found that dismissal was in order. Two days later Forster's wife, claiming that the Curator had forced her sick husband's hand, sent him an intermediary who perused the file only to uphold the arrangement reached. Forster next telegraphed Berlin rescinding his resignation, then telephoned an hour-and-a-half later revoking the telegram "sent at his wife's instigation." The Ministry gave him a week to reflect and ordered the inquiry completed meanwhile. That same day, a Friday, the questioning resumed.[70]

The following Monday, 11 September, Forster took his life with a revolver he had not been known to possess. He had told his wife that his resignation "would not be the end of it," that he "would yet be hauled off at night by the Gestapo." Just after his suicide his wife explained to his elder son that he "had once diagnosed Hitler as hysterical."[71] So he seems to have seen Hitler's hand in the action against him—unrealistically, for such pressure could have provoked him to talk about Pasewalk, though in the event it did not (not even to his visiting brother[72]). He might have emigrated (he had grown up in Amsterdam, worked in Geneva, frequented Paris and Budapest), but he feared that the Gestapo would pursue him abroad.[73] The power of distinguishing imaginary from real appears to have failed him. It may be to the point that "his friends from his student days . . . always considered it possible that he would someday take his life."[74]

Forster's treatment of Hitler found its way via the Café Royal into Ernst Weiss's novel *Der Augenzeuge* (The Eyewitness). According to Walter Mehring, Schwarzschild's coterie had picked Weiss as the "witness" that Forster sought in July 1933.[75] Weiss was a Czech Jew who had trained as a surgeon in Vienna and studied under Freud along the way. By 1914 he had given up surgery for letters, though he then served in World War I as a doctor. He settled in Germany after the war, emigrated when Hitler took power, and killed himself in Paris in June 1940 rather than flee any farther. *Der Augenzeuge*, his last work, was begun late in 1938 and completed the following summer.[76] It centers in the "miracle cure" at "P." of "A.H.," stricken with "hysterical blindness." A.H. claims to have been hit by mustard gas while on a "run of duty up front," and plays the incapacitated war hero while deflecting scarce medical provisions from " 'real' " sufferers. He attracts attention by the trouble he gives ward mates less fired than he by the losing German cause. The chief psychiatrist, repelled by his personality but intrigued by his pathology, draws A.H. out in a lengthy nighttime consultation, then calculates how to utilize his fanaticism to cure his blindness. At a second nighttime consultation he examines A.H.'s impaired eyes and pronounces them medically incurable, but then suggests to him in the darkness that with his preternatural force of will he can cure them for himself. A.H. thereupon strains to see a lighted match, then a pair of candles, while being told: "You must believe in yourself blindly. Then you will cease being blind," and "Germany now needs men like you with energy and blind faith in themselves. Austria is done for, but not Germany," and finally "FOR YOU EVERYTHING IS POSSIBLE! GOD WILL HELP YOU IF YOU HELP YOURSELF!" At this point his eyesight is fully restored and he is put into a dreamless hypnotic sleep until the next morning.[77]

Weiss's hero is "pure Forster" in everything germane to Forster's encounter with Hitler. He is an innovator in brain surgery apart from his special interest in hysteria. He holds hysteria to be all-out simulation that fools the simulator himself. Of A.H. he remarks: "In his lying he believed he was telling the truth"— which matches Forster's "These hysterics talk of their love of country and their courage until they are carried away with themselves like the actor who, in playing Hamlet, takes himself for the Prince of Denmark."[78] He comes to P. from the western front in 1918 with Forster's rank and Forster's Iron Cross First Class; he leaves immediately after the revolution and "miracle cure." The sequel revolves around his notes on A.H., which he takes with him from P. along with some other case histories: "They could be useful if in a scientific study I wanted to give examples."[79] A democrat with close Jewish associations, he is threatened by A.H.'s takeover,[80] the more since A.H. has glimpsed his case notes during the "miracle cure." Even before the takeover a Nazi contact has invited him to hand over his official and unofficial papers "on him" so as to avoid trouble.[81] "I had not taken the official ones along," he specifies in his narrative voice.[82] He guards his notes as a possible weapon against A.H., yet rejects the thought of publishing them—"not from fear of the consequences, which I could not foresee, but from respect for the medical secret."[83] Nor will he destroy them as his wife urges. Instead he drives to Basel in the summer of 1933 and deposits them in a bank safe there. Just as his wife goes to meet him in Bern, he is tricked into returning to Germany and hauled off for thirteen days of interrogation—and to a concentration camp afterward. He "had resolved to resist the temptation of suicide" for his wife's sake.[84] She, though, surrenders the notes in exchange for his being allowed to escape abroad. A bitter life of exile in Paris ensues in which he is slowly estranged from her and their two children. The interrogation represented Forster's real fate as Weiss visualized it, the incarceration the fate Forster had feared, the exile the fate Forster had rejected. Weiss joined his own fate to Forster's for that final sequence. Then he in turn chose suicide rather than flight when France fell. His manuscript containing Forster's secret survived as a rejected entry in an American contest for the best novel by a German emigrant.[85]

Weiss's A.H. in P., while distinctively Forster's "war neurotic," is also distinctively Schmidt's and Westenkirchner's fellow runner of just before the mustard gassing except that A.H. rages against "the 'Yid.' "[86] So presumably the mustard gassing itself induced, or released, that rage in Hitler even before his relapse into blindness and reemergence with a mission to restore Germany. Hitler's "miracle" of recuperation (the term "miracle" is from an authorized biography of 1923[87]) as depicted in the several versions derived from him in the early 1920s is strikingly congruent with A.H.'s "miracle cure." Those versions varied in the mode of transmission of the message from on high (voices, images, sixth sense), as might be expected of a remembrance out of a deep hypnotic trance. Forster held that hypnosis was the achievement not of the hypnotizer, but of the hypnotized—which is just what Weiss's narrator tells A.H.[88] Hypnosis was commonly used by Forster's colleagues for war neuroses.[89] In 1917 Forster condemned this use—but then, the "miracle cure" is expressly devised for A.H.[90] Finally, Forster's having issued Hitler's celestial mandate, or drawn it out of him, would help explain the oddity that it did not implicate the Jews; he did in interpreting it. His received charge was to undo the defeat; to him that meant to remove the Jew.

Even if Weiss took his account of A.H. in P. faithfully from Forster's lips and notes,[91] several key questions remain. Why the innervating effect of the mustard gas on Hitler? Why did Hitler relapse into blindness over the German defeat, and reemerge with a vengeance as Germany's redeemer? Whence his conception, brought out by the poison gas, of the Jew as Germany's undoing? Here two clues leap to mind. First, Hitler ultimately ordered the Jews gassed. He himself drew this connection in 1925: "Had twelve or fifteen thousand of those Hebraic nation-spoilers been put under poison gas at the start of the war and during the war as hundreds of thousands of our very best German workers from all social and professional ranks had to endure it on the battlefield, then the millionfold sacrifice at the front would not have been in vain."[92] Viewed in this light, the gassing of the Jews looks like a massive revenge—and a misdi-

13

rected revenge, since Hitler never supposed that a Jew had fired that British gas shell his way. Second, his ever-recurrent term for the corrosive, lethal action of Jewry against Germany was "poisoning"—a widespread figurative usage at the time, but one he imbued with a peculiar force of literalness in his repeated warnings against "the Jewish blood poisoning and race poisoning"[93] that was "utterly eating our people away."[94] The last words of his two political testaments were for "the deadly Jewish poison" and "the world poisoner of all peoples, international Jewry."[95] This rhetoric likewise points to a Jew behind his gas poisoning. None was behind it in Flanders. But a referent for his conception of the Jew as poisoner stands out from his earlier history: his mother's death in the seventh week of a drastic local treatment with iodoform gauze by her physician, Eduard Bloch, in 1907. As mustard gas is actually a sharp-scented liquid spray that burns through the skin like iodoform, that precedent of 1907 calls for scrutiny next. It will answer more questions about Hitler than those already raised.

Klara Hitler consulted Dr. Eduard Bloch on 14 January 1907 about a pain in her chest.[96] He diagnosed cancer and arranged for a mastectomy that was performed in his presence four days later.[97] On 5 February, after payment of 100 crowns, she was discharged from the hospital as "cured."[98] Her household activities resumed.

The widow Klara Hitler lived with her two surviving children, Adolf and Paula, and her hunchbacked, half-witted sister Johanna. Paula turned eleven that January, Adolf eighteen that April, Klara herself forty-seven that August. Adolf had been idle since September 1905, when he belatedly and barely completed his intermediate schooling in nearby Steyr after nine-and-a-half months' residence there followed by a summer's unidentified illness. His only subsequent separation from his mother had been a few weeks' visit to Vienna in the spring of 1906, his only instruction a few months' piano lessons that ended when she was hospitalized in January 1907.[99] His one known companion was fantasy-prone August Kubizek, who later remembered him

14

passing the time of day fancying himself a great artist- or architect-to-be. He shied away from sex even as, in Bloch's words, "he idolized his mother."[100] She, his doting protectress and provider, indulged his every foible while fretting over him as young and helpless.[101] For all that, he did remove himself to Vienna and a rented room at the end of September 1907, intending to enter the painting school of the Academy of Fine Arts. Before leaving, and for a second time that month, he consulted Bloch just after his mother did. He was clearly concerned about her health, yet saw no cause to give up departing, or for that matter to return home when he failed the entrance test held by the Academy on 1 and 2 October.[102] Possibly he concealed this failure from her; in any event her landlady understood that he had presented himself too late for admission, and Kubizek that he had been admitted.[103] He did return home upon learning from her or from a neighbor—presumably after her visit to Bloch on 17 October, her first in a fortnight—that she had taken a turn for the worse.[104] He was back in time to see Bloch on 22 October.[105] His mother next entered Bloch's record book for two office and two house visits, with a prescription midway. Then he saw Bloch again on 31 October, a Thursday. This was evidently when the iodoform treatment was agreed upon, since Bloch noted payments received against materials the following Monday and applications of iodoform gauze beginning that Wednesday—twice with morphine over four days, then daily without morphine forty times until the fatal issue.

All along Bloch saw the patient's condition as serious, desperate, or hopeless, as he recollected in 1938, 1941, and 1943 respectively.[106] Bloch's dim view is reflected in Hitler's later statement on his mother's death: "It was the conclusion of a long, painful illness that from the first offered little prospect of recovery."[107] Bloch self-righteously refused to discuss the treatment in Linz in 1938 and in Lisbon in 1940.[108] In discussing it after all in New York for *Collier's* in 1941 and for the Office of Strategic Services in 1943, he substituted for the iodoform "an injection of morphine from time to time," then "an injection every day." He did this even with a photostat of his 1907 case record in his hands

15

(he had sent the original to Hitler in 1938).[109] The photostat did not survive him.[110] Clearly the treatment was on his conscience—and with good cause. It was potentially ruinous at about seven crowns a day. And it was worse than futile. Several decades of medical warnings were defied as iodoform gauze was packed onto the suppurating wound at an unexampled, intolerable rate (about a meter of fresh gauze containing some five grams of iodoform daily). Why did not Bloch, a compassionate "poor folks' doctor" and "benefactor of the indigent,"[111] kill the pain with morphine instead at small cost? For he recollected that Klara Hitler's sufferings "seemed to torture her son. An anguished grimace would come over him whenever he saw pain contract her face."[112] And again: "His eyes, otherwise gazing sadly into the distance, would light up whenever his mother felt free of pain."[113] Kubizek's memoirs suggest an answer. According to Kubizek, Hitler stopped by after his first consultation with Bloch following his return from Vienna, and blurted straight out to the friend who had been without news from him since his departure: " 'Incurable, the doctor says.' . . . Fire came into his eyes. Anger flared. 'Incurable—what does that mean?' he exclaimed. 'Not that the illness is incurable, but only that the doctors are unable to cure it. . . . Whenever doctors' wisdom runs out, their next word is: incurable. . . .' . . . Never before had he spoken with such bitterness, such impassioned involvement, as now."[114] Such a Hitler would have urged upon Bloch the drastic treatment that followed, iodoform being chosen because it was advocated here and there as a cure-all did soothe wounds unless and until poisoning ensued. Such urging was the evident source of Hitler's saying later that it would be folly not to apply a desperate remedy, however risky, to a cancer patient who is dying anyhow, and much worse folly for the doctor to apply it only halfheartedly just because of the gloomy outlook.[115] He said this in 1928 by way of justifying his drastic program for Germany. "To cure the national body of deep and grave illnesses," he explained, "is not a matter of finding a prescription that is itself completely nontoxic, but frequently of fighting one poison with another. To remove a condition recognized as deadly, one

*

16

must have the courage to impose and enforce even decisions that themselves harbor dangers."[116] In 1932 he declared in a similar context to the same effect: "Every plight has a root. So it is not enough ... for me to doctor around its edges and try now and again to lop off the cancerous growth, but I must get down to its source."[117]

Iodoform absorbed into the system quickens the pulse and attacks the nerves and the brain, inducing restlessness, headaches, insomnia, fever, and—in severe cases—delirium with hallucinations.[118] It also enters the saliva to bring on a burning thirst coupled with an inability to drink (things taste poisoned).[119] Its sickening odor hangs heavy, and must have infested the tiny rooms in which Hitler nursed his mother during her protracted agony. Three close witnesses to that nursing gave congruent accounts of it in later years: Kubizek, Bloch, and Paula Hitler. "In these weeks it was as if my friend had all at once become an entirely different person," Kubizek related. "... He was exclusively his mother's loyal, helpful son." He took the housework upon himself, Kubizek specified, and rearranged the apartment "so that he would be close to his mother even at night.... Adolf read every least wish out of her eyes and fussed about her ever so tenderly.... In these weeks he forgot himself entirely and lived only in self-sacrificial concern for his mother."[120] As Bloch told it: "In most heartfelt love he clung to his mother, observing every one of her movements so as to be able to render her tiny services rapidly,"[121] and again: "He slept in the tiny bedroom adjoining that of his mother so that he could be summoned at any time during the night. During the day he hovered about the large bed in which she lay."[122] Paula for her part recollected in 1946 (in her interviewer's English): "... my brother Adolf spoiled my mother during this last time of her life with overflowing tenderness. He was indefatigable in his care for her, wanted to comply with any desire she could possibly have and did all to demonstrate his great love for her."[123] Klara Hitler died at 2 A.M. on 21 December 1907. "With his mother," as Kubizek remarked, "Adolf lost the one being on earth on whom his love was concentrated and who had returned it just as completely."[124] Bloch

17

recollected for the Nazi Archive in 1938: "The day after the funeral he came . . . to thank me for the pains I had taken with his departed mother. In nearly forty years of medical practice I have never seen a youngster so *ineffably saddened* with grief and sorrow as young Adolf Hitler."[125] Bloch failed to recollect that it was Christmas Eve and that, as his record shows, he then collected his final 300 crowns. In a reminiscence of 1941 he disingenuously redated the scene with Hitler "a few days after the funeral" and added: "Looking into my eyes, he said: 'I shall be grateful to you forever.' "[126] Hitler redated the scene the same way by implication in explaining to his valet why yuletide depressed him: "My mother died on a Christmas Eve."[127]

Hitler's experience of his mother's last illness looms behind his later tireless diatribes against the Jewish cancer, the Jewish poison, the Jewish profiteer. All his lesser anti-Semitic epithets fall in with those three. The Jewish parasite linked the first and third. The Jewish bacilli, tuberculosis, and syphilis were variants of the first, for in 1907 it was the dominant view that cancer was, like tuberculosis, caused by bacilli and that syphilis was cancerous.[128] "How many diseases have their origin in the Jewish virus!" exclaimed Hitler himself.[129] A good primer for Hitler's Bloch complex in political guise is a passage of *Mein Kampf* arguing that even before the war the profit motive (read: Bloch's) was winning out over the ideal of self-sacrifice (read: his own) in the German people's (read: his mother's) struggle for survival against "forces of decay flaring up in truly frightful numbers like will-o'-the-wisps brushing up and down the national body or, as poisonous abscesses, eating into the nation now here, now there. It was as if an endless stream of poison were being driven by a mysterious power into the outermost blood vessels of this once heroic body, gradually impairing the reason and the very instinct of self-preservation." For all that, the Germans failed to "gain a clear perspective on the destroyer of their existence," namely the Judaic "world pest," Marxism. "Sometimes they doctored around the disease, but then they confused its forms with its instigator, whom they did not, or did not want to, recognize as such. Thus the struggle against Marxism amounted only to bungling quackery."[130] Consciously Hitler bore Bloch no grudges, quite the contrary, from the hand-painted card he sent Bloch from Vienna with "the most cordial New Year's wishes"—presumably for 1909—"from your ever grateful Adolf Hitler"[131] to the request, after the Anschluss of 1938, for Bloch to be photographed in his consulting room in Linz[132] and a decree granting Bloch "all possible alleviations, including monetary."[133] Even unconsciously he exonerated Bloch again and again from his own unconscious charges against him. Thus he answered for a political bloodbath of 1934 by telling Germany: "I . . . gave the order to burn out the abscesses of our inner well-poisoning and of the foreign poisoning down to the raw flesh."[134] Decoded, this cleared Bloch in respect of the breast cancer ("inner well-poisoning") and the iodoform treatment ("I . . . gave the order") while also blaming him for them through a dissymmetrical phrase covering both at once ("of the foreign poisoning").[135] Abusing "the Jew" was for Hitler a means of abusing Bloch while knowing better. This supercharged conceptual device, "the Jew," shaped up and developed latently with Hitler over the decade before it surfaced in October 1918. For in those years he was motivated against a run of evils and evildoers that were disconnected except in having been linked to Jewry in the Austrian and German anti-Semitism of the time. In the men's hostel in Vienna in early 1913 his two cues for fury were "ever and again . . . the Reds and the Jesuits";[136] in a letter of 5 February 1915 to an acquaintance in Munich he looked ahead to a victorious Germany rid of "foreignism" and "internal internationalism";[137] in his last days at the front he would scream like crazy against "pacifists and shirkers."[138] Again, he conspicuously avoided naming Jews when, in his first years in his regiment, he "would rail against the Dual Monarchy, in which every Czech, every Hungarian, every Pole, Croat, and Bosnian, counted for more than a German."[139] The anti-Semitic subliterature that proliferated in Hitler's Vienna must have prompted his choice of "the Jew" as a fall guy for Bloch, what with its big themes of parasitism, poison, and concealed malevolence.[140] This was the truth to his untruth that he left Vienna "as an absolute anti-Semite":[141] the anti-Semitism was absolute, but it was repressed.

In *Mein Kampf* Hitler claimed to have had his father's liberal, cosmopolitan influence to overcome through a long inward struggle over anti-Semitism.[142] The account was designed to boost the credibility of an anti-Semitism so hard-won. Yet it did roughly reflect his unconscious struggle over anti-Semitism—even when he called the anti-Semitism rational and the resistance emotional.[143] Behind his father's influence in that rough reflection lay his mother's. Here was his real deterrent from unloading his guilt and impotent rage of 1907 upon Bloch. She who had laid her life in Bloch's hands to the last was eternally beyond "gaining a clear perspective on the destroyer of [her] existence."[144] And Hitler remained bound, beholden, accountable to her after her death as before. Kubizek had observed "a unique psychic harmony between mother and son" over and beyond all their affinity due to long closeness,[145] and Bloch had the feeling about Hitler after the funeral that "here stands someone before you a piece of whose heart, of whose self, has been torn out!"[146] Logically, bereaved Hitler had either to find a new outlet for his consuming love for his mother or else to perpetuate her in her old role internally—to "introject" her. Psychologically, his job was to do both at once. The surrogate he chose for his missing mother was Germany—not the German state or territory, but the German *Volk*, the nation,[147] the imperishable "people itself as substance of flesh and blood."[148] As an Austrian he was both of the German people and yet separate from it: a son of Germany.[149] There is only his move from Vienna to Munich to suggest, ever so faintly, that Germany may have begun to replace his mother in his heart before August 1914. But then a chance photograph of him in the Munich crowd just as war was being declared documents his attunement to a tense and exalted nation. At once he took up Germany's "life-and-death struggle," making the List Regiment his "home." This transference from his mother was complete as of a letter of 5 February 1915: "... each of us wants only one thing, an early showdown with the pack of them, to have it out whatever the cost, for those of us lucky enough to see our homeland again to find it cleaner and more cleansed of foreignism, and through the sacrifices and sufferings so many hundreds of thousands of us now endure every day, through the stream of blood that flows here day by day against an international world of enemies, not just for Germany's outside enemies to be smashed, but for our internal internationalism to crumble too. . . ."[150] He had begun assimilating the outer foe to an inner infection (inverting his unconscious procedure of blaming Klara's cancer on Bloch) even as once again "he forgot himself entirely and lived only in self-sacrificial concern for his mother."[151]

It was at the climax of that "life-and-death struggle" that Hitler suffered his mother's martyrdom in his own flesh (to adapt his remark about the gas fired his way: "its effects were not yet known to us as far as experiencing them in our own flesh was concerned"[152]). His Jew-hate thereupon erupted amid that medley of symptoms, reminiscent of iodoformism, which Forster diagnosed as psychopathic.[153] Perhaps it breached consciousness on the train to Pasewalk when, as he later put it under oath, "one could hear nothing except about trade and barter."[154] Once it did surface he saw Germany's fatal enfeeblement as due to the Jewish cancer, the Jewish poison, the Jewish profiteer. At the news of the revolution, which sealed Germany's fate, he staggered and reeled, blinded, his "head burning," as if hit by mustard gas again.[155] He also shed tears of self-pity that he had held back since his gas poisoning—or so he himself put it, adding that they were his first since those shed on his mother's grave.[156] His hysterical relapse may have been prompted by the diagnosis of hysteria that governed his treatment.[157] In any event his hallucination fast restored him.[158] To his unconscious mind the summons to revive and avenge Germany came as a summons to revive and avenge his dying mother. More, it came as a summons from her: this is graphic in the authorized version, with the words from on high mediated by a motherly nurse "who holds the twitching, feverish soldier . . . in her arms."[159] Coming from his dying mother, that summons could not itself blame the Jew. Even so, it was uncannily well suited to enable him to take out all his anger and remorse of 1907 on Bloch, alias the Jew, with his mother's vicarious blessings while also arousing anew "all my defiance against the thought of capitulating to a seemingly ineluctable fate."[160] It galvanized his full psychic energy,[161] transforming him from a marginal loner and underling into a dynamic, demonic mass leader.

At the same time his tie to his mother unsuited Hitler for any normal erotic relationship. Kubizek remembered him in Linz romancing in his fancy with a girl he never dared approach.[162] In Vienna he carried his mother's picture in a locket, and in the army against his heart, while shunning women.[163] In the early 1920s he explained his continuing bachelorhood by declaring: "My only bride is my motherland"[164]—this with his mother's picture now over his bed.[165] He cultivated matronly patronesses in his political beginnings—"motherly lady friends," as he called them.[166] His single approximation to *amour-passion* was for a half niece, Geli Raubal, whom he took to live in his flat in 1928 and drove to suicide in 1931, when she was twenty-three:[167] their difference in age approached his father's with his mother, who called his father "Uncle" even after their marriage.[168] Eva Braun, one of his photographer's assistants, was the lady of his Berchtesgaden retreat in his years of power. Yet she was rarely there: she held down her job in Munich until March 1945.[169] This itself argues an asceticism on his part that her boss verified through the Berchtesgaden chambermaids.[170] She joined him in his Berlin bunker against his express wish. He married her on resigning as Führer. The marriage was consummated by a double suicide.

After his gassing, Hitler's 1907 complex surfaced in nonpolitical form as a self-punitive hypochondria that filled his private life increasingly.[171] Around 1907 the books said stomach cancer was the typical cancer for men corresponding to breast cancer for women, and after Pasewalk Hitler generated stomach gas that he insisted was cancerous.[172] In 1932 he confided about his hypochondria, cancer foremost, to an astonished Nazi leader in Hamburg named Krebs ("cancer").[173] As Führer he found a personal physician, Theo Morell, to feed him antigas pills that his two

22

attending physicians said were poisoning him. To an ear doctor who suggested to him in August 1944 that the pills might be causing his stomach pains he objected: "I think the stomach pains are more nervous. . . . Worry over the future and Germany's survival is devouring me daily."[174] When the ear doctor tested the pills anyway and confirmed the poisoning, Hitler dismissed him along with the two attending physicians, declaring: "You can say what you want about Morell. He is and remains my sole personal physician, and I have full confidence in him."[175] To one of the hapless attending physicians Morell confided: "In reality Hitler has never been sick."[176] In this same period a visiting throat specialist found the Führer languishing as if he had lost all will to live: "He can hardly eat, is continually thirsty, is racked by stomach cramps. . . ."[177]

But it was par excellence politically, not medically, that Hitler's iodoform and gas traumas were joined, for his political calling originated in their junction.

Hitler's primary political purpose was the one he took away with him from Pasewalk: to undo Germany's defeat, and to avenge it, by way of "the total removal of the Jews."[178] Down to the word "defeat" this purpose was his hallucinated mandate; the rest followed for him as if it had needed no specifying from on high. In his early career, culminating in the abortive Putsch of November 1923, he left undisclosed the full meaning of his mission to deliver Germany from defeat. Expressly it meant averting the penalties of defeat or, after June 1919, nullifying the Treaty of Versailles. But it implied, beyond this, retrieving the lost victory—an implication close to the surface of all his early speeches and writings, yet never quite drawn in those first years. He said nothing firm about how the Treaty would be nullified except that it would be by force. He discounted resistance to the will of a Germany free of Jewry. "We don't fear heavy arms," he told a contradictor; "if the will is there, the act will succeed."[179] This was, applied to Germany, Forster's prescription to him for surmounting his own physical disablement. He reverted to it in that naïve form to tell his generals, when the ring was closing around his Reich, that victory was strictly a matter of will power. "The objection that there can be moments when technical equipment is decisive is utterly invalid," he affirmed in December 1944.[180]

Of 1914–1918 he maintained: "The power which disabled us then was a Jewish one."[181] By his accounting, the Jews had undermined Germany's war effort by spreading antinational, pacifistic, and defeatist propaganda, by fomenting industrial shirking and strikes, and by financial manipulations and depredations. "The Jewish revolution of 1918"[182] was only the dastardly deathblow. "Not the Revolution, but the systematic demoralization of the people, was to blame for our losing the war. . . . But the Revolution was to blame for our signing that shameful peace."[183] His first programmatic message was that to liquidate Jewry, its accomplices, and its instruments for sapping the strength of nations, namely Marxism, liberal democracy, and finance capitalism, was necessary and sufficient for Germany's recovery— and urgent. "Poison is completely eating our people away," he declaimed.[184] "The abscess on the body of our people must be lanced," he editorialized.[185] "Marxism has been able to eat deep into the national body like a pestilence," he told an interviewer.[186] Sententiously he called himself and his followers "*servants of the German people* fighting for the future of our German people against the mortal enemies of our people, against the Jewish blood- and race-poisoning."[187] More laconically he stipulated: "The fight is with the Jewish race alone."[188] The first need was internal. The Jew and not the Entente, he insisted, was "Germany's gravedigger."[189] His lone refusal to join in the national front against the Franco-Belgian occupation of the Ruhr in 1923 exemplified his political posture. His slogan then was: "Not down with France! but down with the November criminals!"[190] His reasoning then as ever was: "What we long for outwardly can be won only through prior inner cleansing."[191] His conclusion was an attempt to reverse the November revolution on its fifth anniversary: his Putsch.

Quasi-magical like his doctrine of the will was his suggestion that Germany's defeat would be nullified if only its cause, the Jews, were removed. But sometimes he more nearly claimed

24

that revenge against the Jews was what would right the historic wrong of 1918. He enjoined his following to "think of revenge and again of revenge."[192] In cold print he declared in 1921: "If the word justice is not to be empty sound and smoke on this earth, then a judgment must come down upon the race of corrupters such as the earth has not yet known" and again: "Let us pour hate, burning hate, into the souls of our millions of compatriots until at length a flame of anger flares up in Germany to wreak vengeance upon our people's ruiners."[193] The following year he called for "a bloodiest tribunal to punish our people's poisoners"[194] and announced: "From this Germany a people will arise to punish its betrayers as never before."[195] For the tenth anniversary of the November revolution he told the Nazi old guard: "Millions in Germany . . . talk about faith in the future and yet have all failed to grasp one thing, which is that there is also a law in this world that states 'An eye for an eye, a tooth for a tooth,' and that this is the most fundamental law, the most fundamental concept of right, and that a people that goes to ruin from such a crime as the 1918 revolution may not hope to recover if this crime goes unpunished. Here too is a higher right than man conceives. Believe me, if someone asks when Germany will revive, I can answer him: Not until the ninth of November 1918 has been avenged. There is no right so long as this wrong has not been avenged." And he pursued, in heavy prophetic accents: "I believe in my people's resurrection. I believe in the day when the November criminals will be brought to reckoning one way or another. And I have but a single plea to make of heaven: may it grant that our movement be the avenger of the German people, may it make of this movement its arm, and let us promise it that this arm will fall hard and heavy upon the betrayers of our country in its hour of greatest need. And it will be on that day, and through that deed, that the German people recovers its honor. Only then, when that crime is expiated, can the German people venture forth again into the world. Then only will they be Germans again and can expect that heaven will not let them go under again."[196] To the high court in Leipzig he swore in 1930: "November 1918 will be expiated."[197] Retaliation was an old familiar refrain when he

25

announced on the ninth anniversary of his accession: "Now for the first time the true old Jewish law will be applied: 'An eye for an eye, a tooth for a tooth!' "[198] On ushering in World War II he had delivered himself on a variant that went straight to the point: "He who fights with poison will be fought with poison gas."[199] This fell in with his running stress on the retributive means. "The Jews are being fought by us with the same means as they employ against us," he asserted early in his agitation.[200] Here, finally, was his basic formula for reprisal and removal combined: "You can fight one poison only with another."[201]

Hitler's threats against the Jews were not often specific. "Removal" could portend expulsion or extermination.[202] So could language that dehumanized the Jews: "to dispose of the poison mushroom"[203] was just as ambiguous, if more sinister. Nor did metaphors help. "The evil must be grasped by its root," Hitler told his public. "We must provide the people with curative measures. The Jewish question must be settled, not skirted. And there is only one thing to be done about it!"[204] That "one thing" went unspoken then, and repeatedly, amid noisy approbation. It was still more grimly hushed when Hitler declared: "We must take up the fight against this race at long last. Any further compromising there would be poison for ourselves. . . . The *Frankfurter Zeitung* wrote triumphantly on 9 November 1918: 'The German people has made a revolution.' Yes, it made a revolution, but we hope it will also make a second one that does away with the Jew pack altogether."[205] He also cast this hope as a precept: "If you are determined to defend yourself at last, German people, then become *merciless!*"[206] To the Jews he declared correspondingly: "When we have power in our hands, then God help you!"[207]

But alongside such vague and ominous early statements by Hitler, others can be lined up so that they pass over imperceptibly into outspokenness about that "ruthless violence"[208] he foretold. A few may suffice to mark this effect. "We are actuated by the inexorable resolve to grasp the evil by the roots and eradicate it to the core. To attain our end, every means must be right by us, even a pact with the devil."[209] "There are only two possibilities:

we shall be sacrificial lamb—or victor!"[210] "In the life of peoples, whoever will not be the hammer must be the anvil."[211] "Short work must be made of Jewry."[212] "Jewry as a people confronts us as a deadly enemy."[213] "Anti-Semitism is worthless unless it is implemented in truly bloody earnest as the precondition for our people's inner convalescence."[214] "Solving the Jewish problem is for us National Socialists the core problem. This problem cannot be settled by tenderness, but in view of the enemy's fearful weapons only by brachial violence."[215] ". . . fight to the knife against Jewry . . . ."[216] "No humanity toward the Jews . . . ."[217] "May we be inhumane! But if we save Germany we have done the world's greatest deed. May we be unjust! But if we save Germany we have rectified the world's greatest injustice."[218] "The army command made one mistake: that it did not string up in good time all the filthy Jewish rabble that drove our people into the dreadful calamity in 1918."[219] ". . . their heads will roll. . . . The wheel will roll over [them]."[220] "Let us swear today that we will not rest until our goal is reached, until our oppressors lie smashed on the ground."[221] "The Jew's skull will be smashed by Germanic will."[222] Hitler's "one thing to be done" about the Jews required no more specifying than this. He allowed that the Nazis were indeed "anti-Semitic rowdies" pending the takeover.[223] But after the takeover, he stipulated, they would act by due process. "We want no pogroms. . . . We want a firm organization of the national will that can then effect our purposes."[224]

Even consciously his public can only have understood those purposes as deadly. Yet they intermingled with alternative purposes that were less than deadly. "Out with the Jews, who are poisoning our people," he cried in those same early years,[225] and "away with the racially alien rabble."[226] Or again, he called for "removal of the Jews from our nation, not because we begrudge them their existence, we congratulate the whole rest of the world on their visit."[227] Alternatively he proposed: "The Jewish undermining of our people is to be prevented, if necessary by its instigators being locked up in concentration camps."[228] In one instance he schemed: "Upon the takeover of the state the Jews

27

would be held hostage until treaties of guarantee are concluded to prevent interference with the National Socialist movement."[229] And in another: "The criminals of the November revolution must be removed, Jewry expelled from Germany, and its property used to back a new currency."[230] Asked in confidence once in 1922 just what he would do to the Jews if he had his way, he screamed: "If I am ever really in power, the annihilation of the Jews will be my first and foremost task"—and he detailed in a mounting fury how they would be strung up in every public square.[231] As against this *cri de coeur*, his interest within his terms of political reference was for Germany's Jews to resettle among Germany's enemies and poison *them*. But his professed aim of reversing Germany's defeat concealed a purpose deeper than that of saving his mother after all—a two-way tendency to avenge and to repeat the fatality of 1907. He would avenge it by poisoning Germany's poisoner. And he would repeat it by a partial removal of Germany's cancer (applied to the Jews, his surgical terms "removal" and, as in 1907, "extirpation"[232] denoted expulsion, though they connoted worse) and by a drastic "special treatment" of the remainder, with Germany succumbing in the process.[233]

Poisoning Germany's poisoner required an international act. Hitler indicated the international dimensions of the mortal peril to Germany as early as April 1920—"We must efface the poison outside and inside of us if we want to recover"[234]—even though Germany was then powerless to act abroad in any foreseeable future. And in 1928, when Nazi business was slow, Hitler told the Party that at least the anti-Semitic idea was alive: "It has been laid on the table, it will not disappear any more, and we shall see to it that it becomes an international world question, we will never let it rest until one day the question is resolved. We think we can yet see that day."[235] But only until the Putsch did Hitler profess that "one thing alone matters: one must concern oneself solely, entirely, and exclusively with the Jewish question."[236] After the Putsch, even with his death sentence against the Jews in full force,[237] he charted a second, parallel course for discharging his Pasewalk mission, one with

Germany's claim to more "land and soil" as its rationale and with the goal of reversing Germany's defeat explicit. He soon came to treat of the "core problem" less and less, and then obliquely and (as in 1913–1918, when his anti-Semitism was latent) through cover terms, particularly "Marxism" and "Bolshevism." Thus the retribution called for in his speech of November 1928 to the Nazi old guard was against the "November criminals," identified with Jewry only deviously through one mention of "our Hebrew poisoners," one of enemy propaganda by "the German Jews," and one each of "the Jewess Rosa Luxemburg" and "the Jew Kurt Eisner" as arch culprits.[238] "From him who cared to hear," Albert Speer affirmed long afterward, "Hitler had never concealed even his intention to exterminate the Jewish people."[239] Even on those who did not care to hear, the message was not lost in being conveyed by hints after *Mein Kampf* of the mid-1920s. On the contrary, it found its own psychic level below that of clear consciousness, as it did formerly through his speeches that had muted it. Besides, his speeches that had not muted it were remembered and reprinted —uncensored in the latter case. And brutal *Mein Kampf* sold over 50,000 copies a year in Germany beginning in 1930 and close to a million a year beginning in 1933.[240]

The message retained its outward fuzziness for some years after Hitler established his dictatorship—even when he told Nazi district leaders in April 1937, by way of refusing to quicken his moves against the Jews: "The final aim of our whole policy is perfectly clear to all of us."[241] Joseph Goebbels mistook that final aim when he launched the *Reichskristallnacht*, a huge pogrom of late 9 November 1938 that proved "devastating" for all concerned.[242] Reichsbank chief Hjalmar Schacht mistook that aim his own way and a month later began negotiating in London for Jewish emigration from Germany to be financed by an international loan on Jewish properties in Germany. When Schacht came close to succeeding, Hitler fired him from the Reichsbank on 20 January 1939. The conflict between them had broken over Hitler's alternative of a currency issue to be based on those Jewish properties—one of his pre-Putsch schemes.[243] "You don't fit into the whole National Socialist picture," he explained to Schacht.[244] He thereupon extended to the Reich proper a procedure developed in Austria by Reinhard Heydrich since August 1938 for despoiling and expelling Jews.[245] He had rationalized this "Operation Reinhard" (as it was nicknamed) in telling a visiting South African on 24 November 1938 that he was "exporting anti-Semitism."[246] He assured this same visitor that "the problem would be solved in the near future" and that "the Jews would one day disappear from Europe."[247] How can he have meant that solution and disappearance if, as he claimed, the Jews would not leave voluntarily and if, as he boasted, he was making them undesirable everywhere? Alfred Rosenberg provided an answer five days before Schacht's dismissal: that the goal was a Jewish reservation outside Europe.[248] Five days after Schacht's dismissal a Foreign Office circular stated that the point of the Reich's spoliations and expulsions was to force the Jewish issue toward that very goal.[249] In between, Hitler himself brought up the Jewish reservation as he was telling the Czech foreign minister that in Germany "the Jews were being destroyed. The Jews had not made the ninth of November for nothing, this day would be avenged."[250]

The Jewish reservation under international administration—later the SS-run Jewish penal colony—was mere masking for Hitler's final aim.[251] He proclaimed this aim on 30 January 1939, the sixth anniversary of his accession, after sneering at the crocodile tears shed for Germany's Jews from behind the closed borders of the democracies. "Should international finance Jewry inside and outside Europe succeed in plunging the nations into a world war again," he declared, "the consequence will be, not the Bolshevization of the earth and therewith the victory of Jewry, but the annihilation of the Jewish race in Europe."[252] He recalled this "prophesy" insistently before, during, and after its near fulfillment. On the next-to-last occasion he said: "I played fair with the Jews. I gave them a final warning before the war." And on the last: "I left no one in doubt that this time . . . the real culprit would . . . have to expiate his guilt."[253] The prophesy connects back to a warning he issued while establishing his dictatorship, "Jewry must recognize that a Jewish war against Germany strikes

Jewry itself in Germany with full sharpness,"[254] and farther back to his pre-Putsch scheme for holding the Jews hostage.[255] The prophesy was also designed to spread the guilt across those closed borders for the annihilation to come. It was inherently contradictory. If the democracies' borders were closed to the Jews, then for the democracies the Jews were no hostages. Or if the Jews were strong enough in the democracies to plunge them into a war against Germany for the sake of their own "interests" and "Old Testament vengefulness,"[256] then they would open up the democracies' borders first. Either way, the war that then came with those borders still closed was no "Jewish war." But the prophesy was cynical anyhow, as only eleven days later Hitler told a military group that "he must wage war . . . soon" for "a) mastery of Europe, b) world mastery for centuries."[257] He nonetheless called that war a Jewish war to the last, as when in February 1945 he claimed that, before it, he had faced up to the "problem" of the Jews "by chasing them out on all sides in order to cleanse the German world of the Jewish poison. For us," he added, "this was an indispensable disinfection treatment undertaken at the last minute. . . . With this operation a success in Germany, we had a chance it would spread. It was even bound to, since health normally prevails over disease. The Jews were at once alert to this hazard, which is why they decided to go all-or-nothing and launch a fight to the death against us. They had to bring down National Socialism at whatever price, even should the planet be destroyed. No war was ever so typically or so exclusively a Jewish war as this one."[258] This rationale of his prewar Jewish policy only compounded its illogic. For its avowed result was not that "health" prevailed over "disease" in the democracies (as it was "bound to"), but that the democracies were incited to a "fight to the death" against Germany—which was cleansed of the "Jewish poison" and yet succumbed in a purely "Jewish war." But psychologically the inconsequence was consequent. As in 1907, so now again the "operation" left a residue of "infection" within Germany to be poisoned out in that losing "fight to the death."

The transition to this poisoning-out was provided by the Euthanasia program, launched even as the expulsions practically ceased with the start of hostilities in Europe. Hitler first whispered about setting up a secret Euthanasia program in wartime just as he was striking a pose of moderation toward the Jews during the drafting of a racial law at the Nuremberg Party Rally of September 1935:[259] here already, then, his radicalism toward the Jews was rechanneled into Euthanasia.[260] In the spring of 1939, in a prologue to the program proper, Hitler seized on a parental request for an infant that was blind and "seemed idiotic" to be put to death.[261] That summer he already began instructing his future operatives.[262] Late the following October he signed a personal order backdated to 1 September 1939, when his Polish war had started, charging Philipp Bouhler, chief of the Kanzlei des Führers (his private office), and Karl Brandt, his senior attending physician, with administering the selection of "incurables" for "mercy killing."[263] Orally he restricted the order to mental incurables.[264] Theirs were lives not worth living, he explained in briefing sessions—and besides, medical resources ought to be economized in wartime.[265] He excluded Jews and the mental casualties of World War I—contradictorily, in that by the one exclusion he implied that Euthanasia was a benefit and by the other he implied the opposite.[266] The mechanics of the killings were administered by Viktor Brack of the Kanzlei des Führers: a commission from Berlin arrived in Grafeneck on 17 October 1939 to set up a gas chamber there while the chief of Stuttgart's criminal police was devising one independently in Brandenburg.[267] Hitler himself ran the program closely at the outset through oral instructions.[268] As the means of killing he prescribed gas in early October, with a tentative choice of carbon monoxide in November that he finalized after eighteen or twenty victims died swiftly, painlessly, and unsuspectingly in a first experiment in Brandenburg early in January 1940.[269] He required that doctors only should pull the gas levers. Throughout he saw watchfully to the exclusion of the war casualties: early in 1941 he ordered some rumored slip-ups investigated at once (it turned out that the mental condition predated the war service in every instance).[270] But Jews were, on the contrary, removed from mental institutions to the gas chambers beginning in the summer of

1940, and with decreasing medical pretense[271]—then from concentration camps as well beginning in March 1941, and with decreasing regard for fitness to labor.[272] In July 1941 the mass execution of Jews and of derivative political and racial enemies began behind the German battle lines in Russia as provided by a directive of Hitler's of the previous 13 March.[273] Then on 24 August Hitler called off the Euthanasia program as of that fall.[274] Over the following months Bouhler and Brack stepped up the removal of Jews from the concentration camps to the gas chambers while also transferring Euthanasia equipment and personnel piecemeal to Poland for the Final Solution.[275] On invading Poland in September 1939 Hitler had ordered Jews from the Reich massed in a few specified Polish cities having good rail connections—for "the final aim," which was "to be held *strictly secret*" and "will take some time," as Heydrich told SS commanders on 21 September (that was not the *open* aim of a Jewish reservation).[276] Jewish egress from all German-controlled Europe was halted in 1941—stark proof that "the final aim" was not a last recourse. Once the Final Solution was under way in its Polish compound, Hitler's involvement in its details slackened even as its implementation gradually passed from the Kanzlei des Führers to the SS. Thereafter Hitler applied himself instead to extending its compass to Germany's satellites—by diplomacy so long as this availed. When his Reich was collapsing he boasted: "We have lanced the Jewish abscess."[277] And he managed some positive thinking against all odds: "In a world that will be increasingly infected by the Jewish poison, a people immunized against that poison must prevail in the long run."[278] He had meanwhile refuted with a vengeance his postulate that Germany's 1918 defeat, being the Jews' doing, would be undone by their undoing. That refutation covered the subpostulate that his mother's death was Bloch's doing.

The secret sense of Hitler's secret Euthanasia program as he initially framed it at the Nuremberg Rally was to rectify 1907 with a mercy killing of his incurably sick mother by Bloch that would, incidentally, obviate wasteful expense. But through the program as he applied it he identified himself in Pasewalk with his mother dying in Linz. His own gassing of 1918 was the referent for his Euthanasia gassings; he was, by the terms of Forster's diagnosis, the original mental patient; the consideration of saving scarce medical resources for the war wounded was Forster's toward him (it did not yet figure with him in 1935). More, his precursive little victim, a blind mental defective, was a dream-style manikin of himself at Pasewalk.[279] Yet even at the planning stage of the program he meant the "mercy killings" for his mother, given his dual, vicarious exclusion of himself and, initially, Bloch (of the mental casualties of the war and, initially, Jews). Euthanasia was thus like a last defense, psychologically speaking, against that further program it led into after all— against that "final aim." Through this climactically ghastly finale, Hitler repeated his mother's terminal treatment—applied it to Germany, that is—while also taking it out on Bloch alias the Jew. That was the ultimate meaning of his advance billing of his politics as a desperate eleventh-hour treatment of a dying Germany.[280] Once again the treatment helped ensure that the patient would perish, for the mass executions in Russia fired resistance there,[281] and the exterminations that followed for the rest of German-controlled Europe deflected crucially needed manpower, materials, and transportation from the German war effort.[282] Actually these exterminations outside Russia were undertaken only after Hitler had acknowledged in closed councils (after the Russian counteroffensive outside Moscow and the Japanese plunge against America in early December 1941) that his war was unwinnable.[283] Thereafter the losing war covered the removal of Jewry, originally proposed as a means to victory.[284] At the same time Hitler took to remarking that for Germany the wages of defeat was death, and increasingly with the addendum that those wages were well earned.[285] "Get one thing straight, Schellenberg," he snarled at the SS counterintelligence chief in mid-1944, "in this war there is only . . . victory or ruin. Should the German people fail, it will go to ruin." And after a pause: "Yes, then it should go to ruin, then it should perish."[286] In the end he issued scorched-earth orders designed to make sure it would perish[287] (they went largely unheeded). Here was the nether side of that positive thinking he managed *in extremis*, the hate hitherto buried beneath his consuming love for a mother who had unfitted him to outgrow that consuming love for her.

Hitler's politics was his anti-Semitism—exclusively until his Putsch of November 1923 and still decisively thereafter. His anti-Semitism was his reaction against his guilt for his mother's agony of 1907 following Bloch's ministrations that he prompted. That reaction, long repressed, was released by a gas poisoning reminiscent of his mother's agony—a reminder of traumatic intensity that impelled him to relive the unassimilated experience behind it. Such traumatic reliving involves patterned revisions of the original experience—reversals, and tendencies both to undo the outcome and to carry it to its final consequences.[288] Poisoning the poisoner was a reversal; to undo mother Germany's demise was Hitler's ostensible aim; the culprits of 1907 both came to grief the second time around. But these revisions were subordinate to Hitler's straight reliving through his dire false cure for Germany's supposed mortal ailment. That reliving was no less straight for his assuming Bloch's old role on top of his own, beginning with the "operation" he ordered in 1938 "to cleanse the German world of the Jewish poison."[289] It was no less straight either for bearing Forster's impress in Hitler's insistence that Germany's seemingly physical incapacitation could be overcome by will power, and perhaps also in Hitler's use of hypnotic techniques with the national patient.

Where Forster had given him a new lease on life, Hitler in turn could only renew an old one for Germany. This renewal will be considered next.

II

TOMORROW THE WORLD

Suddenly the dream of German world
dominion is dreamed out. Maybe it
was not such a lovely dream anyhow.

German lieutenant's diary entry
for 15 October 1918.[1]

We'll keep on marching before us
  Though everything's shot to hell,
For Germany's ours today and
  Tomorrow the world as well.

(*Wir werden weiter marschieren
  Wenn alles in Scherben fällt,
Denn heute gehört uns Deutschland
  Und morgen die ganze Welt.*)

Nazi marching song.

Hitler's myth of the toxic Jew amounted to a denial of the 1918 defeat. For the force of it was that there would have been no defeat except for the treachery of Germany's Jews—that is, of un-Germans mistaken for Germans. As Hitler put it: "Heroically our people won the war. It took four-and-a-half years to poison our people to the point that it then defeated itself."[2] His implied denial of the defeat led straight into his proposal for undoing it: "If we took care of all the trickery and devilry of the outside enemy four-and-a-half years running, we shall take care of the devil on the inside too."[3]

While such transparency was exceptional even on Hitler's part, denial was a widespread German response to the 1918 defeat. Official welcomes addressed to troops repatriated from France and Belgium were all of a kind with that of the new Socialist chancellor Friedrich Ebert on 10 December 1918: "No enemy vanquished you."[4] Technically Ebert spoke the truth. The German government had opened armistice negotiations to forestall a debacle when German strength was exhausted in the face of practically unlimited Allied resources being mobilized. To the German people this final outcome was unacceptable after four years of overstraining, starving, and bloodletting in supposed self-defense combined with expectations of gain, unbelievable after four years of victories in the east and victory bulletins from the west.[5] Discouragement did mount earlier as the all-out spring and summer offensives of 1918, launched by the Reich's warrior chief Erich Ludendorff, ended in so-called strategic retreats.[6] But the worst expectation was that occupied Flanders, and the very worst that Alsace-Lorraine as well, would have to be surrendered in a negotiated settlement that would leave the Reich's eastern gains untouched./Because the Reich had been born of military victories, military victories were felt to be its birthright.[7] As Ludendorff's frantic disclosure of 29 September 1918—that the army was on its last legs and the front could crack momentarily —filtered down, the Reich did not rally:[8] it panicked as if it were all at once laid open to savage depredation. An archaic terror sounds through the insistent, shrill silliness with which for years afterwards Germans right, left, and center called the lost war a struggle for national survival and charged the victors with intent to enslave and annihilate. The shock effect of the defeat was truly pervasive: no Reich German escaped it (not even Ludendorff himself)—least of all on the extreme left, where the fear had been rather that German soldiery might subdue all Europe.[9] That effect was largely drained in the first instance by domestic turmoil and turbulence. Sailors and soldiers, workers and even peasants, set up "councils" styled after the Russian soviets, which had snatched revolutionary victory from military defeat.[10] At the other extreme, Freikorps formed that refused to be done with the lost war.[11] The republic arose at Wilson's bidding— unresisted,[12] and in the put-on mood of a reconciliation of peoples.[13] Its institutions were then fashioned in the perfected image of those on the victors' side. The theory was that the onus of defeat was on the Empire, so that with the Empire disavowed, Germany was out from under.[14] When the victors shattered this theory, the republic was thrown on the defensive, and defended

only as a provisional or transitional regime.[15] For five years the
battle raged internally behind Germany's diminished borders—
except for one electric instant of solidarity in May 1919 against
the *Diktat* issued in Versailles, another in March 1921 behind a
foreign minister who said "no" in London,[16] and a third in
January 1923 against the Franco-Belgian invasion of the Ruhr.[17]
At those moments the war reopened in German hearts. Notwith-
standing the wrangling and scuffling, moreover, all Germany
was revisionist, or averse to paying for a defeat it would not
own.

The classic myth about the defeat, the army stabbed in the
back by civilians, originated even before the armistice was
signed.[18] Ludendorff, its loudest mouthpiece, had laid the
groundwork for it himself by installing a parliamentary regime
with a coalition government to negotiate the armistice in his
stead.[19] The putative stab in the back started out as the bid for an
armistice, turned into the revolution entailing needless concessions in the armistice negotiations,[20] and wound up by the end
of 1919 as the revolution causing the defeat. The stab was supplemented increasingly in political parlance by a "poisoning,"
meaning the revolutionary subversion of the fighting army from
the rear echelons and home front over long months before the
defeat.[21] These twin legends gave ground after the Versailles
Diktat of May 1919 to the legend of a Germany duped by Wilson
into surrendering.[22] The Wilson legend accorded better with the
postwar policy of revisionism in that it entailed plaints and recrim-
inations abroad while the stab and poison legends only helped
divide Germans against themselves. Yet it was as infelicitous as
its two older rivals: it said Germans were fools where they said
Germans were self-destructive. And no more than they did it
permit hope for a national comeback or point a way out of the
international bind.

Hitler's was the going legend of a poisoning, but with "the
Jew" as poisoner. Occasionally he employed the stab and Wilson
legends as well for side effect. He had the Marxist leaders
"already reaching for the dagger" while still clutching the
Kaiser's outstretched hand after August 1914 and "the great

army ... struck by a sneak attack" from behind in November 1918.[23] "The German front would have held fast," he affirmed, "had not the front of pimps and deserters stabbed Germany from the rear."[24] Or again: "Not from the fighting front but from the rear" they "plunged the dagger and brought the front down."[25] And he pronounced Wilson "a conscious, systematic deceiver" and "thorough scoundrel who with his fine promises tricked our people in the foulest way."[26] "We Germans," he claimed, ". . . believed Wilson's promises of a conciliatory peace and were so bitterly deceived."[27] He also combined the stab and Wilson legends with his own in varying proportions. Once he maintained that the poisoners had promoted Wilson's Fourteen Points, whereupon "the 'glorious' revolution broke out, and on 12 November 1918 the enemy, exploiting Germany's inner distress, posed fundamentally different demands."[28] And another time: "How could a people that waged such heroic battles lose its national spirit all at once? Through moral contamination by the Jews. Their systematic undermining of the front and the rear made it possible for the nation to cast aside its tried and proven leaders and throw itself into the arms of a trickster like Wilson."[29] But his own legend predominated, and with good cause, for it alone was cogent as legends go. It entailed a simple, practical measure—to rid Germany of Jews—with treaty revision to follow from the strength of a Germany thus purified. And he never said "revision" but that he meant revocation. Even in raising a demand for "revision of the peace treaty," he declared: "*The Treaty of Versailles must go.*"[30] More pointed was his call for: "Not revision, but smashing, of the Treaty of Versailles."[31] But to revoke the treaty was to revoke the defeat, with the implication— undrawn, but unavoidable—of putting all of eastern Europe back under Germany's control or at Germany's mercy as in 1917–1918. This undrawn, unavoidable conclusion would be reached by force of arms: "The German yoke must be broken by German iron," he stipulated.[32]

Fully as primitive as Hitler's proposed proceeding against the Jews was his logic of a resultant racial regeneration retrieving the victory lost in 1918. Even in a Germany with its constitutive

39

values destroyed by defeat, revolution, inflation, and the war guilt clause, such a message was too crude and fantastic by common standards to resonate beyond the beer halls and stadia where Hitler delivered it. It enabled him to gain a fanaticized following of some tens of thousands in the Munich area, with its concentration of ideological cranks and its memories of Jews leading a half year of tragifarcical revolutionism in Bavaria following the defeat.[33] "What were Eisner, Levien, Toller, and consorts?" asked Hitler. "Purely Jews!"[34] For what little difference it made, Max Levien was purely German Lutheran.[35] That rhetorical line led Hitler not to Berlin—where, at his Putsch in Munich's Bürgerbräu beer hall, he announced he was headed—but only to the Odeonsplatz across the Isar River and to jail in nearby Landsberg. His Putsch fiasco was like a last mad fling in Germany's postwar political free-for-all. Therafter quiescence set in overnight, and Hitler, who had been widely dismissed before then as a fringe agitator or political psychopath,[36] was discounted by all, himself included, until further notice.

Hitler's first formula for delivering Germany from defeat—to poison the international poisoner—pointed beyond mere revisionism as did that intended deliverance itself. His second formula, worked out between his post-Putsch imprisonment of 1923–1924 and his unpublished book of 1928, left revisionism behind.[37] It was a program, complete with an excuse, for Germany to seize the world power that had eluded her under the Empire and, to top it off, world rule. The excuse was that peoples do each seek world rule anyhow in an ongoing contest among them for feeding ground, and that this fundamental law of life is its own justification even with its provisions for victors to enslave or annihilate the vanquished on pain of decadence. The program was meant to correct Germany's hapless play for world power of 1914–1918 by replaying it in installments.[38] Germany would first subjugate the European continent and transform it into an autarkic, blockade-proof arsenal.[39] British acquiescence, which was indispensable, and perhaps even British cooperation could be gained in return for a temporary renunciation of German naval,

40

maritime, and overseas colonial ambitions. In due course Germany, as master of continental Europe, would supplant Great Britain—by force of arms if need be—in dominating the Eastern Hemisphere preparatory to challenging the United States for world dominion. The objective of the first installment, Europe's subjugation, would itself be pursued piecemeal. To avoid a two-front war, Germany would knock out France before turning on Russia. For the same reason Germany would neutralize or liquidate the Central European successor states—France's eastern allies—seriatim before turning on France. This last was at all odds the intent behind Hitler's actual procedure of the late 1930s. Those successor states went unmentioned in his planning of the 1920s, where his frame of reference was the configuration of powers prior to World War I—minus the Hapsburg Empire, which he had already written off before the war.[40] Within that frame of reference, his planning for the first round of the German power play was that of Imperial Germany before World War I, updated: alliance with Italy, arrangement with England, then a quick knockout blow against France preliminary to a life-and-death struggle with Russia.[41]

The accord Hitler proposed with England was unobtainable if only for a reason implicit in its very terms: the danger to England from a German conquest of continental Europe. England was to countenance that conquest if Germany merely renounced all further ambitions. The present renunciation indicated the future danger. And if that were not enough, Hitler advertised the ulterior motive of the projected unequal arrangement even after the national limelight was on him beginning in September 1930. Thus the following November he sounded his old familiar theme before faculty and students of Erlangen University in an address entitled "Our People Will Forge Its Own Future," which was included in a popular volume of his speeches issued just after he liquidated Czechoslovakia in the spring of 1939: "We have close to seventy million people crowded together in a relatively small area. We must sustain and nourish this compressed human mass. We are therefore compelled to expand our living space. . . . Every people strives for world dominion. Only he who keeps his

41

eye fixed on this final goal finds the right way. A people that is too timid, or no longer possesses the courage or the strength, to set itself this goal enters upon the second way, that of renunciation and self-surrender ending in extinction."[42] He went after the deal, or double-deal, with England neither forthrightly nor beguilingly when the time came, but in the self-defeating Wilhelmian way—by nuisance threats, or pressure without leverage, in the naval, maritime, and colonial spheres.[43] He did enlarge his intended offer in the latter 1930s to a guarantee of the British Empire against non-German threats. But he did so while he was already "smashing" the peace settlement of 1918–1919 in central Europe by way of bringing Germany up to his planned starting point for his expansionist push.[44] That smashing destroyed the worth of a German guarantee many times over before he even brought out the enlarged offer, which "had no chance of being accepted" anyhow—and which he brought out only in a fit of last-minute nervousness on 25 August 1939 as Britain stood by its guarantee of Poland despite his startling conclusion of a pact with Stalin two days earlier.[45]

Before this fit he had maneuvered himself, since 1933, through a devaluation of the proposed British entente into an acceptance of the risk and finally even of the desirability of forcibly disinteresting Britain from continental involvement.[46] Nominally he was thereby only revising the first installment of his counteredition of World War I. Actually he had begun scrapping his installment plan itself—his winning combination. As his appointed adversaries began rearming, he forced events with the idea—Chancellor Bethmann Hollweg's of the years before World War I—that if a general war was inevitable, then the sooner the better.[47] On the eve of his Polish campaign he concealed his nervousness about England to tell his entourage: "This time the mistake of 1914 will be avoided."[48] After the British ultimatum to evacuate Poland was read to him, he sat petrified a while, then turned upon his muddled foreign minister, demanding: "What now?"[49] He had frequently cited the 1914 precedent himself with a sneer at Bethmann Hollweg: "On the morning of 3 August [1914] he knows for sure that England will not declare war on us."[50]

He scrapped his installment plan definitively in practice when, with the British refusing to be intimidated even after France fell, he attacked the Soviet Union anyhow. This attack of June 1941—Barbarossa—opened the "two-front war that Hitler had repeatedly thrown up to the Imperial leadership as its greatest strategic error."[51] His rationale for the attack was the topsy-turvy one of obviating a two-front war. His argument ran: "We are threatened with a two-front war because England (or America) is beyond our reach. So the adversary within reach (Russia) must be beaten preventively."[52] But at times he justified the move by the need to bring the British to terms by eliminating their last prospective ally on the Continent.[53] He refuted this justification in advance by telling his generals after France fell that he wanted the Russian war before settling with Britain.[54] Through the fall and winter of 1940 he nevertheless made a show of exploring alternatives in the war against England and finding them wanting (Channel crossing, Mediterranean strategy, Continental Block, partnership with Russia or Japan) until the attack on Russia came to look like a last recourse (the same procedure as he had followed to arrive, concurrently, at the Final Solution). The effect of the attack on Russia was to telescope phases one and two of his programmed play for world rule —and indeed phase three, since the increased danger to Britain meant increased American involvement, as he well knew. He jumped the gun by declaring war on the United States himself at the very time he whispered that his continental war was unwinnable.[55] Right out of 1917 he asserted that German U-boats would clean American shipping out of the Atlantic, cutting off American supplies to England.[56] With his corrective for World War I now fully cancelled, his new war threw back for him to its prototype more and more overtly. "Thenceforth—and definitively after his last effort to 'turn fate,' his summer offensive of 1942 in the east, had failed as of September 1942—Hitler saw himself in the role of the Third"—Ludendorff's—"Supreme Command of World War One."[57] But in the end he did not just reiterate, he also implemented, Ludendorff's dictum that, if his great gamble lost, "then Germany must go to ruin."[58]

Hitler's focus in articulating his second, expansionist message was "the conquest of new living space in the east and its ruthless Germanization,"[59] it being considered only natural for a great people hemmed in to expand along the path of least resistance. Premise and conclusion here were distinct from those of his Jewish politics if also compatible with them.[60] Despite this logical distinctness, his second political course connected directly back to his Pasewalk mission just like his first, for it too was aimed at reversing the 1918 defeat. And it was plainly as hopeless as the first. Killing Jews would not win the lost war: this Hitler himself now acknowledged by implication in denouncing the pursuit of world power simultaneously by land and sea as Imperial Germany's fatal error. But neither could Britain be expected to let Germany conquer the Continent in return for Germany's forswearing, or rather deferring, a threat to British naval supremacy if Germany could not pose that threat until after that conquest. Worse, that conquest could be undertaken only after a forced revision of the victors' peace on Germany's terms that itself already required British compliance.[61] As it was, Hitler went astoundingly far in his programmatic direction, yet did not even reach phase one proper before England declared war. This killed his chances of correcting World War I, and not just by the terms of his unrealistic program. He was not equipped to defeat England any more than he was minded to. Even weakening England would, he knew, only benefit Soviet imperialism in Asia, just as his efforts to force England out of the fight would only increase American involvement with England and his own dependence on the Soviets for supplies.[62] Nor could he beat Russia militarily while engaged even defensively against England.[63] And time was working against him on both sides.[64] He moved his armies into Poland nonetheless, then Scandinavia, the Low Countries, France, the Balkans, and Russia. "Let no one doubt my determination to carry out preconceived plans one way or another," he had once warned the world.[65] But his game was up before it ever began.[66] *That* was the preconceived plan beneath all his farflung planning. In Golo Mann's formulation: "Seriously speaking, there was no attempt that failed to the regret of the attempter; there was only an insane enterprise that was *bound to* fail, that in the depths of the monster's consciousness was *intended* to fail."[67]

In those depths of consciousness Hitler was reliving his tragedy of 1907 through his Jewish policy: the two match up all the way. In contrast, the elements of his power politics—east and west, land and sea, Russia and England—correspond to nothing in his personal history. All of them are, though, conspicuous in Germany's previous thrust for world power culminating in the 1918 catastrophe. Indeed, the power-political venture proposed and conducted by Hitler related to the Wilhelmian global misadventure quite as if it were unconsciously calculated for *Germany* —as was his Jewish policy for *him*—to relive an unassimilated disaster. Not only was it expressly a replay for world power, but his intended corrective of the earlier misplay harked back to Germany's earlier failing efforts to keep England and then America neutral and to escape the two-front war and the "hunger blockade." His program recast in the future tense the consideration widespread in Germany after the 1918 defeat that the eastern victory had been futile for want of time to exploit it and that it might have been underwritten by the Allies at the beginning of 1918 in return for the evacuation of Flanders and, if need be, the retrocession of Alsace-Lorraine to France.[68] "We had attained a tremendous extension of power to the east, and the perfectly obvious thing for us to have done was, as I see it, to offer concessions in the west so as to make peace." The terms of this reflection of March 1925 by a Democrat on the Reichstag committee investigating the defeat are precisely those of phase one in Hitler's program: a tremendous extension of power to the east leaving the western territorial settlement of 1918–1919 undisturbed. A Nationalist committeeman inquired fittingly: "But how can we ascertain whether our adversaries would have gone along?"[69]

So Hitler's foremost power-political aim, to conquer land from Soviet Russia, linked back with 1917–1918, when the German armies did just that.[70] Barbarossa renewed and intensified Ludendorff's eastern campaign of 1917–1918, which reduced Lenin's rump Russia to dependence on Germany: in September 1918 the German line stretched from the Gulf of Finland southeastward into the Caucasus, where a new advance was impending.[71] It was, above all, the very vastness of this conquest that rendered defeat inconceivable to Germans and, when it came, incredible. A later remembrance by Gustav Stresemann bespoke a general state of mind well forgotten by others: "My sense of it was that after the collapse of Russia we could not be vanquished militarily."[72] Ludendorff's fluid line advancing eastward reappeared in Hitler's successive schemes for conquering Soviet territory just so far and no farther, with the hostilities to continue indefinitely on the eastern periphery. Even so, he took a jump on Ludendorff in those schemes of conquest—up to the lower Don, the middle Volga, and the northern Dvina already in his first request for invasion plans, on 3 July 1940.[73] Those hostilities slated to continue on the periphery foredoomed the projected conquest, which turned on the expectation that the Soviet regime would, like its predecessor, collapse before the German invaders. Hitler's unwillingness to move on Moscow or Leningrad during the actual invasion, in August 1941, repeated Ludendorff's desistance of 1918. His drive for the Baku oil fields instead renewed Ludendorff's last offensive. His harsh plans for the areas conquered from the Soviets took off from Ludendorff's approach, outlined on 29 December 1915, to "the Polish and eastern question generally," which was to "divide and rule" after annexing lands to serve as "breeding places for men needed for further struggles eastward."[74] His actual eastern occupation practices were anticipated on a smaller scale by Ludendorff's of 1917–1918: confiscations, deportations, Germanization.[75] The original of the infamous Commissar Order and related instructions of 1941 for executing Russian prisoners of war[76] is to be found in an Oberost directive of early 1918 for hanging all captured Red Army "bandits" without exception.[77] When the Independent Socialist Georg Ledebour protested in the Reichstag that this directive condemned the entire Red Army to the noose, the Vice-President of the Reichstag silenced him, declaring: "Such a thing is unthinkable."[78] The Bolsheviks had been Imperial Germany's partners only the year before—in a remote counterpart to the Germano-Soviet Pact of 1939.

It was when he launched Barbarossa that Hitler ordered European Jewry exterminated. This shows that on his own traumatic level ("he lived continually on several levels of consciousness at once"[79]) he took for granted that Barbarossa would fail. For he realized that it could succeed only as a blitzkrieg.[80] But he also realized that the massive extermination of Jews would be possible only in a climate of all-out war and would take long months just to prepare.[81] As his closest military adviser avowed after the event: "Earlier than anyone in the world Hitler sensed and knew that the war was lost."[82] "No one doubts ... that I meditated more than anyone on Napoleon's Russian experience," declared Hitler himself apropos of his choice of the same day of the year as Napoleon to invade.[83]

The eastern land grab was anticipated in Hitler's occasional pre-Putsch considerations of power politics alongside of his prepossession with Jewry. On 10 December 1919 he proclaimed that "might ... decides right. Is it right that for instance eighteen times as much soil should fall to a Russian per capita as to a German?"[84] The ratio took a sly cut when he returned to this loaded question on 6 March 1921: "Today the German people is taxed with being imperialistic and believes this nonsense. No one will face the fact that eighteen times as much land and soil falls to every adult Russian as to every German inclusive. ... Is it perhaps imperialistic if we demand land and soil for all our countrymen?"[85] That was ten days after he explicated the Nazi Party program for its first anniversary, its Point 3 being: "We demand land and soil (colonies) for the nourishment of our people and settlement of our surplus population."[86] At a Party meeting the following 31 May he declared in a speech entitled "Versailles and the German Worker" (as reported in outline by the Party newspaper) that Germany in 1914 was catching up with England in foreign trade and that "in this fact lies the inner cause of the outbreak of the war." From this tired disclosure[87] he went on: "There are only three ways for a dynamic people to preserve itself insofar as it does not want to become more of a plaything than ever of the other rising nations by deliberately restricting births. Colonization. Germany came too late and found no room left in the world to discharge its excess vitality. Emigration. What people wants to give its children away as cultural fertilizer for other countries? As the German people was deprived of these first two possibilities, it set about creating a means of survival by developing industry and exporting goods." This said, he served up one of his favorite old propaganda themes—with a new twist. That old theme was "the truly boundless humanity" of Germany's *Diktat* to Soviet Russia at Brest-Litovsk in early 1918 as against "the inhuman cruelty" of the Allies' *Diktat* to Germany at Versailles a year later.[88] The new twist was anomalous: "Under the peace settlement with Russia, Germany's nourishment as well as the existence of work were to be supplied through *the acquisition of land and soil*, through raw materials imports and friendly relations between the two countries. Versailles: the opposite. Rape of the territories that assured Germany's nourishment. . . ."[89] That punch line about land and soil checks with an outline by Hitler for a similar speech with a similar title, "Workers and Peace Treaties": "Brest-Litovsk was to assure German people's nourishment through I. soil II. securing of raw materials for industry and trade."[90] Behind that punch line lay—preformulated—Hitler's stock oratorical buildup of the late 1920s to his call for acquiring "living space" in eastern Europe for Germany's human overflow: the elimination of the alternatives of birth control, emigration, overseas colonies, and increased industrial trade.[91] From his later message he dropped that "existence of work" invoked on 31 May 1921—it was merely a courtesy to his title "Versailles and the German Worker"—and with it those "raw materials imports and friendly relations" (which he nonetheless actualized for a brief spell under the Germano-Soviet Pact of 1939–1941). His later conclusion was all but reached in that speech outline headed "Workers and Peace Treaties": "German colonization: 8th–13th centuries. First the eastern march, then the northeastern march. Is our people fit for that? Prerequisite: *power*."[92] It was reached by late December 1922, when he revealed his program for a German dictatorship to a confidant of Chancellor Cuno: ". . . Abroad, Germany would have to go over to a purely

48

continental policy, avoiding any damage to British interests. The breakup of Russia with England's help should be attempted. Russia would provide enough land for German settlers and a broad field of activity for German industry. Then England would not butt in when we settle with France."[93] The derivation of this policy from Germany's eastern conquest of 1917–1918 was no longer showing. It remained to be covered over in *Mein Kampf* when Hitler asserted in expounding the need to expand the "motherland" eastward: "In this we National Socialists consciously put an end to the course of Germany's prewar foreign policy. We pick up where Germany left off six centuries ago."[94] Unconsciously it was more like six years.

In *Mein Kampf* Hitler called his old repertory piece vindicating Brest-Litovsk against Versailles one of the two "very most important" speeches of his "agitational" beginnings, both of which he delivered "in ever new versions" that incorporated "running," "living" corrections read off his "listeners' faces."[95] The other such speech refuted "that downright monstrous lie"[96] about German war guilt. Germany had no more started or wanted the war, he insisted, than Germany had been acquisitive or brutal at Brest-Litovsk. The point of both these companion speeches was that the defeat was undeserved and hence unacceptable. Yet that same *Mein Kampf* contained Hitler's first public bid to launch a new war for seizing land in the east to be ruthlessly Germanized. This incongruity marked a turning from unconscious denial toward unconscious repetition with a vengeance.

With the war that Hitler proposed to wage for Germany—he called it a "struggle for existence" which "originates with the people itself"[97]—he was responding unawares to a need he dimly sensed for Germany to work through the agonizing past a second time the way a traumatized individual does. With his aim of infusing one will into Germans individually went his claim to have elicited that one will from them collectively. As aspirant dictator he professed to heed only "the natural inner will of the people" as against "public opinion," which, he affirmed, "can never be identified with the people's will proper. . . . The more public an opinion is," he added, "the less it corresponds to the real inner will of the people."[98] Later, as dictator, he manipulated "public opinion" by way of implementing the people's "inner will."[99] Even so, he repeatedly invoked a mystic bond with the people during his years of power. Heedless of logic, he declaimed: "I have grown out of the people, I have stayed in the people, I return to the people," and "that is the source of my entire power."[100] The truth to this began just where logic left off. Already in his political incunabula he could establish total rapport with an audience of thousands addressed as a nucleus of the nation at large. His speeches would gradually key up listeners into a single, taut sensibility that seemed to be prompting him, and it took a practiced observer to keep what he said conscious.[101] He would start off a speech, remarked a contemporary, by sounding out an audience "with instruments of various metals and various weights. When a resonance issues from the depths ... the masses have given him the pitch."[102] More pointed was a characterization of him in an anonymous postmortem as the "accumulator of the national wrath over the lost war."[103] His political calling came from a personal breakdown synchronic with the national breakdown—a gas trauma within the national shock of defeat. Both his political messages resonated with this national shock. The first was a myth designed to explain the defeat away, dashed with "devilry"[104] to conjure it away and so restore German dominion to its extent of August 1918. The second, cast as thoroughgoing realpolitik, was at once a critique of Wilhelmian overreaching and a program for reaching even farther in a pretended new departure that was none. Unconsciously, the thrust of the second was to repeat the fumbled Wilhelmian play for world power, while the thrust of the first was to repeat the futile surgery and counterproductive poisoning of 1907. And in the second repeat, when it came, liberties were taken with the original experience that paralleled those taken in the first. The bogged down offensive in Flanders and eventual breakthrough in Russia were transposed in World War I-bis.[105] Efforts to "turn fate" prolonged the new war to the bitter end after the scheme to serialize the old war had become a dead letter. Indeed, the hopeless struggle to fend off the forced outcome the second time around was also the means whereby that hopelessness was driven home with gruesome finality.[106] But the most conspicuous liberty taken with the bygone war as Hitler refought it for Germany was just this tendency to carry it to a full finish—to fashion "a new war a hundred times more dreadful and cruel that will complete what the old one started."[107] In the process, the defeat was shown to be Germany's due—materially in that every potential scapegoat was savagely sacrificed in advance,[108] and morally in that every crime charged and overcharged to Wilhelmian Germany by the victors of 1918 was committed and overcommitted by Hitlerian Germany: authoritarianism, militarism, planned aggression, deceitfulness, brutality in conquest, "acts of inhumanity, spoliation, and desolation" (thus Wilson in October 1918).[109] And the defeat was made total, final, indisputable, in a foregone conclusion corresponding to Hitler's impassioned slogan: "Never again a November 1918!"[110]

The Hitlerian replay remained just that through all these variations on the original. Hitler's post-Putsch title to leadership, his program for that replay, was on the surface a program for guarding against one. Thus he clung to that program even after September 1939—unrealistically until the invasion of Russia, then downright absurdly.[111] The replay was the great hazard he was seemingly set on avoiding, the dread fate that is conjured up in the process of being warded off and with a feeling that every move that way is forced.[112] This is precisely the traumatic syndrome. The former League of Nations High Commissioner in Danzig, Carl J. Burckhardt, caught its mood in a reflection on his futile efforts to mediate between the western powers and Hitler in August 1939: "The German word 'fate' [Verhängnis] is a very expressive word. It conveys the idea of a chain reaction which, once set off, can no longer be halted. Paradoxically, the mechanical process under way worked through Hitler's decisions. Running its course outside of his will, it became a seeming act of that will itself. Remarkable was his fixed vision—the set goals of his dream. Quite incomprehensibly, he always announced straight off what after many detours, reverses, and false departures he then did actually wind up doing. And it is not far out to

51

assume that the insatiable hate in him linked up in the unconscious part of his being with the concealed, yet ever-present certainty that awaiting him at the end was the most dreadful failure and a personal demise such as was in fact reserved for him in the Reich Chancellery on 30 April 1945."[113] That "ever-present certainty" emerged from concealment once in the winter following the fall of Poland as Hitler was railing against foreign journalism as Jewish. "For almost fifteen years this propaganda was made against us," he cried. "My old Party comrades, you remember this propaganda! It's the same words and the same phrases; yes, if we look more closely, even the same faces and the same dialect! I dealt with these people as a solitary unknown who drew a handful of men around him. For fifteen years I dealt with these people, and today Germany is the greatest world power." This outburst of hubris brought on the ironic prophesy: "It is not true that age of itself makes one wise. Age does not make the blind see either. But he who once already *was* stricken with blindness *is* so now too. But he who *is* stricken with blindness, him would the gods destroy."[114]

A huge question has been tacitly reserved about the Germans' felt need to lose World War I over again. Did that need exist outside of Hitler's psychic system? The question can be approached only through a consideration of the precedent that dominated Hitler's experience of sensing and supplying Germany's traumatic need. This precedent was his experience of a traumatic need of his mother's that he was literally born to meet.

III

THE LOUD-SPEAKER

He is the loud-speaker which magnifies the inaudible whispers of the German soul until they can be heard by the German's conscious ear. He is the first man to tell every German what he has been thinking and feeling all along in his unconscious about German fate, especially since the defeat in the world war.

CARL G. JUNG, October 1938.[1]

He does not dominate the minds of millions, his mind belongs to them.

KONRAD HEIDEN.[2]

Adolf Hitler's mother, Klara Pölzl, was born of peasant stock in Austria's Waldviertel on 12 August 1860. Her marriage on 7 January 1885 required a papal dispensation because on paper the groom, imperious Imperial customs inspector Alois Hitler, was her second cousin. Alois was born on 6 July 1837, also in the Waldviertel, to an unknown father and Anna Maria Schicklgruber, an unwed peasant's daughter aged forty-two. Anna Maria married a mill worker named Johann Georg Hiedler in 1842, and Alois was raised afterward by Johann Georg's elder brother, Johann Nepomuk, a peasant proprietor with three daughters slightly older than Alois. The oldest, Johanna, became Klara's mother. In 1876, well after his mother and stepfather had died, Alois had himself legitimated in his stepfather's name at Johann Nepomuk's instigation, apparently for the sake of an inheritance. Oral tradition has it that about then Klara became a member of Alois's busy household in Braunau am Inn on the Bavarian border. Alois's first wife, who was fourteen years his senior, died

53

separated from him and childless in 1883. He thereupon married a housemate just under Klara's age, who by then had one child by him and was expecting another. A further mistress and illegitimate child are known.[3] The memoir involving Klara that goes back farthest is one dictated in 1940 by Alois's cook of 1884 and 1885: it incidentally shows Klara living with "Uncle" and "often" visiting his second wife, then laid up with tuberculosis in the country nearby.[4] Alois was again widowed on 10 August 1884. It must have been just afterward that Klara conceived her first child, born on 17 May 1885, for the chance that the gestation exceeded that 280-day interval is well under one in ten.[5] Alois, who had kept Klara, lacked the necessary concern and restraint to have kept her childless until then by the only effective contraception known in those parts, *coitus interruptus*. The indication is that Klara's fertility had been blocked spontaneously until her last rival was eliminated, then unblocked overnight.[6]

Her fertility was blocked again in the aftermath of her fourth delivery, that of Adolf on 20 April 1889. Of her six deliveries in all, five were spaced closely, in strict accordance with the norm for their time and place. But the one following Adolf's birth was some forty-and-a-half months late.[7] This oddity is unique in scale for a settled marriage such as hers with aging Alois proved to be. Behind it lay the loss of her three previous children by quick turns from "infant diseases"[8] just after the third birth and within forty-and-a-half months of the first conception. No mother could escape the traumatic effect of such a loss, and Klara Hitler the less since her two stepchildren survived the diphtheria epidemic responsible for at least two of her own children's deaths. Twenty years later Kubizek observed "the muted sorrow that ... spoke out of her features": it was, he discovered, due to the "fearful trials" of her young motherhood. "Whenever I saw her," he later related, "I felt ... compassion and the need to do something for her."[9] Such a blow of fate as befell Klara Hitler is unconsciously felt as a punishment. And unconsciously a punishment entails guilt, for which Klara Hitler had ample grounds: she had married "Uncle" after having

54

waited out the deaths of his two previous wives and then having begun her childbearing with unseemly promptitude. She conceived Adolf on schedule next—but when she was due to conceive again, she relived her traumatic maternal experience instead by not having (suppressing) children for an equal stretch of time. And she lavishly overprotected and overindulged Adolf in the process as if thereby to repair her tragic loss. She later remarked that "she had lived in continual worry lest she lose him." So Kubizek recollected, adding that this worry only "ended with her death." [10] Her unconscious reliving fed into her anxious pampering, so that Adolf drank in the maternal trauma with his mother's milk. [11] He was given, and took, the breast long and lustily enough to be fixated on it at the stage of oral aggression that follows teething. Thence the regular payoff of his later rounds of exertion for Germany: when he would sink into blissful contentedness gorging himself with sweets after routine runs at the front, or would work himself into a trancelike rapture through fierce oratory day after day in his political infancy. This was a nursling's regalement revived, and not a deprived nursling's hankering. But breastfeeding was rare and then exceedingly brief in the vicinity of Braunau. [12] Also, the chronology rules out any lengthy suckling by Klara of her earlier children. She was herself the seventh of eleven children, whose dates argue lengthier nursing, especially in her own case. [13] With Adolf she may have reverted to her mother's practice or acted on information then spreading about the benefits of breastfeeding. [14] Either way she overcompensated for her earlier omission.

Klara Hitler's breast cancer meets all the specifications for a psychogenic factor yet suggested by medical researchers. In one close reckoning, breast cancer requires "a serious separation experience" in childhood and a similar one "in the six-month to five-year period preceding the manifestation of the malignancy." [15] Klara lost two brothers and a sister successively in 1,491 days beginning when she was thirty-two months old; she lost father, husband, and mother successively in the 1,491 days ending on 6 February 1906. Even so, if her breast cancer was meaningful it meant self-punishment, with her traumatic loss of

55

her three children (beginning just midway between those other two triple losses[16]) as the big "separation experience" behind it —twice removed. Behind it once removed was her reliving of that traumatic loss through her nursing symbiosis with infant Adolf. This reliving was culpable several times over. To begin with, breastfeeding was naughty in the Hitlers' neck of the woods. Just across the border from Braunau an enumerator for an official Bavarian inquiry on breastfeeding noted in 1905: "Many a mother believed that to confess she was suckling her child herself was something to be ashamed of and admitted the performance of this duty only after repeated questioning and then with blushing."[17] Worse, the nursing bond between Klara and Adolf was intensified and perpetuated, in fact and then in reciprocal fancy, beyond all normal limits. Still worse, through this breast-and-mouth incest Klara was using and abusing Adolf for her traumatic reliving. She must have felt how she was holding back his development in her protective, possessive, permissive embrace. "The spoiled mother's darling, the fellow who knows that things will never go wrong for him: he will never confront life like someone who is thrown back upon himself," Hitler later remarked.[18] And worst of all, in this process she deserted her husband emotionally even as she failed him procreatively. A decade later his death restored her old twosome with Adolf, then entering adolescence. A new spell of overmothering ensued for her under the sign of duty. Through her established associative channels it set the guilty breast tingling under her widow's robes. This second round of tender, fretful, guilt-ridden clinging to her baby boy ("But for me he is so young!" she would protest as he was approaching nineteen[19]) issued into a self-punitive breast cancer at the point where the first round had ended in a pregnancy. For the onset of the cancer must be dated after her visit to Bloch—presumably for a checkup—on 3 January 1906, the third anniversary of Alois's death. It would fall in mid-May 1906 if this reliving of a reliving was likewise of the exact same length as the original traumatic experience. That was just when Adolf was off in Vienna by himself for a few weeks' sightseeing, his first time that far from his mother. His next time was when

56

he took the art test at the Academy and her condition plummeted in his absence. By then the guilty breast had been removed—to no avail. The son ended up nursing the mother night and day while having medication applied that ate into where the breast had been.

The symbiosis with his traumatized mother that dominated his infancy was a formative experience that Hitler could never outgrow. His emotional development was on the whole arrested at his later nursing that following teething. From this aggressive orality flowed his frenzied tirades no less than his craving for sweets—or his phobias (bedeviled cravings) against tobacco, then alcohol, and later meat as well.[20] Thence too issued the lust to conquer and assimilate in brutal fashion, which drove him forward to recover the breast-fed bliss of a fledgling self dissolving into the world it imbibes. His deep sense of special election and protection came from his nutrient mother's oversolicitude and overindulgence as she used him to repair—and indeed fail to repair—the loss she was unconsciously reliving. His mission, hallucinated in Pasewalk, of repairing Germany's loss threw back to that mission of repairing his mother's loss. So he was as if reborn in Pasewalk. As he declared on revisiting there in 1932, "I took my life back as a gift of Providence."[21] Undaunted in his political limbo of the latter 1920s, he styled himself "a man . . . whom Providence . . . has destined to be the leader."[22] He added, on the last anniversary of his Pasewalk relapse before taking power: "I also have the conviction and the secure feeling that nothing can harm me, because I know that I have been appointed by Providence to fulfill my task."[23] By way of fulfilling his task he recreated his infantile situation, with Germany in his mother's place. He made himself into Germany's chosen means of reliving a previous traumatic reverse in a futile effort to reverse it. And he did so with his mouth opened on Germany— through "the violence of oratory," as he put it.[24] As dictator (the very term spells oral aggression raised to the highest power) he intoned the symbiosis in scriptural accents: "Whatever you are, you are through me," he told his followers, "and whatever I am, I am only through you alone."[25] He talked, or indeed screamed, his way to that new symbiosis. "Stop his mouth and you destroy his drawing power": this was the logic of the temporary prohibitions leveled against his speaking in most German states after he served his term for the Putsch.[26] In haranguing a mass audience he would work himself into a crescendo of fury, foaming at the lips—an oral-sadistic orgasm.[27] He had presumably felt it as an abandonment, a betrayal, when his privileged position collapsed with his mother's new pregnancy—and these deathly feelings revived in him against Providence and Germany respectively when his Putsch collapsed in 1923 and when his Reich collapsed in 1945. The failed Putsch left him with a "very severe traumatic neurosis," as diagnosed by the prison doctor.[28] It also turned him back into a spoiled baby crossed: in his first interrogations "he was fresh at times and for the rest would break into crying fits."[29] Meanwhile he tried to starve himself to death; next he insisted that the food offered him was poisoned; finally he fed himself fat with sweets from his "motherly lady friends" while he talked himself out of this oral crisis at his trial.[30]

It was then that he began publicizing his new aim of eastern conquest.[31] The single reason he gave for that aim from the time it germinated in 1921, that the "Germanic mother" could not feed her children adequately,[32] expressed his mother's maternal trauma as he had absorbed it through her compensatory overfeeding of him. But the aim itself expressed his oral-aggressive side of that absorbing. He said as much when he asked: "How can we feed the nation?" then answered: "We either export people or goods, or else we strive to adjust land and soil to population. Nature lays this possibility at every living creature's cradle. That is the self-preservative instinct. The child does not ask, when it drinks, whether the mother's breast is being tortured. Hunger and love are healthy instincts."[33] Universalizing his oral-aggressive input into his eastern course of conquest, he called all history a fight for feeding ground.[34] And he projected the eastern land grab beyond itself to world conquest—half circle back to his all-enfolding ecstasy at the breast.

It has already been shown that the conquest of feeding ground

Hitler called for was for him unconsciously the lost eastern conquest of 1917–1918.[35] But now a second, closer look is needed.

In an address to the Party on 31 May 1921 Hitler ruled out birth control, emigration, and industrialization to cope with Germany's human increase and praised the short-lived Brest-Litovsk settlement for having provided the additional land and soil that Germany needed. By then he had long since internationalized the Jewish peril and identified Jewry with Bolshevism.[36] Yet on 12 April 1922, after an hour's raging against the Judeo-Bolshevik world peril, he declared: "There are only two possibilities in Germany! . . . Either victory of the Aryan side, or its destruction and victory of the Jews."[37] He developed this same theme in a memorandum of 22 October 1922 on building up the Party: "What is involved here is not winning a majority or even so-called political power. What is involved is a life-and-death struggle between two world views that cannot coexist. Their clash will leave only victors and victims. This conception has become second nature to Marxism (witness Russia). A victory of the Marxist idea means the total extermination of its opponents. This basic sense of the struggle has not yet been grasped on the so-called bourgeois side, where the intractable resolve that such awareness would bring with it is consequently lacking. So the brutal power colossus on the one side is faced by, in part, most deplorable inadequacy on the other side, where the consciousness of a fight to the death is altogether lacking."[38] Such a "life-and-death struggle between two world views" was the logical grounding for the scheme Hitler hatched of destroying Soviet Russia with England's help. Conversely, logic pushed for carrying that "fight to the death" from German to Russian soil. If the Jews were a deadly international danger with their power center in Russia, that danger could not be met within Germany's borders alone. By destroying Jewish power inside Germany alone, Germans would only incite Jewry to revenge. "To grasp the evil by the roots and eradicate it to the core"[39] meant moving on Moscow.

At Hitler's maiden mention of his eastern scheme, as reported by Cuno's confidant in late December 1922, the anti-Bolshevik grounding for it lay close to hand. "With the suppression of Bolshevism in Germany," Hitler began, "iron-fisted dictatorship must rule."[40] But then, in expounding the scheme, he reverted to his problematical "land and soil" premise of nineteen months earlier. Subsequently he buttressed this premise by considerations of the right of Germans to grow at others' expense. He promoted the eastern conquest on this basis beginning in *Mein Kampf*—routinely until a few weeks after the Nazis' electoral leap forward of September 1930, then guardedly in public, and yet quite starkly again in his political and military councils after his accession. To Reichswehr commanders on 3 February 1933, after four days in office, he foretold "the conquest of new living space in the east and its ruthless Germanization."[41] On 28 February 1934, before roughly the same group enlarged by SA and SS leaders, he pointed ahead to "creating living space" for Germany in the east.[42] On 5 November 1937 he briefed his five top political and military assistants on his contingency planning "to solve the German space problem."[43] In a military conference of 23 May 1939 he held forth about "expanding our living space in the east and securing our nourishment."[44] And all along he kept the racial-ideological (anti-Semitic, anti-Communist) motive for war against Soviet Russia to himself—or almost. In *Mein Kampf* he cited Judeo-Bolshevism's mortal designs on Germany only as the last of many reasons for Germany not to ally with Soviet Russia.[45] In his secret book of 1928 he merely observed in an extraneous context that, populous as it was, the Soviet Union was not a military, but only an ideological, menace.[46] In his memorandum of August 1936 initiating economic mobilization, he cited separately the threat from international Jewry based in Russia and Germany's need of more living space for a "definitive solution" of its economic problems.[47] The Anti-Comintern Pact that Germany concluded with Japan in November 1936 and with Italy a year later carried a hint of secret aggressive designs. In reality it was spineless: the sham mutual defense was merely propaganda to justify German rearmament.[48] But the preliminaries did prompt Hitler to remark to the Japanese negotiators in June 1936 that he had "always seen Europe's sole salvation in

60

the uncompromising fight against Communism," and in July 1936 that the Bolshevik threat could be met only by a dismember- ment of the Soviet Union.[49] On 2 June 1940, with France falling, Hitler told an army headquarters group in Belgium that he expected a "reasonable peace settlement" with Britain that would free him "at last" for his "great and proper task: the showdown with Bolshevism."[50] Only when Barbarossa was mounted, however, did Hitler reopen in full that parenthesis of 22 October 1922—"(witness Russia)"—which had followed his assertion that the fight against Bolshevism was a "life-and-death struggle between two world views." On 30 March 1941, in handing down Barbarossa to 200–250 assembled army commanders, he called the upcoming eastern war "a struggle of two world views against each other" and pursued: "The struggle must be waged against the poison of decomposition. . . . What is involved is a struggle of annihilation."[51] Then, while he ordered the army to kill captured Communist officials (the "Commissar Order"), Heydrich instructed his SS henchmen that "eastern Jewry is the intellectual reservoir of Bolshevism and in the Führer's view must therefore be annihilated."[52] With the start of the invasion, secret instructions went out to the press to switch its tack to "the annihilation of Bolshevism" and some days later to the link between Bolshevism and Jewry.[53] Living space had taken second place.

The immediate source of Hitler's "feeding ground" rationale for repeating Germany's eastern conquest of 1917–1918 was that conquest itself, specifically the establishment of a satellite Ukraine from which a starving Germany expected bread that never came.[54] He could even justify his new war as necessary to prevent that starvation from recurring in a new war[55]—truly an argument from hunger. (Fittingly, his own attempt to exploit the Ukraine was to prove more counterproductive than Ludendorff's of 1917–1918.[56]) Hunger as a military and political weapon appears to have been the opening theme, filling two out of eleven pages, of his outline for "Workers and Peace Treaties," the speech resembling his "Versailles and the German Worker" of 31 May 1921.[57] In both speeches the "land and soil" gained and then lost in 1917–1918 was his basis for deploring the outcome of the last war in terms that were to carry over into his pitch for the next war. His choice of that basis appears to have been prompted by Ludendorff, whom he first met only weeks or even days before that 31 May and who had stipulated in his directives for Brest-Litovsk: "Annexation of Lithuania and the Courland, including Riga and the islands, as we need more land for our people's nourishment."[58] But the choice was governed by his nursing complex. For his mother's trauma of loss, on which that complex centered, had presensitized him to Germany's trauma of loss primarily in its alimentary aspect. His coverup for Germany's reliving—the proposal to conquer feeding ground—threw back to his nursing also in that his nursing had been his mother's coverup for her reliving. He updated accordingly his own, impassioned input into that coverup, his oral aggression. Even so, the foregone conclusion from his "land and soil" premises of 31 May 1921 took some nineteen months to follow in its established eastward direction. And by the time it did follow, in December 1922, he had developed a likelier grounding for that eastern reconquest, a racial-ideological grounding informed by his trauma of 1907: the fight to the death with Judeo-Bolshevism operating from Moscow. He could barely contain this fight within Germany's borders, as when he declared in 1923: "It will be bigger than the World War. It will be fought out on German soil for the whole world."[59] Yet he missed all his own cues for projecting it beyond Germany's borders. Thus on 21 April 1922 he exclaimed, with reference to the Germano-Soviet treaty newly concluded at Rapallo: "What can help? Not to negotiate with Russia's despoilers, but"—of all things—"to summon the Russian nation to cast off its torturers so that we can then draw closer to it."[60] He did not so much as add the racial-ideological argument to the "land and soil" one when he came to publicize and elaborate his case for conquering Soviet Russia—not even in 1925–1926 to argue down the Nazi partisans of a Soviet alliance then in revolt against his policies. "Such an alliance," he objected, "would entail the immediate Bolshevization of Germany and is thus to be rejected as national suicide"; the Nazis' business was rather "to see to it that we obtain enough land and soil to nourish every compatriot, and that means embarking on easterly colonization as in the Middle Ages," the more since "only a farsighted colonial policy, not in other continents but in Europe, on our eastern borders, will enable our race to recuperate."[61] For all this singleminded territorializing, he did preformulate in 1922 the racial-ideological grounding for the war on Russia in the very terms in which he formulated it in 1941.[62] More, by 1928 he had forged a doctrinal link between this latent alternative argument for the war on Russia and the argument from Germany's need for "living space": the conception of the Jews as nonterritorial parasites with whose ascendancy, spelled Bolshevism, the territorial competition of virile peoples, namely history, would cease.[63] This doctrinal link, the conclusion of his unfinished, unpublished book of 1928, was even anticipated by 1923 (with statelessness in lieu of nonterritoriality) in an outline for a book he never wrote.[64]

Why did Hitler work out an alternative, racial-ideological reason for that eastern war, and take pains to square it with his original, territorial reason, only to keep it to himself while he solicited and achieved dictatorial power over Germany for the express purpose of waging that war? The answer begins, and almost ends, with a reminder that the reason so long withheld came of his own trauma of 1907 and not Germany's of 1918—that it was his reason and not his constituency's. The argument from "land and soil" spoke to Germany's traumatic purposes as he was programmed to sense and serve them in nursing his mother's trauma at his mother's breast. His racial-ideological argument was a device for according Germany's traumatic purposes with his own derived from 1907. Not with his nursling's purposes: these he indulged through his rough thrust for feeding ground along the German traumatic line. That thrust enabled him in due course to recreate his nursing symbiosis vicariously with a traumatized Germany in his mother's place. He met his own traumatic need concurrently through his global thrust against the Jew. Of the two, his traumatic thrust was much the stronger: it encroached on his oral-aggressive one sub rosa from the start, and at length confidentially in remarks to Japanese

63

negotiators, before prevailing outright once Barbarossa was mounted. Joseph Goebbels gave German journalists their first, dark hint of it when he told them in secret on 5 April 1940: "Today we are carrying out in Europe the same revolution that we carried out on a smaller scale in Germany." That sprang the national confines of the racial-ideological fight to the death. And Goebbels added: "Today we say 'living space.' Everyone can make of that what he wants. We shall know what we mean by it when the time comes."[65]

Why, rather than simply extend his projected racial-ideological showdown eastward beginning in 1921–1922, did Hitler bill the proposed reconquest of Soviet Russia as a war for feeding ground? Tracing this new, power-political line cost him the more trouble since he had to coordinate it with his old, racial-ideological line both intellectually and psychologically. Its overriding value to him was that through it he aligned the new war on the old one, taking off from the lost eastern conquest of 1917–1918. He chose the concept of feeding ground as a battle cry because it evoked that eastern conquest as perceived by the Germans in its time. He chose it also because his mother's trauma was the prototype of Germany's for him, and she had breastfed him out of her trauma to the point of fixation and beyond. But he did not need the call for feeding ground to cry for the breast politically; this he had done from 1919 on in the undertone of his call to remove the Jew. The world all his, like a sated suckling's, was the goal implied by his universalizing of the Jewish peril and personalizing of the power required to remove it. Indeed, the trauma animating him against Jewry came of his loving violence of 1907 against the guilty mother breast, or rather against its cancerous residue. His thrust against Jewry followed on the same attunement to the 1918 calamity, and the same mandate hallucinated in Pasewalk, as did his later drive for land and soil. And it took some straining to evoke Ludendorff's lost eastern victory, and with it the 1918 calamity, through agrarian terms alone, such as "land and soil." Thence the later variant, and at length substitute, "living space" or just "space," which spoke more to the German sense of a national encirclement broken for a brief, dizzying moment in 1917–1918.[66] "Living space" was, then, only secondarily an outlet for Hitler's orality. First and last it was his answer to the unconscious national need to turn from denying the defeat to reliving it. He registered this need, and prepared his programmatic response, early. After December 1922 there followed nearly another year's agitation against the Jew as the culprit behind the defeat and its consequences, then his abortive Putsch and crisis of abandonment by Germany, before he released his new, power-political message to the public. And he released it as if he were coming to it rationally step by step, from his courtroom orations through a magazine article to Mein Kampf.[67] He responded to Germany's need, as originally to his mother's, for his own sake. His own reason for the new eastern war was to kill Jews. This reason surfaced as the way to that war was clearing, and edged out the German reason as he handed down the marching orders.

Now to the crucial point. Between 31 May 1921 and late December 1922, even as Hitler was projecting the past, lost conquest of feeding ground from Soviet Russia into the future, he supplied that proposed reconquest with an alternative, racial-ideological reason that was to emerge as his preferred reason for it when, after two decades, he was ready and able to proceed. It follows that through his program for world dominion featuring that reconquest—a program related to the lost war of 1914–1918 like the conscious expression of an unconscious design to relive the loss—he was responding to a collective German trauma that was real in its own right, beyond his mental universe. For his personal, favored premises for the new eastern venture were not the ones he used to promote it, the arguments from land and soil linking it to the old eastern exploit; rather, they were the racial-ideological premises he developed betweentimes, then held in abeyance until he could draw the easterly conclusion in deeds as well as words. He did produce his arguments from land and soil out of his nursling's posture as his mother's instrument for working through a trauma of loss. This was both because he aspired to recreate that privileged instrumentality with Germany in his mother's stead and because that formative relationship, persisting unconsciously, was what alerted him to the German traumatic need and enabled him to absorb it open-mouthed as he discoursed on Brest-Litovsk in continual, intensive, vital interchange with his mass audiences. But had his nursling's nostalgia suggested to him a German traumatic need where there was none, his preferred reason for the war to meet that need would have been the one imbued with his nursling's libido. And in that case he would not have come up with an alternative, racial-ideological reason relatively removed from his nursing complex, held it in abeyance through two decades of promoting and preparing that war, then overwritten the land and soil reason with it when the way to that war finally lay open before him. Nor did he stand so long on his land and soil premises, and on those alone, from calculation. He devised and adopted them even while, by his agitation along the racial-ideological line, he was building up a following in Bavaria sufficient, as he thought, for him to launch a "national revolution" meant to spread overnight from Munich to Berlin on 8–9 November 1923. Conversely, his representations of 31 May 1921 about the feeding ground won and lost in eastern Europe in 1917–1918 left no discoverable impression with his listeners, and his call of the late 1920s for conquering feeding ground in eastern Europe met first with strong resistance in the Party, then with surface incomprehension and indifference among Germans at large.[68] As for the British, on whose favor his program turned, he adopted precisely the other, anti-Comintern line when he turned opportunistic toward them in 1936–1937.

It has been shown that the stimulus for Hitler's expansionist program came to him unconsciously from outside himself—from a German trauma of defeat dated 1918. The German trauma of defeat has thus been evidenced indirectly—through Hitler registering it and reacting. That evidence counts. Many a physical entity is first known, or known only, by inference from its presumed effects. (Helium was first known from spectral lines in the sun; a venerable subatomic particle, the neutrino, is still known only from an apparent disappearance of energy in nuclear de-

66

cay.) But now the question arises of a direct approach to the German trauma. Before it can be pursued, though, a further consideration remains to complete the picture. This is that Hitler's expansionist program was the secret of his success in Germany. The simple, salient facts are these. Beginning in 1925 Hitler solicited dictatorial power from Germany for the declared purpose of applying that program, unique in Weimar politics, and for no other purpose except to remove the Jew—his controlling purpose, which, however, he outwardly subordinated to German expansion until further notice, proposing to wipe out the Jewish poison in order to restore German strength for that new external push. And Germany obliged him. His following mushroomed, resistance right, left, and center collapsed before him, and within ten years absolute power over Germany was his.

It is true that other Nazis, national and local, enunciated other aims.[69] But Hitler never left off reminding all concerned that the organic principle of his Party as reconstituted in 1925 was "Leader command, we follow," that its sole reason for existing was to extend that principle to all Germany in the form of "one Reich, one People, one Leader," and that if he did not always call the tune it was only because he did not always care to. Whenever he saw fit to condemn a given tendency within his Party or later his Reich, allegiance against it was his; its proponents knuckled under, sometimes even jubilantly. The Party itself did hold attractions in the line of camaraderie, pageantry, marching, and violence,[70] but all in a cause from which they could never be fully disassociated—to which indeed their appeal was integral. In 1925 Hitler told regional Party leaders that "drill" was needed (or again "unity, authority, and drill") for "an army of warriors of the new world view" to triumph over the leveling, debilitating Weimar system.[71] Nazi militancy and the Nazi alternative to parliamentarianism—"Subordinate!"[72]—carried forward the spirit of the national battle of 1914–1918. The projected "folk community," so seductive to Germans of Hitler's day, updated "the mystic all-rank communion of the trenches"[73] or "the 'ideas of 1914' and the ideology of trench warfare, the feeling aroused by propaganda and self-deception that the war

67

had torn up all class lines and social barriers forever."[74] Hitlerism was that very feeling rearoused. "In kindling the national fighting spirit and refashioning first the Party, then the state and society, into an all-inclusive fighting community, National Socialism unfolded its true force and skill.... War was in this more than a mere pragmatic means. National Socialism therewith returned to itself, so to say—back to its proper element."[75]

It is also true that Hitler's foreign aims won little clear understanding, let alone consequent acceptance, from Germans individually.[76] He did call for the conquest of "living space" baldly enough throughout Germany beginning in 1927–1928, as the speaking bans imposed on him regionally after he left Landsberg were lifted one by one. His call was well reported too. To illustrate at random: the local press in Dingolfing summarized point for point a stock speech he delivered there on 30 September 1928, culminating in the "power concept, to which the German people must rally, for life is combat and will remain so as long as the world lasts. Without combat, no victory. There is only one right in this world, and that right is might. There is only one aim: honor, freedom, and bread for the German people. And the way to this is combat. Therefore the German people should close ranks to become a power factor in world history fit to gain the feeding ground necessary for its growth."[77] Again, the folkic weekly *Deutscher Michl* gave just as straight a synopsis of his speech of 23 October 1928 in Augsburg: "The law of force will always determine a people's chance to survive.... The German people have more space and soil coming. Therefore they must solve their land problem to assure their nutrition.... Only through combat will the German people rise again. That is our wish and aim."[78] No jaws dropped when he forecast that combat to Reichswehr chiefs in closed sessions hard upon his accession.[79] Even so, when he briefed his foreign minister, his war minister, and the heads of the army, navy, and air force on 5 November 1937 on the practicalities of "gaining a larger living space,"[80] he nonplussed at least four of the five. The fifth, air force chief Hermann Göring, himself stood for a no-risk power play in central Europe.[81] Joachim von Ribbentrop, who took over

68

shortly thereafter as foreign minister, saw England as the mortal enemy.[82] Propaganda minister Joseph Goebbels was at heart for an understanding with the Soviets against the West—openly so at the start and finish of his Nazi career.[83] Farther afield, SS chief Heinrich Himmler drifted from Ribbentrop's side to undercover advances toward America in 1944–1945.[84] Nazi ideologue Alfred Rosenberg saw the colonization of Europe as the terminal stage of German expansion.[85] Of Hitler's collaborators however fanatical, one at most, financier Hjalmar Schacht, grasped his foreign program with full clarity.[86] And none of them heeded it except Hess when Hess went mad. Hitler's second in command of the Party, Rudolf Hess, crossed the Channel in the eleventh hour before Barbarossa to negotiate on Hitler's terms of guaranteeing the British Empire in return for a free hand in continental Europe, whereupon Hitler repudiated him in an animal rage.[87] Hess's case dramatizes the point that Hitler's program was not meant for implementation. It was a reworking of World War I that Hitler made it his business to prove unworkable. The obsolete Wilhelmian language of world power or ruin[88] was respoken in Hitler's raucous accents out of the national trauma of 1918. At that aural frequency, "living space" signified the eastern conquest of 1917–1918 and stirred associated visions of German continental sufficiency and invulnerability in the unequal struggle for equality with England—of a barbed-wired German continental *Grossraum*. The program sounded at that pitch "did not penetrate the consciousness of the German public":[89] it penetrated deeper.

It is true too—indeed it is crucial—that Hitler took to mincing his public words about living space soon after the Nazis' great leap forward in the national elections of 14 September 1930.[90] *Mein Kampf* remained in full force nonetheless and was sold ever harder. Its expansionism came across sufficiently for the joke to be whispered around Germany, following the Germano-Soviet Pact, that Hitler gave Molotov a copy with deletions in his own hand.[91] Hitler did also re-echo his old cries for feeding ground sparingly, but tellingly, after September 1930. On 8 November 1930 he spoke of the Germans' need to expand their "living space," if not their "export trade," by the "use of force"; [92] five days later he dropped that export trade and added the aim of "world dominion." [93] In January 1932 he told a group of industrialists: "If we want to develop a new domestic market or to solve the space problem: ever and again we shall need the concerted political strength of the nation." [94] A year later, shortly before being named chancellor, he declared: "Once Germany has been successfully purified and regenerated, it will soon enough be brought home to the outside world that a different people now confronts it. And with that the preconditions will have been created for putting our land and soil in proper order and securing the life of the nation on its own for a long time to come." [95] Some two weeks after his top-level briefing session of 5 November 1937 on procedures for expanding Germany's living space, he congratulated destiny on having chosen him to serve his people even as he announced: "New tasks await us today. For our people's living space is too narrow. . . . I am convinced that the most difficult preparatory work has been accomplished. . . . If the whole Party and with it the entire nation stand solidly behind the leadership, then it will be possible for the leadership, backed by the collective strength of sixty-eight million people vested in the last resort in their armed forces, to defend the nation's interests and solve the problems facing us." [96] Two days later he supplied the historic referent for those "new tasks" to a gathering of junior Nazi officials: "We held Europe once already. We lost it only because we lacked that force of leadership which was necessary for us not merely to hold our position, but to extend it." [97] These were reminders of a purpose once openly defined that completed their meaning. He also evoked the course of conquest through terms long associated with it in his distinctive usage, particularly "freedom" ("to gain freedom, to gain land and soil, that is our goal" [98]). But mainly he suggested it through a proposition previously established as, in his mouth, complementary. Throughout the late 1920s he argued that national unity was necessary for foreign conquest, whereas Jewry in a covert, concerted, parasitic power play had split the nation down the middle by means of Marxism, fragmented both sides by Weimar parliamentarianism, and atomized the fragments by democratic liberalism. He would heal the multiple cleavage for the sake of national survival, meaning world power and ultimately world dominion. He even tied together the three stages of the proposed operation by the fall of 1928: he would cleanse Germany racially to restore German unity for the necessary war ahead.[99] This treble project was inchoately his in the early 1920s—not so schematically, that is, and with only a revisionist war foreseen. "What can help us now?" he asked in March 1920, while raging against the victors' peace. "Only the greatest unity of all breeds of Germans," he answered.[100] And a month later he cried out: "Merciless war on those drones who brought us to grief! We want a single German people back however much the whole Jew pack kicks."[101] He struck a long familiar stance in the Ruhr crisis of 1923: "Do we want to restore Germany's freedom and power? Then let us first rescue it from its spoiler!"[102] His call for a racial housecleaning was toned down in his post-Putsch oratory earlier than was his cry for feeding ground—possibly in the first instance to oblige the Bavarian government when it provisionally lifted the ban on his public speaking in March 1927.[103] Even muted, the racial housecleaning remained more than a mere means to national unity in his political discourse, whereas national unity figured from first to last as merely the means of conquering feeding ground. Take his presentation of 26 March 1927. "Even the beaten Communist," it ran, "is my compatriot as soon as he is down. I want nothing more than for civil strife to stop, for Germans to stop being two classes, for a new army to form out of both classes and, bridging the gap, plant above and beyond it a new banner that is both national and social, so everyone can see that in fighting for the idea I am fighting for each of my compatriots to get bread for life, for them each someday to get the proud feeling of being German." In this isolated passage, the gap-bridging can look like an end in itself—army, bread, and all. But this clarion call for unity followed up a bugle call for the eastern land grab: "To conquer land and soil, strength is needed. That lies in unity. That is, if a people sees the necessity for being able to preserve its life only through a policy

71

of expansion, then it must put all its vital energy into such a policy. And it may not be distracted by other problems. It must have a single goal. If it pursues other goals, then it lacks the strength to fight outwardly." The clarion call led up to a recall besides: "We [National Socialists] are convinced of the necessity for struggle. The peoples of this world have to struggle for their existence. If a people no longer does so, then history takes no further notice of it. History does not say: 'All right, if you won't have it that way, then have it some other way.' It says: 'Then you drop out.' Yes, the creature that stops defending itself goes under." (Through all this, Hitler reminded his listeners only in passing that "the international Jew has become master.")[104] Never did Hitler invert his means and his end by promoting the foreign land grab in order to drain domestic tension. He came closest once in his fever year for theory, 1928, when, bypassing the Jews, he blamed Germany's civil strife on the shortage of land and soil: "Social diseases appear that then gradually assume an ideological character, until at length bloody civil strife erupts internally, a consequence of the disproportion between people and area."[105] But after September 1930 he evoked the end as a rule by citing the means only—intoning the first bars of his familiar refrain and leaving the rest to be hummed unthinkingly. That is, he sounded the aim of conquering feeding ground *through* the theme of terminating social and political divisions. And this pitch to heal the civil rifts and restore a "community of fate"[106] became his basic, constant pitch in the two years before he took office. As he put it on 31 July 1932, the issue was "whether Germany is to keep these twenty-five and thirty or forty parties, or whether Germany is to be pulled back together once and for all into a single formative will."[107] Or again on 23 January 1933: "If we succeed in turning proletarian and bourgeois back into Germans, the German future is ours."[108] This was his set piece in office too while public life was Nazified.[109] The sequence was the same in his politics as previously in his rhet-oric: first came the Nazification, then—and all Germany felt it coming—the expansionist war. The Nazification began, moreover, with the exclusion of the Jews from public life and the

72

suppression of Marxism, parliamentarianism, and liberal democracy.[110]

Given its national character, Hitler's appeal is in no wise explained by its social variance in the course of his rise to power.[111] In particular, Hitler was not the recourse of the frightened middle classes against Bolshevism. The Bolshevik peril was patently, blatantly bogus in Germany after 1923 at the latest —and doubly so in Hitler's mouth, where it fronted for the bogus Jewish peril.[112] After the speaking bans on him were lifted in 1927–1928, Hitler built up a mass party by drawing former Nationalist voters in the first instance; converts from predominantly middle-class parties came later. He also gained disproportionately large worker support: a third of the Party's members were common laborers by the start of 1933[113] (as against roughly eleven percent factory workers in the Communist Party at that same time[114]). His apocalyptic Nazi-Communist antithesis was a word game: the two parties exchanged members and voters wholesale down the years before his takeover,[115] and then Communist stalwarts joined the SA by the cell-load.[116] Susceptibility and resistance to Nazism did vary fractionally this way and that with class, age, sex, religion, and much else from region to region and from election to election—here perhaps most closely with previous political commitment. In brief, Nazism spread helter-skelter on its way to engulfing Germany, so local zigzags tell nothing of why it spread. The Depression certainly eased its way,[117] but by no means in the sense that people turned to Hitler for the sake of the economic recovery that was then accomplished under him. He had small use at most for economics. "World history teaches us that no people grew great or went under by economics," he proclaimed.[118] On taking office he told an assemblage of generals that the crisis was one of human laziness: "So the masses must be trained to work again as fast as possible."[119] His approach in office, insofar as he had one, was that of his predecessors, especially his immediate predecessor, Schleicher. His contribution to the recovery already under way was an unplanned side effect of his step-up of secret rearmament and related public works.[120] He never promised prosperity before

or after he took power, but always called for sacrifices instead—
"and," as his Minister of Finance remarked, "thereby proved
himself a good connoisseur of the German psyche."[121] He proposed no remedies for the Depression, but capitalized on it by
representing it as merely the latest catastrophic consequence of
the domestic and international order that had issued from the
mistaken defeat of 1918.[122] He stood for repudiating that order
and with it that defeat. Otto Dietrich's later claim to have been
won over to him in April 1929 by the "national community" he
preached amid "economic duress" and "national depression"[123]
is illustrative: April 1929 was long months before the duress
and depression began. That spring and fall the Nazis' upswing
to a mass party was clearly registered in provincial elections,[124]
whereas in the thick of the duress and depression the Nazis suffered a severe temporary electoral setback (November 1932).[125]
Besides, nothing like Hitlerism arose in other countries hard
hit. Hitler's following did not batten in those lean years because
his dictatorship beckoned as the only practical alternative to a
regime that had proven ineffectual; rather, the regime proved
ineffectual because his impractical alternative beckoned and his
following battened.[126] His appeal was then as always to the
pathology of nonacceptance of the 1918 defeat—a piece of
traumatic unreason that surfaced the more readily in conditions
of hunger and fear such as had attended the defeat itself. In
June 1920 Hitler complained: "It is hard to bring a people that
is sick onto the right track."[127] Right track or wrong, the Depression helped.

Hitler called the establishment of his dictatorship a "seizure of
power" both before and after the event. That virile term first
served to placate the revolutionaries in his ranks, particularly the
paramilitary SA, while he steered his legal course after the
Putsch. Then it stuck—right down to misguided, misleading
post-Nazi studies of the techniques and stages of his takeover. In
reality his takeover was a pushover. To quote one overview, "In
whatever direction Hitler moved, nearly everything crumbled
without significant resistance":[128] the "nearly" here is intrigu-
ing. Nervously anticipating resistance where none was forthcom-

74

ing, he had hasty recourse to intimidation and terror before they proved unnecessary. He had no preconception, and little sense, of how to proceed. Far from grasping opportunities with diabolical cunning, he just struck out as the spirit moved him, and all too recklessly to succeed except that the spirit moved his opponents correspondingly. Seeing the Reichstag in flames on 27 February 1933, he went wild at the seeming materialization of the Communist confrontation he had foretold. At two governmental meetings that night he could only issue heedless, unheeded orders for police violence against Marxism. The Reichstag Fire Decree for "defense against Communist acts of violence," drawn up at a cabinet meeting the next morning for President Hindenburg's ready signature, abrogated civil rights—an impulsive, impolitic gesture on the eve of elections for a new Reichstag intended to vote him an Enabling Act. To quote one historian of the event: "Hitler had no way of knowing that he would gain unlimited power without a struggle, at the very first try. In response to the supposed signal for total Communist resistance, he put down all his chips like a poor roulette player, and won." [129] The power he gained at that juncture was hardly unlimited, but no matter. In presenting his Enabling Act on 23 March 1933, he called on the new Reichstag "to grant us for the sake of law what we could have taken anyhow"; [130] the Reichstag did even that. The fact that the Nazis polled less than a majority (43.9 percent) in the elections of 5 March 1933 even as the institutional Nazification of Germany went unresisted only bears out Hitler in his distinction between public opinion and national will. [131] Whatever the head count against him, a despot's power was conceded to him on all sides. In the conscious forms it took, his opponents' compliance can be called variously timeserving and miscalculation and naïveté. [132] But consciousness does not run very deep: remove the wearisome sound track and a spectacle of precipitous surrender emerges. That surrender was due to no German tradition of bowing to authority: authority had been flouted in Weimar Germany as nowhere else in Europe at the time. Compliance toward Hitler was continual for twelve years. To explain it by his dictatorship is to confuse cause and effect. A fit symbol of the "seizure of power" is Communist chief Ernst Torgler delivering himself up to the police to prove his innocence of the Reichstag fire. Nine months later, in a miscarriage of Nazi injustice, Torgler was acquitted of the charge of complicity. Göring had him detained nonetheless to protect him from the Gestapo,[133] which Göring himself headed.

Torgler's "protective custody" was no sinister joke of Göring's, but a minute instance of the mess of overlapping and crossed competences through which Hitler ruled—of the *"Führungschaos"* within the *"Führerstaat,"* as his press chief, Otto Dietrich, styled it in 1946.[134] For all its tangled lines of authority and policy, Hitler's regime could project such an image of concerted action in its heyday that it took historians long years to break through the illusion of a masterminded totalitarian machine. But this illusion harbored a reality now emerging from close studies of single offices or concerns of Hitler's state: that it cohered through its pursuit of the racial and expansionist objectives that Hitler had set for it.[135] This means through the expansionist objective, as expansionism was Hitler's justification for his domestic racial policy, whereas his racial aim abroad was *"strictly* secret."[136] That reality within the illusion held, beyond Hitler's state proper, for his Reich as a whole.

The fact that Germany followed Hitler to rerun the disaster course of 1914–1918 does not of itself prove that the 1918 defeat was traumatic: that fact alone could as well be put down to a national vocation for disaster. It does mesh with the indirect proof already provided, but this proof is difficult, special—and indirect. Direct proof is wanted. But so are comparable case studies, without which only guesswork is possible about the signs of that collective trauma or any other.

There is no reason to suppose that a collective trauma can be evidenced from the event itself any more than an individual trauma can. Similar experiences will traumatize one person and not another; one person just traumatized will appear frantic, another numbed, another nonchalant. The present collective case is complicated by the fact that the spontaneous, concerted reaction to the 1918 defeat produced an auxiliary shock effect of its own.[137] That reaction was the November revolution, in which all Germany was implicated inasmuch as no one lifted a finger to defend the old order.[138] As Hitler told a gathering of industrialists in 1932: "Believe me, our entire German people, all walks of life, bear a full measure of guilt for the collapse, some because they willed it and deliberately brought it about, the others because they looked on and were too weak to prevent it. In history, failure to oppose is weighed exactly as the intent or the deed itself." [139] (By so saying, he unweighted his own concept of "November criminals.") Hitler owned outright at his Putsch trial that he himself had not batted an eye when Red sailors poured into his ward at Pasewalk, as "I was loath to cry out at a time when one felt the collapse coming." [140] This completed his symbolic figure-cutting: disabled at the front [141] and overwhelmed by the revolution, then resurrected. Authority impressing order from above was the second of the two organic principles of the Prussian-made Reich that collapsed in 1918; [142] military supremacy was the first. Because the Reich had been forged by blood and iron under authoritarian Prussian leadership, the sequel to its military defeat was a ground swell against the Imperial social controls accompanied by strong regionalist, even separatist, impulses.[143] (The persistence of the regional identities overlaid by the Prussianized Reich after 1870 was, as much as the numbers of non-Germans included and of Germans excluded, what had lent that Reich its fatal proneness to annexations and Germanizations combined.[144]) The shock of authority and order crumbling merged with the shock of defeat in the concept of a "*Zusammenbruch*" (collapse or breakdown) covering, *au choix*, the revolution as cause of the defeat or the defeat as cause of the revolution.[145] The revolution had come off unopposed only to generate bloody divisions afterward as long as the Weimar system lasted. Through these divisions the patriotic fever of August 1914—the jubilant battle cry in chorus, the thrill of Germandom outing—took on a mythic, magic lure. "In 1914, confronted with the hatred of 'a whole world of enemies,' we experienced an intoxicating intensification of our whole being," Ludwig Dehio remembered.[146] The Germans went out of battle array in 1918 as they

77

had gone into it in 1914: by a convulsive composite movement. With his pitch to restore authority and unity with a vengeance, Hitler spoke to the November shock of hierarchies tumbling and the Reich disintegrating, and behind that the "August days" symbolizing a national oneness to be recovered over against the November oneness of disarray.[147] Hitler's "national revolution," as he called his takeover, repeated the November revolution in simple reverse, with the submission from below instead of above. His Bavarian bid to reverse the November revolution on its fifth anniversary had been styled after that revolution unreversed, from the beer hall oratory behind it to the street march meant, like Kurt Eisner's five years earlier, to touch off a national ground swell that would wash away the regime identified with the defeat (and therewith in effect the defeat itself).[148] Hitler was, like Eisner, an outsider to Bavaria, a mass agitator, and a political visionary bent on regenerating Germany—all, to be sure, in point-for-point antithesis to Eisner's image and message.

Direct evidence of an individual trauma includes the transparent repetition of the experience that brought it on. This line of evidence is complicated in the German case by Hitler's having been in charge of the repetition. His personal input can be factored out of his warmaking, but this is the indirect approach again. Empowering an uncontrolled leader may itself be indicative of a collective trauma, like the singlemindedness and unrestraint that mark a traumatized individual's reliving. With a dictator to act for it, Germany was better able to dominate events and inflict its unaccepted fate upon itself anew. Hitler dominated events up to, precisely, the telescoping (in June–December 1941) of the three stages (continental, hemispheric, global) of his program for repeating World War I while reversing its outcome. But Hitler's dictatorship was also part and parcel of that traumatic replay. It renewed Ludendorff's de facto dictatorship of 1916–1918 with one turnabout: Ludendorff had built up his power within the military and then extended it to politics. Hitler's dictatorship, unlike Ludendorff's, was overt and all-out, but to intensify the key elements of a traumatic experience is routine in replays by individuals. Similarly, Hitler's acting for Germany in secret councils reflected and enlarged the distance between official and public consciousness in the war Germany refought. For the German public, that war of 1914–1918 began in self-defense.[149] The annexationism that promptly came to the fore was more or less distasteful to more or less of the nation according as victory appeared more or less remote.[150] Not until the final debacle were any inferences drawn from annexationism to war guilt, and those then drawn were wiped out by the unanimous indignation over the war guilt clause of the treaty imposed on Germany. This reflex of national solidarity with the repudiated regime was an early portent of Hitler's reversal of the revolution and repetition of the war.

Only Hitler would have issued the marching orders (like the killing orders) he did: thence his following. But the fact that the marching orders were his leaves only their execution as direct evidence, for what it is worth, of the national trauma behind them. They were taken as they were issued: in a spirit of fatality. "We were condemned to wage war," said Hitler at the end point of the course he had traced.[151] As Barbarossa was handed down, only its provisions for shooting "commissars and Ogpu types" gave a few officers brief pause.[152] When it went into operation, Germans at large accepted it, after a momentary jolt, "as a new, but ineluctable, burden that had to be borne with the Führer's help."[153] Its initial success took the public by surprise. As it bogged down afterward, a sneaking sense of hopelessness set in. Conspiracies against Hitler waxed, particularly in the military, but they were all paralyzed by telltale passivity, indecision, and blundering. Stauffenberg finally planted his bomb at Hitler's side on 20 July 1944 only when his fellow conspirator Carl Goerdeler was slated for arrest, which meant exposure in any case.[154] The intended signal for action against the regime was one for savage repression instead.

The direct evidence for the 1918 trauma seems strongest in the German national equivalent to the early attempt of a traumatized individual to elude or refute the traumatic facts. This effect of the shared shock was manifest, paradoxically, in discord. To quote Hitler on the November revolution: "They ended the fight all at once only to take it up at home. Our people's perpetual unrest dates from then; since then we have been rent asunder."[155] Weimar Germany's intense, ceaseless wrangling and scuffling were over degrees of willingness to live with the defeat and its consequences. For a decade and a half the debate raged in the Reichstag and the courts, in scholarly journals and the popular press, over domestic responsibilities for the outcome of a titanic, hopeless, ruinous four-year struggle.[156] "We brooded over our defeat," Ludwig Dehio recollected, "but in order to prove to ourselves that it was undeserved, not to understand why it was deserved."[157] Ludendorff had thrown Germany's last material and human reserves into an all-out offensive to take Paris against ever-increasing odds. Afterward he led Germany in resisting the simple lesson of the war: that it was unwinnable— that even taking Paris in 1918 would not have made it any less unwinnable.[158] As Arthur Rosenberg put it in 1927: "The colossal tragedy that ran its course in 1918 is being completely effaced by superficial twaddle about stabs in the back and the like."[159] Weimar politics spent itself in smarting at the liabilities and disabilities imposed on Germany, notably disarmament and reparations. Then Hitler rearmed Germany to the amount of the unpaid reparations.

Direct evidence that the German defeat was traumatic must abound, for it is hard to find a detached, informed account of the event that does not describe it that way. In one historian's view, "Germans never recovered from the shock produced by the revelation that further fighting was hopeless."[160] Other historians speak of "a blow never absorbed," "an incomprehensible deep outrage," "tremendous psychological repercussions," and the like.[161] Their perceptions rejoin participants' recollections of a "paralyzing terror" or a "genuine panic" or a "fearful moral breakdown," with "effects so catastrophic and consequences so fateful."[162] Eloquent among the mementos of the defeat is this diary entry of 3 October 1918 by a German seaman: "We have lost the war as if overnight. As always in such cases, the German people were completely in the dark about developments down there. Now all at once the crash comes. Utter despondency is settling over the best of us like a nightmare. Yet"—and here was the traumatic rub—"a certain feeling impels me not to believe in the complete collapse of our hopes.[163] Arresting testimony came from many a moral casualty of the crash. Thus Franz Schauwecker: "With one blow the most tremendous expectations were dispelled. Suddenly everything had been in vain. The world appeared senseless."[164] Ernst Jünger felt weak and vulnerable at first, then developed "symptoms that, as in a chronic illness, were now more, now less pronounced without ever vanishing entirely. Among them was a sense of constriction, of being tight pressed, about like that of a culprit at times and a trapped soldier at others, and of a rustic too who thinks he has been taken in by shrewd lawyers. Stalingrad," Jünger adds, "was for me more of a confirmation, like sediment settling in a turbid solution."[165] But did an Ernst Jünger fall in with that national traumatic effect while, say, a Bertolt Brecht fall out with it? It was distinct from any individual German's reaction to the defeat, yet it must have been felt by Germans individually. Perhaps C. G. Jung can be believed here. "I could have predicted the Nazi rising in Germany through the observation of my German patients," Jung claimed in old age. "They had dreams in which the whole thing was anticipated, and with considerable detail. And I was absolutely certain—in the years before Hitler, before Hitler came in the beginning; I could say the year, in the year 1919—I was sure that something was threatening in Germany, something very big, very catastrophic. I only knew it through the observation of the unconscious."[166]

The German trauma of defeat was detected through its causation of Hitler's expansionist politics. But little headway could be made toward evidencing it directly. And by now the search for distinctive signs of its workings has thrown it out of historical focus. Its interplay with Hitler's own trauma behind his politics and, after that, Hitler's action on his traumatized public remain to be considered. But first some historic perspective must be restored.

The Germany traumatized in 1918 had for four years been

blockaded and besieged while also fighting beyond its borders. However mixed and confused the Germans' intentions, the logic of their struggle was to break their enemies' bind on them, and that necessarily meant to dominate the continent. The game was won in the east by late 1917 with the help of subsidies to the Bolsheviks. But in the west by then the Allies held a clear, strong advantage that was steadily mounting. The Germans' great—and only—chance at that point was to bargain for a delayed victory whereby Germany would give ground freely in the west in return for the Allies' acceptance of German supremacy in the east. However, Ludendorff would not hear of evacuating Belgium, let alone renouncing Alsace-Lorraine. Instead he launched a ruinous offensive.[167] When that offensive turned into a retreat, Germans were discouraged. But they had not begun to feel vulnerable before Ludendorff's staggering announcement that the game was up. Hard upon that announcement Ludendorff called a parliamentary regime into being to sue for an armistice. The armistice was just being concluded when the Imperial establishment fell before a sudden popular upheaval animated by naïve, escapist Leninism and Wilsonism combined. As soon as this momentary revolutionary impulse was spent, a model democratic republic was constituted. It was promptly discredited with the German public by the harsh peace the victors handed down: that shows where its credit had lain. It survived on sufferance as long as Germany was out for concessions from the victors. Even so, it turned authoritarian in practice with the President's ongoing exercise of emergency powers beginning nearly three years before Hitler's accession. The President was then Hindenburg, nominal chief of the army in Ludendorff's prime, senile symbol of the unacceptably lost cause.

In working through their defeat, Germans passed over the simple sense of it: that they had been fighting beyond their strength. The eastern conquest of 1917–1918 was disowned or glossed over, then forgotten, at least as regards the dizzying vistas of expansion it had thrown open. It was even excluded at first from the purview of the Reichstag committee investigating the causes of the defeat. "Here clearly is a gaping deficiency in the committee's work," observed a subcommittee chairman in the sixth year of the deliberations. Eduard Bernstein added: "It is dangerous when important facts go unmentioned." [168] Mentions followed to the final effect that the subjugation of eastern Europe, besides tying down troops, had violated the spirit of a peace resolution passed by the Reichstag in the summer of 1917, when the war had seemed issueless. Some subcommitteemen also blamed the eastern conquest along with annexationism in the west for having prevented a compromise settlement. All saw the German struggle begun in 1914 as properly defensive and expansionism as aberrant. [169]

That multipartisan subcommittee concluded unanimously against the stab in the back. But through its conclusion can be glimpsed the same national ill from which the legend arose: against that ill, information and insight availed little. To quote the subcommittee's summary verdict: "Only in the reciprocal action of numerous causes . . . is the blame for the collapse to be found." [170] Domestic causes were implied, as if the defeat were due to a national failing rather than to enemy power—an implication conspicuous in the very fact of that prolonged, intensive inquiry into "the causes of the German collapse in the year 1918." The issue was not the reason for the defeat, but the "blame" for it (or the "guilt": "*Schuld*"). [171] And defeat was "collapse," since the revolution was meant as well. This ambiguity helped the implication of shared domestic failings behind the defeat to get by. [172] The double meaning was the more treacherous since it was no mere trick of wording: the defeat and the revolution did go closely together in historic reality. Indeed, this conjunction enabled nationalists to take out on the revolution their outrage over the defeat. The revolution did not much alter Germany beyond collapsing the dynasties; the victors' exactions did, which were underwritten by the Imperial armistice commission and inescapable in any case. As Arthur Rosenberg said of Ludendorff's institution of a parliamentary system: "That was the decisive thing; the ninth of November was just decoration." [173] But nationalists, mistaking the revolution for the defeat, construed it as a deathblow dealt to Germany by antinational forces. Extremist imaginings reduced the revolutionaries to Jews and Jews' henchmen the more readily since an international people was even better fitted than an international party to double for the outside enemy. And Jews on their side often redoubled their native internationalism in the psychological scramble to escape the defeat.

The defeat permeated that scramble on the extreme left as elsewhere. The seizure of power rashly attempted by the Spartacists in Berlin in January 1919 would have put Germany at the head of the revolution launched by the Bolsheviks (as Lenin thought vital for its success) and thus salvaged in a new form the German dominion over eastern Europe won by means of those very Bolsheviks in 1917–1918. Leninist revolutionism failed grimly in Germany well before it built up the massive following that exchanged blows and members with the Nazis beyond the two ends of the Weimar coalition. That tight-pressed coalition's efforts to normalize Germany's postwar situation culminated in the Locarno agreement of late 1925 between Germany and her European victors, whereby Germany recognized her western frontier as retraced in 1918–1919. This left her eastern frontier open. At Locarno, Germany did symbolically what earlier in the year a Democrat on the Reichstag committee had called "the perfectly obvious thing for us to have done" after the eastern conquest of 1917–1918.[174] Hitler had just begun proposing to correct that same omission in the same sense, only more so.

IV

THE DOUBLE TRACK

New and fantastic dreams have arisen
in which constantly figure Barbarossa
and his two-edged sword awakening
from his rock-bound sleep to put to
flight the enemies of Germany.

TRUMAN SMITH, November 1922.[1]

Everything recurs,
And what is to happen
Has run its course.

*(Es kehret alles wieder,
Und was geschehen soll,
Ist schon vollendet.)*

FRIEDRICH HÖLDERLIN.

Hitler's two political tracks both took off from his mission hallucinated in Pasewalk. They ran to Auschwitz and Stalingrad respectively. His main line, traced first, was the one to Auschwitz.
For its sake he laid the other, German line as well and rode it for
the longest stretch as if *it* were his main line.

 His hallucinated mission was to resurrect Germany by undoing and reversing the 1918 defeat. The first means he envisaged
was, in his parlance, to remove Germany's Jewish cancer and to
poison out Germany's Jewish poison. The latent sense of this
means was to undo and reverse his mother's death—the conclusion, in 1907, of a toxic treatment that he had urged upon her
Jewish doctor after a mastectomy proved unavailing against a
cancer spreading from her breast. His mission to undo and reverse an accomplished fact was unrealistic from the outset. So
was that first means, which turned on misplaced blame for the
1918 defeat matching his misplaced blame for his mother's
death. But he never fooled himself deep down. Practically speak-

ing, to remove the Jewish cancer and poison out the Jewish poison would mean—in his unconscious frame of reference—to repeat rather than rectify his traumatic experience of 1907. An inner compulsion to repeat this experience was one earthly source of the unearthly command he received.

This command later served him well to meet a corresponding need for Germany to relive the traumatic sequence of 1914–1918 in disguise. But his first political message was attuned more to a prior German need for unconscious denial in that it blamed the defeat on non-Germans mistaken for Germans. This blame came from him, and took him into politics. He did not feel it out of his mass audiences, though he did suit it to them continually. And he stuck with it even after he had drawn from his mass public, in 1921–1922, a new policy that met the national need to relive. In brief, he went after Jewry on his own account conformably with his mission. This conformation was as when he had indulged, and overindulged, himself at the breast in serving his mother's attempt to absorb her traumatic loss of her three children before him.[2] His nursing mother's mute injunction to help her over her loss and then through it again was the original of his mission. The specific terms of the mission—to undo and reverse Germany's defeat—did not cover her traumatic business as they did his.[3] But the Providence that conferred that mission was, transparently, his nursing mother: the version he authorized even had him receiving the mission in a nurse's arms.[4] And the mission left the way open for a second mode of fulfillment, this one suited to his experience of his nursing mother rather than his dying mother.

That mode was his war policy, conveyed by his message for Germany to win more feeding ground for more progeny. He sensed and, with that policy, served Germany's traumatic purposes by way of plying them to his own, just as he had made his own use of his nursing mother's use of him for her traumatic reliving. His dominant motivation toward Germany was the traumatized son's, not the suckling sweetheart's: his Jewish policy came first. But his nursing complex underlay his instrumentality to Germany, which lay with his war policy, and he could apply

86

his Jewish policy only if he might apply his war policy. So he gave the German policy top public billing from the Landsberg jail to the Berlin bunker, from near start to near finish. And he traced it solely according to German traumatic needs even if his nursling's libido did lend it a personal motive force along with its special rhetorical form.

Into Hitler's anti-Semitism went, then, his traumatic thrust aligned on Germany's; into his expansionism went Germany's traumatic thrust steeped in his nursling's libido. The premises beneath the two policies—Germany's Jewish cancer and poison, the feeding ground won and lost by Germany in 1917–1918— were as different as the drives behind them. He gradually coordinated the two in theory and later in practice. Psychologically they remained quite separate: few nursling's motives came into his Jewish politics, few 1907 motives into his program for world power.[5] And yet he did the coordinating for himself rather than for his public, for he kept its high points secret—his book of 1928 and later the parallelism of Barbarossa and the Final Solution. In practice, his programmed misplay for world power complemented his designs on Jewry and Germany even before any coordinating. Only in conditions of war could Germany's Jews be transported and liquidated. To go after Jewry outside Germany called for military action outside Germany. And mother Germany could be destroyed only through a new defeat carried to a full finish, as *Mein Kampf* already provided: "Germany will be a world power or will cease to be."[6] He could at least have publicized the confluence of his two courses in the direction of Moscow, whereas he held his side of the Moscow run secret before Barbarossa. In any case he needed, in order to coordinate his two courses in theory, not just a confluence between them but a common doctrinal source from which they would flow.

He was out to devise such a unitary doctrine before he plotted that second course in public during his incarceration for the failed Putsch—possibly even before he indicated it in private to Cuno's confidant in late December 1922, during the seventeen months he took to project into the future the feeding ground Germany gained at Brest-Litovsk and lost at Compiègne.[7] That quest for a unitary doctrine was implicit in his outline for an unwritten work labeled "Volume I. *The Germanic Revolution.*"[8] This outline certainly predates the Putsch and *Mein Kampf*, as will be seen. It cannot predate August 1920, when the Nazi flag, which dominated Hitler's sketch for a title page, was created.[9] It also departs too far conceptually from his speech of 13 August 1920 on the Jews, which survives in manuscript (and mentions the new emblem[10]), to be from the same period. This speech represented the Aryans as history's only state builders and the Jews as nomads from way back, with attributes the opposite of the instinct for labor, the racial purity, and the artistry required for state-building (the opposite given for "racial purity" was "in-breeding").[11] The outline featured the same stock antagonists: "The Jew, the Aryan," and "Germany—An Antipode of the Jew,"[12] and again "2 races. Aryan. Jew." The antithesis was spelled out only in the notation: "2 human types—Toilers and drones—builders and destroyers—children of God and humans." (These were standard epithets of Hitler's for Aryan and Jew except the last, puzzling pair.) Nomadism and artistry were miss-ing—nomadism more significantly, for by 1924 Hitler found that the Aryan rather than the Jew had once been a nomad, defined as a worker who carries his living space around with him.[13] But the stress fell on racial purity: "Basic racial principle ... Earliest history of peoples (on the basis of) with clear exposition of the racial law ... Racial purity Highest basic law ...." And this time the Jews epitomized racial purity and took a decisive advan-tage over the Aryans. "Bible: original sin—A dreadful fact—Its consequences, misfortune forever. The Bible teaches two facts: I. All peoples of the Bible (cultural area Asia Minor, Mesopotamia, Palestine, Egypt) perished from it (i.e. racial mixing). One people not: The Jews. Why? Racial purity. Not wars destroy races, only original sin—blood poisoning alone.[14] II. All peoples had states of their own—One people not, the Jews. So: the other peoples (Aryans) had their own 'states' and could not preserve them-selves. The Jew had no state of his own and still preserved him-self. Only at first sight incomprehensible—why?"[15] The question was left dangling.

In "The Germanic Revolution" Hitler was after historic laws covering the Jews along with the rest of humankind and featuring continual warfare among peoples, laws from which his anti-Semitism and expansionism would follow as a twin necessity. But until his "Workers and Peace Treaties" speech like the "land and soil" one of 31 May 1921, his only stated generalizations about the human lot were that right is worthless without might [16] and that human solidarity would be against nature: [17] neither afforded sufficient reason for Germany to remove Jews and conquer land. And until that same speech his only admission of the Jews to a universal law of life was a concessive and partial one in a remark of 13 August 1920 about the Jew in the Middle Ages: "Even he gradually had to conduct a struggle for survival against the increasingly wary and angry peoples." [18] (He had begun using the phrases "self-preservative instinct" and "struggle for survival" only a few weeks earlier.[19]) The "Workers and Peace Treaties" speech took up this Darwinist notion for a first, false start in the same theoretical direction as "The Germanic Revolution." His notes for the speech read: "The struggle for one's own survival is justified. But the individual's survival requires the nation's political power." [20] Putting the individual before the nation, as here, was inimical to his conception of peoples as the stuff of history.[21] He must have been fishing around in handbooks of political theory for a start. "The Germanic Revolution" marks an advance toward an amalgam of individual and national necessitation: "Nature is relentlessly harsh, which means: victory of the stronger because he has victory coming to him by reason of his strength or his will Prerogative of strength as basis of nature as a whole The man of genius aware of nature does not seek to depart from this basis which is the cause of his favored position in this world but puts his conduct too within the compass of this law". For the rest, this outline for a "monumental history of humankind" dealt only in races or peoples or nations (terms Hitler interchanged).

Hitler's few pre-Putsch texts that link up with distinctive pieces of "The Germanic Revolution" all date from early 1923. That 3 January he called his Party "the bearer of the Germanic revolution"—a verbal equivalent to his design for a title page.[22] A few words later he anticipated his eventual conjunction of the thrust against Jewry with the thrust for world power: "If Germandom is to cure the world one day, that can only mean: Germany can and will be the victor in the fight against the golden dragon Judah." That 13 April he reiterated his old view that, in world history as elsewhere, might decides right, then added: "All of nature is a violent struggle between strength and weakness, a perpetual victory of the stronger over the weaker. All nature would be rottenness otherwise. All the states that transgress this basic law become rottenness"—a dig at the Weimar Republic.[23] Within the hour he also spoke of Jewry as "at bottom . . . mortally averse to all national states."[24] This, then, is about where, chronologically, "The Germanic Revolution" fits into Hitler's advance toward the theoretical scheme he developed after the Putsch and finalized in 1928. He retook an old step toward that scheme the following 3 May by representing Jewry as a menace to all peoples equally. Urging "emancipation from Judah," he declared: "For that is in the last resort the question of the convalescence of peoples."[25]

Peoples alone figured in the completed rationale of his politics: what was good for a nation was good for everyone in it. That rationale, worked out in *Mein Kampf*, was refined in his unfinished book of 1928, which he then had locked up in a safe for the rest of his days.[26] The rationale comes to this. History is a perpetual contest among peoples for feeding ground. One people can grow only at another's expense. The alternative to preying on others is to stagnate and become a prey to others. The Jews alone do not live off land of their own; they live off other peoples instead, debilitating them increasingly and thereby endangering the entire human breed, themselves included. Ergo, to kill Jews and conquer land is a double duty. It was unclear why killing Jews was a nation's duty when exporting its Jews instead would ease its expansion. And Hitler violated his own scheme by the world conquest he projected for Germany ("in the end the fittest people will rule the earth"[27]): that would stop history dead. But he did accommodate intact his demographic premises of 31 May 1921 for Germany's eastward expansion as well as all his old charges against Jewry except nomadism. And that was no mean feat.

Politics emerged from this theoretical perspective as an ongoing struggle to adjust territory to population in a global economy of scarcity. Statesmanship was accordingly the art of conducting a people's struggle for survival [28]—of fulfilling that "most exalted mission to guard and protect the mother of all life." [29] This formulation betrays the sense behind Hitler's synthesis. Jewry unfitting the nations for their life-and-death struggle to expand: here was, universalized, his view of Germany's experience in World War I. Universalized, it was charged with his traumatic fury of 1907 short of the infinitive "to expand": this was Germany's traumatic input. Beneath the tie between his two political tracks, which balanced them evenly, he gave the edge to his own trauma and hence to the Jewish track. The tie was no less tidy, with a new, perfected triad of antithetical qualities opposing Aryan to Jew: the Aryan's national fiber and spirit, capacity for leadership and followership, and "healthy natural self-preservative instinct," as against Jewish internationalism, egalitarianism, and pacifism. [30] Under the third count the Jews wound up where they had started out in 1920: not quite inside or outside the universal law of life —the law of the jungle that Hitler ratified.

The threefold antithesis between Jew and Aryan also went into Hitler's speeches of the late 1920s tending to join his Jewish and expansionist policies in the argument that removing the Jew would, by restoring national unity, ensure German expansion. [31] He even carried the antithesis along with this means-end conjunction of his anti-Semitism and expansionism into his rhetoric of the 1930s except that he substituted Jewry's instruments, usually Marxism or democracy, for Jewry itself. [32] The antithesis reinforced the means-end relationship hyphenated by Germanic strength. [33] Both fell in with the military mood that came over Germany beginning about 1930. [34] But coming from Hitler, the call to eradicate Jewry for the sake of German expansion—or, as rephrased in the early 1930s, to eradicate the Weimar system and spirit for the sake of readying Germany militarily—was misleading twice over, for it restricted the eradicating to Germany and presented the military-expansionist aim as the determinative one of the two. In a speech of January 1932 published as a pamphlet, Hitler set forth the three Aryan virtues as Nazi-held values confronting their opposites in a fight to the finish for control of Germany. For the Nazis' "inexorable resolve to exterminate Marxism in Germany down to the last root" he gave a single, insistent reason: "With today's body politic, no active foreign policy can be conducted any longer. . . . Forming the will of the nation as a whole is essential; it is the point of departure for political operations [abroad]."[35] On 4 December 1932 he spelled out for a Reichswehr officer the first measures necessary to capacitate Germany for such political operations: "1. Repression of Marxism and its effects to complete extinction. Preparation of a new national unity of mind and will. 2. General spiritual and ethical rearmament of the nation on the basis of this new unity. 3. Technical rearmament. 4. Organization of national strength for national defense. 5. Attainment of formal recognition from the rest of the world for the new situation brought about."[36] Four days after taking office he extended this short list in a talk to Germany's top brass (as noted by one of the generals present): "Overall political goal solely the recovery of political power. . . . Internally: complete reversal of present domestic situation in Germany. No tolerance for any manifestation of sentiments (pacifism!) opposed to the goal. He who won't bow must be bent. Extermination of Marxism root and branch. Youth and entire nation must be attuned to the idea that only struggle can save us. Everything must yield to this idea (actualized in the Nazi movement's millions: it will grow). Toughening of youth and strengthening of will to defense by any and all means. Strictest authoritarian rule. Removal of the cancer of democracy! . . . Buildup of the armed forces most important requirement for reaching goal: winning back political power." Once this goal were reached, Hitler concluded, expansion would begin.[37] The proposed exterminating, though displaced from the Jews to their institutional and intellectual mischief, was no less confined to Germany as a first step toward a new German power play. Hitler shortly proceeded as he proposed, from reversing the German "domestic situation" to rearming for German expansion. And Jewry was not wiped out beforehand; it was separated out meanwhile. The military themselves were fooled on the whole, and increasingly, right down to the decisive juncture. "In the preparation of the attack against the Soviet Union and during its initial phase . . . cooperation between Hitler and the military leadership attained a maximum of unison. Working from a supposed consensus on goals between themselves and Hitler, most of the higher officers had not realized that . . . only an ancillary function fell to militarism by the terms of the radical universal anti-Semitic racial doctrine that determined policy as a whole and that was now, in 1941, to be translated into full-scale reality."[38] This was the harder to realize inside or outside the army since Hitler did not divulge his priorities before then. An exception that proves the rule was made for the Italian ambassador as an angry Hitler told him on 21 March 1933, in rejecting Mussolini's representations against an impending boycott of Jewish businesses: "I do not know whether my name will be held in high esteem in Germany two or three hundred years from now for all that I hope to be able to do for my people, but of one thing I am absolutely certain: in five or six hundred years the name of Hitler will be glorified everywhere as the name of him who will have extirpated the pestilence of Jewry from the world once and for all."[39]

In presenting the destruction of Jewry as a worldwide imperative concurrent with the fight for feeding ground, Hitler's secret rationale of 1928 had been more nearly forthright than his oratorical means-end conjunction of the two. But this conjunction did put the means first in time, and that was more than mere precedence in that the means was false. In no way could removing Jews be expected, for all Hitler's talk, to conduce to conquering land. That talk was like a tacit assurance beyond his expansionist program itself—and beyond his person, first known throughout Germany from his Putsch fiasco—that with him in charge of the means, the end would fail. Tacitly again, his naming Jewry's devices (democracy, Marxism) in place of Jewry itself as the national evil to be rooted out only signified to Germany that the rooting out of Jewry itself was for later. This rescheduling was politic. Jewry having been no part of the German war trauma, he could relate the two for few Germans beneath the level of talk.[40] In effect he stopped trying after 1928 as his political fortunes mounted. Instead, the ending of divisions among Germans became his cover theme both for (his) removing the divisive Jew and for (their) rallying to conquer living space.[41] "Our fight is . . . for the German person, whom we want to and are going to join back into an indissoluble community of fate":[42] here was, capsulated, Hitler's charged summons to mass folly that proved irresistible.

The killing of Europe's Jews was rescheduled to begin with the invasion of Soviet Russia.[43] This synchronization was prefigured when Hitler predated the order for the Euthanasia program, forerunner of the Final Solution, to the start of the invasion of Poland, forerunner of Barbarossa.[44] It was postfigured repeatedly as, beginning in 1942, Hitler repeatedly recalled his grim prophesy of death to Europe's Jews and each time postdated it to the start of the Polish war.[45] The Polish war brought a practical end of the expulsion of Jews from Hitler's area of control,[46] his order for transporting Jews instead to the future killing centers,[47] and special directives from him for SS atrocities behind the battle lines.[48] This was not yet his full racial-ideological extermination program, but neither was that war yet his long-heralded one for living space. Barbarossa first made his prophesy practicable by creating the requisite climate of war to the death and putting virtually all of Europe within his grasp. He assigned the first full-scale Jewish exterminations, under the label "special tasks," to SS commandos operating in a reserved zone behind the battle lines.[49] This provision of Barbarossa got by his military commanders unexamined as he hit them on their side with orders to kill captured Communist officials in an ideological war of annihilation.[50] The racial war half hid behind the ideological war in these preliminaries to Barbarossa as in his rhetoric of the early 1930s. Occasionally he reverted to this rhetoric after Barbarossa was launched, as when in 1944 he told his ear doctor that in

June 1941 he "took up the fight against the Moloch Bolshevism."[51] But he betrayed his lesser interest in killing Communists
than Jews by remarks of October 1942 noted by an army adjutant:
"He knows all right that the orders issued to the army such as
the 'Commissar' Order (June 1941) have been carried out only
haltingly if at all. . . . If he didn't have his SS, just think of all
that would be left undone."[52] The army invading the USSR
shielded the killing operation behind the lines:[53] here the land
grab fronted for the Jew kill as in his rhetoric of the late 1920s,
but literally now. Goebbels, in his speech of 18 February 1943
calling for total war, depicted this arrangement in reverse: "Behind the Soviet divisions charging ahead we already see the
Jewish liquidation commandos."[54] The battle also screened the
killings of Jews in that they could be assimilated to executions of
partisans.[55] And it obliged the military to look the other way.

The battle shielded those killings no less when they were displaced to the death camps in 1942. The preparatory deportations
were presented to the army as serving the military interest. Typically Hitler told the German military attaché in Budapest in October 1942: "All Jews must be removed from the [Czech] Protectorate . . . . This is unfeasible just now only because of the military's big need for transportation. At the same time as the Jews
from the Protectorate, all Jews are to disappear from Berlin and
Vienna. The Jews everywhere are the conductor that conveys all
the enemy's news with the speed of wind to the farthest reaches
of the population."[56] But by the winter of 1943–1944 Himmler
was haranguing the generals and admirals as well as the high
officials of state and Party on the overriding necessity for exterminating Jewry down to the last child.[57] On one such occasion
Himmler paid special tribute to armaments minister Albert Speer
for cooperating in this higher interest despite the critical need
for the Jewish laborers left in war industries.[58] The death mills
drained off other vital resources besides Jewish labor, primarily
transportation, from the war effort and thereby quickened the
catastrophe that Hitler had long since foreseen at the end of his
own traumatic course and Germany's.[59]

So Hitler's expansionism emerged as instrumental to his anti-

Semitism once they came into full action together:[60] his rhetorical reversal of means and end was unreversed in practice. Ostensibly, however, to increase German power was all along the objective that Hitler pursued in eliminating Jewish influence and then Jewry itself from Germany. Either way, the two tracks ran wide apart in his mental landscape. On the Jewish track it was axiomatic that the Jews would, and then did, cause a new world war. But on the German track that war was expressly, even ostentatiously, his. His it was par excellence in his briefing sessions with political and military aides. Hardly had he prophesied on 30 January 1939 that a new war begun by Jewry would mean the end of Jewry in Europe[61] when he told a gathering of army commanders that he must go to war soon because he was aging and "the others" were arming.[62] Here for once his anti-Semitism fronted for his expansionism.

Hitler did not scrap his old means-end formula when he launched Barbarossa. Nonetheless Barbarossa signaled an ascendancy of his ideological style, recessive until then, over his power-political style, previously dominant.[63] His style in this German line was ever Machiavellian and in his own line fanatical.[64] True, before 1941 he imposed on his racist policy a semblance of pragmatism backed by cunning. On 29 April 1937 he told a gathering of Nazi district leaders, by way of justifying a tactical slowdown of his moves against the Jews: "I don't want to start an opponent fighting right away by force, I don't say 'Fight!' because I feel like fighting, but I say 'I will destroy you! And now Shrewdness, help me maneuver you into the corner without your making a single thrust, and then you get the thrust straight to the heart.' That's it!" But he delivered himself of this Machiavellian rhetoric in a telltale crescendo of frenzy.[65] The change in his controlling style from Machiavellism to fanaticism with the start of his war proper in the spring of 1941 was in effect foretold in a passage of *Mein Kampf* about workers deserting Marxism for the national cause in the August days of 1914: "But now was the time to proceed against the whole fraudulent fellowship of these Jewish nation-poisoners" and "make short work of them without the slightest regard for any clamor or

96

lamentation that might arise. . . . All of the instruments of military power needed to be ruthlessly employed for the extermination of this pestilence."[66] Here already, in this inverted prophesy, the terminal action against the Jews starts punctually with Germany's life-and-death struggle. And fanaticism takes over ("without the slightest regard . . .") as that action claims absolute priority over the military struggle covering it ("All of the instruments . . ."), which it ostensibly subserves but transparently disserves (again: "without the slightest regard . . . All of the instruments . . .").

With this change in Hitler's ascendant style went one in his state as devices of arbitrary rule cut sharply across previously normalized channels of authority.[67] Here too his Euthanasia program, based on a personal order rather than a law, was a symbolic foreshadowing.[68] His line of personal command was by and large the racial-ideological as distinct from the power-political one. In practice, as formerly in theory, he linked the two without ever merging them. When his controlling anti-Semitic investment in Barbarossa emerged in the guise of anti-Bolshevism in his military councils of March 1941, it emerged outside the purview of the military. "The tasks are too demanding to be laid upon the army" was Hitler's first mention to the army of the SS's "special tasks" ahead.[69] And when the chief of the army nonetheless proposed a military administration of the areas to be conquered, he came in for a tongue-lashing from Hitler to the effect that "the army understands nothing about politics."[70] The generals accommodated themselves to those rear-line operations; some justified them in Hitlerite diction to the troops; a few even cooperated with the SS in rounding up partisans and Jews together for execution.[71] But Hitler never treated his racial enterprise as the generals' business. To Heydrich and Himmler he had spoken the language of racial struggle and contamination and annihilation from the first; with generals and, as a rule, ministers, functionaries, and foreign statesmen as well he was the calculating, if increasingly miscalculating, Realpolitiker to the last. Only in rare instances did he hold forth both ways in the same company and then ordinarily by distinct turns.[72] His doctrinal integration of his two approaches to Moscow had not survived his long discretion about both. As he remarked in a military conference of 1943, apropos of a confrontation over occupation policy in the Ukraine between Eastern Minister Alfred Rosenberg and Reich Commissioner Erich Koch, ideologue and *Machtpolitiker* respectively: "Ideological issues and ordinary practical issues are not so easy to reduce to a common denominator."[73] Here his slightly ironic phrasing already gave the edge to power politics for the generals' benefit. Ever so much more so did his account of Koch besting Rosenberg that followed and that exposed in full the fiction of Jewish parasitism and the counterproductivity of the Final Solution: "He [Koch] said: Here I lose 500,000 Jews," Hitler related. "I must remove them because the Jews are the insurrectionary element. But the fact is that in his area the Jews were the only craftsmen."[74] Hitler could shelve his doctrines just as well while dining with political personnel, as he did on 23 September 1941 to remark that "Stalin is one of the greatest people alive in that he succeeded in forging a state out of this Slavic rabbit breed—only by the most brutal coercion, to be sure. He was obliged to use the Jews to do it, since the thin Europeanized layer of Russiandom proper that had run the state before was wiped out and not about to be replaced."[75] That was time off from Bolshevism as rule by Jewry decomposing the body politic.

The ascendancy of Hitler's racial politics over his power politics once Barbarossa was under way was reflected in the rise of the SS over the other agencies of government, the rest of the Party, and the army.[76] Before 1941 German power, ultimately German military striking power, was the raison d'être of the Nazi state, the direction of its dynamism, the rationale of Hitler's ill-rationalized apparatus of rule. To heighten that power was a Darwinist enterprise in which ever new bureaus, procedures, and personnel competed with the old under his supreme control[77]—below the level of the armed forces themselves until Barbarossa. Symbolically, he justified Euthanasia as a war economy at the prewar planning session for it.[78] In the face of the SS his other instruments of rule, multifarious and tangled, amounted to a regular governmental establishment. The SS, which embodied,

98

enforced, and elaborated his racial values,[79] was his principal vehicle of lawlessness. Its functions were relatively confined before the Polish and especially the Russian war, so long as his anti-Jewish action was still public and most of Europe was still beyond his reach. They broadened enormously thereafter even as the SS was—"more or less conspicuously to the top echelons of the military, the administration, and the diplomatic corps—pushed to the mid-point of the Nazi system now directed to continental rule."[80] Yet with Himmler himself, not to mention Himmler's henchmen, ideology yielded to expediency in the end. The equation of Bolshevism with Jewry had come apart for Himmler by April 1944, when he angled to contact "world Jewry" for an exchange of Hungarian Jews slated for extermination against trucks to be used solely against the Red Army. He was obscurely seeking acceptance by the western Allies as Hitler's prospective successor who would fight Bolshevism with world Jewry's support.[81] In September 1944 he shut down the last extermination camps behind Hitler's back before their grim job was finished.[82] On the night of 20 April 1945 he went from Hitler's last birthday party to meet a representative of the World Jewish Congress invited from Sweden and propose "to bury the hatchet" between Nazis and Jews.[83]

Hitler for his part put his Jewish politics above his power politics ever more outspokenly once Barbarossa was launched.[84] His old means-end formula survived only with the means term enlarged to enclose the whole. As of 1942 he maintained that eliminating Judeo-Bolshevism from Germany had been, besides a precondition, a rehearsal for the present war for living space, since then already the enemy had been the same. "Thus we are now waging a fight that had its prelude in the harsh internal showdown that could leave only a single surviving force to unite the entire German people. And we are waging this fight outwardly now with the same object again."[85] He hinted at a new rhetorical integration of the two terms of his politics in his address of 28 December 1944 to a group of division commanders. "Such struggles as are being fought out in our time," he declared, "are inherently ideological" and in this regard unlike

Germany's formative struggles of the eighteenth century. Then Germany had been out to win acceptance as a great power, whereas now "the German Reich is waging an ideological life-and-death struggle which, if won, will definitively stabilize this great power already established as such through its numbers and value—or, if lost, will destroy and shatter the German people."[86] His routinizing of ideological warfare had cost it none of its racial character, at least for Germany ("for Germany" Bolshevization would mean the destruction of her "racial substance"[87]). But now the competition of peoples by numbers and ethnic value was acquiring a self-stabilizing tendency. This was just interim wishful thinking. The two terms of his politics came wide apart again, with the Jewish term foremost and topmost, in his apologetics toward the last. In a memoir dictated in mid-February 1945 he represented his domestic Jewish policy of the 1930s as an urgent, vital necessity, the western war as Jewry's reaction, and his annihilation of European Jewry in turn as retaliatory. "The world of the future will be eternally grateful to us," he added.[88] In another such memoir he made out the attack on the Soviet Union to have been necessitated by the war against England, by his dependence on Soviet supplies, and by the danger that Stalin would attack first.[89] His expansionist program was forgotten. So was his racial-ideological crusade except that the war he had made came out invertedly as "an exclusively Jewish war" (as on his side it tended to be), with his own purposes projected onto the Jews: "they resolved to throw everything they had into a fight to the death against us."[90] On 2 April 1945 he reverted to his old means-end argument in a final memoir to affirm, amid the wreckage of his Reich, that the German people cleansed of Jewry would prevail in the long haul.[91] The means had more priority than ever.

In a signed and countersigned political testament of 29 April 1945, the eve of his suicide, Hitler vindicated the revenge he had taken on "the real culprit" behind "the murderous struggle" and concluded: "Above all, I bind the national leadership and following to scrupulous observance of the racial laws and to merciless resistance against the world poisoner of all peoples, international Jewry."[92] The other term of his politics was relegated to a postscript dictated a few hours later: "The goal must still be to win living space in the east for the German people."[93]

Hitler's expansionism was, then, accessory to his drive for retribution against the world poisoner. Yet through it he supplied in full the German need to reexperience the struggle for world power that had been traumatically lost. He did so by renewing that German struggle and losing it conclusively. This was decisive in that traumatic line; the rest was so much side effect.

He continually recalled the first war as he led Germany into and through the second. He recalled it as a rule by insisting that it would not be, or was not being, repeated. Here the outcome was stressed in a rhetorical form cast by Goebbels when, to top off a bellicose speech of Hitler's at the height of the Czech crisis of September 1938, he compacted it into an oath of fidelity centering in the words: "Never will a November 1918 be repeated among us."[94] "Hitler looked up to him"—so noted the American broadcaster—"a wild, eager expression in his eyes, as if those were the words which he had been searching for all evening and hadn't quite found. He leaped to his feet and with a fanatical fire in his eyes that I shall never forget brought his right hand, after a grand sweep, pounding down on the table and yelled with all the power in his mighty lungs: 'Ja!' Then he slumped into his chair exhausted."[95] On 1 September 1939, after announcing that Germany was "returning fire" on the Polish border, Hitler declaimed: "Never again will a November 1918 be repeated in German history!"[96] When England declared war two days later, he declaimed further: "The Germany of 1939 is no longer the Germany of 1914! . . . Only the disunity of 1918 led to the collapse. Therefore whoever transgresses against national unity now can only expect to be destroyed as an enemy of the nation."[97] Anyone who expressed doubt about a German victory was to be arrested forthwith under a decree of 1938 providing a death penalty for seditious talk in wartime: these instructions of 3 September 1939 for implementing that decree were rapidly amplified in practice.[98] Hitler sounded the Goebbels refrain about November 1918 over and again in ever new variants on the order of "No capitulation outside, no revolution inside,"[99] or "A different country stands behind the front and a different front stands before the country."[100] He was as shrill as ever about it when he cried to a gathering of munitions workers a few weeks after the Anglo-American landing of 6 June 1944 in Normandy: "It will never come to a 1918! Never! So long as I live and so long as one of my guards lives, whoever so much as thinks that will be destroyed. . . . A ninth of November will never be repeated in German history. And because a ninth of November will not come again, we shall win this war."[101]

The bomb blast in his East Prussian headquarters that 20 July perturbed the refrain. Over the radio that night he styled the feckless conspirators behind the blast "a tiny group that believed it could deliver the stab in the back now as in 1918."[102] But at a military conference eleven days later he called their act "a symptom of an inner systemic disturbance, of an inner blood poisoning, that has taken place in us" and fulminated against "that outfit that kept spreading poison," that "damned little clique" of "absolute destroyers and traitors" occupying "the most important positions in the rear." Probably they were to blame for all of Germany's military reverses in the east, he exclaimed. Then he added incoherently: "But even if that did not prove to be concretely so, it would be quite enough that people are sitting here in the most decisive place who instead of continually exuding strength and spreading confidence and above all else deepening the absolute awareness of the fatefulness of this struggle—a fateful struggle that can't somehow be broken off or traded away by some clever political or tactical stunt, but that it really is a sort of battle of the Huns in which either you stand or you fall and die, one of the two. If these thoughts are not present in the higher echelons, but instead these idiots imagine that their situation would improve because today the revolution is being made by generals instead of by soldiers as in 1918, then simply everything just comes to an end, then an army must be gradually decomposed from the top down . . . betrayal . . . ongoing betrayal . . . traitors . . . traitors. . . ."[103] Another military conference a month later found him still castigating rear-line officers for infecting front-line officers with defeatism.[104] But the July bomb blast was again just a failed dagger thrust in his proclamation for the next anniversary of the November revolution. [105] And for front-line commanders in his Ardennes offensive of December 1944 he drummed up his old motif intact: "Today the entire German people stands unshakable and will stand unshakable. In 1918 the German people capitulated without any need."[106] That New Year's Day he assured both army and nation that, since he had mercilessly purged them both after 20 July, the byword of no defeat without or within was more valid than ever.[107] On 30 January, in his last radio address, he ruled out a new capitulation, declaring: "History does not repeat itself!"[108] As late as 11 March 1945 he was still proclaiming: "1918 will not be repeated."[109]

Eight days later he ordered Germany destroyed in the wake of its retreating armies.[110] In his political testament he claimed that "our resistance is gradually being sapped by creatures as deluded as they are unprincipled,"[111] and in his addendum to it that "disloyalty and treachery had undermined the force of resistance during the entire war. It had therefore not been granted to him to lead his people to victory."[112] This hollow updating of the legendary defeat from within perfected his full-scale refutation of it. This time around, moreover, the defeat was driven home, and the collapse of the established order was unmistakably its result.

"No new November 1918" was like a motto for Hitler's entire approach to World War II. His program for the new war turned on precautions against the old one being repeated: proceeding against the old adversaries by stages (continental, hemispheric, global), successive localized blitzkriegs in the first stage, Britain's advance acquiescence in the continental conquest. And he promoted his Jewish policy as a precaution against the internal poisoning he blamed for the old defeat. Those were respectively two kinds of precaution he took against renewing the 1918 defeat: ineffective preventions of true causes of that defeat and effective preventions of false causes of it. Under the latter head, removing the Jews and repressing defeatism were only the first and last steps in the logic of his domestic politics, which was to avoid a new self-defeat in the old war. He retraced a few of the steps in between for a gathering of young officers and officer candidates on 15 February 1942. "August 1914: the whole German nation is of one mind, seemingly of one mind. Unfortunately they neglect to lock up the inside enemies in good time, to seize that great moment of national exaltation to dispose of those who must by their very nature be averse to such exaltation. The nation is united, and then in four years the nation begins to be disunited again. . . . And so this people disintegrates, and at the same time as it disintegrates its outward strength wanes. . . . For that reason I then laid the foundations for a movement with the absolutely extreme and intransigent goal of destroying party after party in Germany, removing all manifestations of that disunity, suppressing the several states, extinguishing their parliaments, breaking up trade unions, dissolving employers' syndicates—in short, reducing this whole inner Germany to a single common denominator. And now there is no doubt about it, my young officers: to the very degree that this succeeded, the German flag slowly rose back up from half mast, and today it waves again over Europe. That was the result of this development. We thereby overcame Versailles, knocked piece after piece out of that devil's pact . . . from one cause alone: because we succeeded in gradually removing all the elements of inner German dissolution, in setting a single commanding will at the head, in seeing to it that through our unitary organization the recurrence of such fragmentation and therewith of a dissolution of German strength is avoided for all future time."[113] He expunged much besides from his Reich to the same end, such as the cultural modernism widely held to have undermined Germandom. And apart from removing causes of the fabled self-defeat, he guarded against a new dupery like the fabled one by Wilson. Six weeks after the unwanted Munich Agreement he compared British appeasement to Wilsonian hypocrisy and concluded: "The German people has learned its lesson, and a collapse such as Germany underwent at that time thanks to her credulity will not be repeated in the next thousand years!"[114] With every new move abroad thereafter he worsened his chances of ever falling back on a negotiated European settlement even as he lengthened his record of damage and deceit.[115] In this he achieved the cumulative effect that Wilson had cited in October 1918 in declaring it impossible to negotiate peace with the then "masters of German policy."[116] He himself drew the connection in asserting, on New Year's Day of 1940, that "the Jewish-capitalist world enemy" (the Jewish-Bolshevik world enemy was his ally just then) "knows only one aim, which is to destroy Germany, the German people," but had professed to pursue another, "the removal of my person—that is, the extermination of National Socialism"—until it emerged "that after the experience of 1918 the German people simply no longer falls for this stupidest swindle."[117] He downright intended the extermination of the Jews to cut off his approach to the west. To the Rumanian chief of state, in April 1943, he put it (to quote his interpreter's record) that "the more radically one proceeds against the Jews the better. He . . . prefers to burn all his bridges behind him, as Jewish hate is gigantic in any case."[118] And to the Bulgarian council of regency in March 1944: "He believes that one should cut off all possible lines of retreat oneself: then one fights with greater ease and resolve."[119] He made a virtue of ruling out negotiations even when in full military retreat. In the early summer of 1944, some weeks after the Anglo-American landing in Normandy, he assured armament workers: "I would not think of some rotten compromise or other."[120] In private councils later that summer he called it "just plain naïve" to imagine that Germany could come to terms with either England or Russia against the other, let alone play them off against each other.[121] His interpreter observed that, while he consistently rejected suggestions from foreign visitors for extending peace feelers either way, in Stalin's case "this rejection was expressed with none of the same wild, indeed almost fanatical, vehemence as in the case of the 'plutocrats.'"[122] His last recorded refusal to try making a deal with the "plutocrats" was the incongruously worded one of the night of 20–21 April 1945: "I am done making deals."[123] His concern to obviate a new Judeo-capitalist swindle had helped deter him from approaching England as his program for correcting World War I required. Instead he could only hope for his projected pact with England to materialize of its own—or toward the last, with his bridges all burned behind him, for a clash between the Soviets and the West "if Germany held firm."[124] So the stab-in-the-back and Wilson legends served for repeating, as well as denying, the 1918 defeat since they indicated safeguards against it that were illusory and worse.

Insistent denials that an experience would be repeated and multiple precautions against its being repeated: these evince a reliving in process unconsciously. But how did the second experience reflect the first in externals? The chief elements of both were the same—the chief nations and territories involved—as does not ordinarily happen with a traumatized individual.[125] They could hardly have been much different once the event was duplicated outright, as another world war, but this it presumably did not need to be. It might have been relived in another sphere of endeavor, like Hitler's own trauma, or else at least by symbolic equivalence, like his mother's. As it was, the second war rendered the first the more starkly. But it did so through permutations that are routine in unconscious reliving, and serve to keep the reliving unconscious by distancing the second experience from the first on the surface. Chief among such permutations are reversals, as befits the straining in vain to reverse the traumatic outcome. Thus Russia was as much underestimated militarily in the planning and initial phase of Barbarossa as it had been overestimated in 1914.[126] Hitler's intended knockout campaign in Russia following the fall of France—Barbarossa—inverted Ludendorff's in France following the fall of Russia. At the same time Barbarossa mirrored the Germans' western offensive of 1914, which was likewise designed to avert a two-front war by smashing the enemy on the one side before a real threat could be expected on the other—and was likewise mired. (In this, minus the miring, Barbarossa was prefigured by the Polish war, and earlier by the Czech war of which British appeasement deprived Hitler in September 1938.[127]) Hitler's theory and practice of the blitzkrieg, which foundered with Barbarossa, reversed Ludendorff's theory and practice of total war.[128] Even Ludendorff's panic of 29 September 1918 was reversed. At that point Ludendorff cast off his political power while calling for an armistice six months after having launched his all-or-nothing western offensive. Hitler in turn saw the inevitability of defeat six months after having launched Barbarossa, whereupon he issued a strict no-retreat order in Russia and took personal command of the army. Thereafter he repeated the 1918 civilian government's alleged betrayal of the army by lying in the opposite way about the prospects of victory—down to his eleventh-hour insistence that victory was solely a matter of nerves not cracking.[129]

Akin to reversals were Hitler's unavailing correctives on the order of his installment plan for expansion. Notable under that head are his turnabout alliances with Germany's old enemies. The Italian was the first such to be envisaged (1920) and likewise to be achieved (1936). It brought him no help against France, trouble in the Balkans, and a "feeling of insecurity" in Africa and Russia that kept him awake nights [130]—rightly. Italy's defection in September 1943 delivered him.[131] Similarly, his successive pacts with Japan (1936, 1940) failed to cow Britain as intended; instead they helped to involve America against him.[132] His single reversal of a pivotal World War I alignment, his pact of 23 August 1939 with Stalin, was itself reversed by Barbarossa. In February 1940 he pointed to the realignment of Italy, Russia, and Japan and boasted: "Today the situation has changed fundamentally in several respects as compared with 1914." [133] He came around in February 1942, after having invaded Russia and declared war on America: "Thus fate determined us to fall in against the same coalition that fought against us once already." [134] A professed corrective that was none was his Four Year Plan of 1936 for autarky: it postulated expansion.[135] Again no provision was made for a long war on the ground that Germany could not sustain one—that the only possible victory was a quick one.[136] "Today the attempt is frequently made to present things as if Germany had entered the war in 1914 with goodly provisions of raw materials. This is a lie": thus Hitler's memorandum on his Four Year Plan.[137] Hitler did thereupon prescribe a departure from World War I: to invest in today's arms output rather than in increasing tomorrow's, and with a minimum of economic controls. That was blitzkrieg economics. Once Barbarossa had foundered, he directed Germany after all into a centralized war economy aimed at maximizing productive capacity, one coordinated along lines laid down the first time around by that Prussianized personification of the Judeo-capitalist world enemy, Walther Rathenau.[138]

As World War II reverted more and more openly to its prototype, Hitler followed along. In December 1942, just before the encirclement of the German Sixth Army at Stalingrad, he justified to his generals his standing order not to surrender a foot of land in Russia[139] by the consideration that the German retreat "after the Marne idiocy" of September 1914 had been in danger of turning into a rout.[140] After that retreat of September 1914 from the Marne the German offensive had resumed in Flanders for some weeks with Hitler's regiment out front. That winter Hitler had told one correspondent: "I dare say I risked my life and stared death in the face every day," and another: "As if by a miracle I remain safe and sound."[141] "Then began the positional war," Fritz Wiedemann later recollected. "As hopes ran high in the winter of 1914–1915 of resuming the offensive the following spring where it had been mired in the mud of the autumn rains, the rule was that terrain once won was to be held firmly. So just where the attack had ground to a halt ran the line of trenches sinking ever deeper into the mud. In those months we lay south of Lille, to the west of a hilly ridge containing the village of Fromelles.[142] The flat terrain was as unfavorable as could be for a fixed position. When the winter rains began, the trenches were flooded, so that the breastwork had to be set up above ground with sacks of sand. At times water became a worse enemy of the companies than the English facing them. It would have been most sensible to move the front line a few kilometers back to the dry, elevated terrain. And we submitted requests to this effect. But they were always rejected by the High Command on the ground that terrain once won was not to be lost again. So every salient reached by an advancing group was held with senseless losses. There is no doubt that Hitler made this principle, false even then, his own: No voluntary retreat under any circumstances. Later he transferred this tactical principle to strategy and therewith among other things sealed the fate of the Sixth Army in Stalingrad."[143] And yet Hitler appears to have come to that principle independently of the High Command, to judge by his discussion of that very salient in a further one of his letters of that winter of 1914–1915: "Through the perpetual rain (we have no winter) the closeness of the ocean and the low level of the terrain, the fields and meadows resemble bottomless marshes while the roads are covered with mud a foot deep, through these swamps run the trenches of our infantry, a mess of dugouts—trenches with firing slits, communication trenches, wire entanglements, covered pits, booby traps, in short a nearly impregnable position. . . . Our troops took the town by storm. The English resisted desperately. . . . Only when it went up in flames with its huge cloister did our regimentals carry off the assault, streaming with blood. Now the French are bombarding the ruins. Day after day for two months air and earth here have been trembling from the howling and crackling of the grenades, the bursting of shrapnel. . . . But no death and no devil will budge us from the spot. We shall stay put till Hindenburg has softened up Russia. Then comes the reckoning."[144] Some twenty-eight years later he told his chief of staff: "I have thought something over in the broad view, Zeitzler. Under no circumstances must we give *that* up."[145] "*That*" was the German foothold in Stalingrad.

In an address of May 1942 to newly commissioned officers Hitler declared, after fusing the second war with the first in a higher historic continuum: "I too know this fight. I was in it for over four years."[146] His identification of the two wars climaxed in his last-hope Ardennes offensive of December 1944, inspired by Ludendorff's last-hope western offensive of 1918. Literalizing the equivalence, he weakened Germany's eastern defenses in order to launch it[147] and practically forgot about the Red Army in the thick of it. Midway, while reviewing its difficulties to date before division commanders, he betrayed its futility by an unguarded turn of phrase: "And yet for a moment the situation almost permitted the hope of our holding out."[148] He added: ". . . Here 1918 must be a warning to us. In 1918 the pauses between successive attacks were much too long. . . ."[149] The next day he remarked at a military conference: "Something just occurred to me because people are always complaining they get reinforcements too late. We marched off for the second offensive in 1918 on the 25th [of May]. On the 26th we slept in a forest. . . ."[150] From then on, the strategist's planning of 1944–1945 was informed by the foot soldier's experiences of 1914–1918—with horses and bicycles, with artillery rationing, with transporting ten- and fifteen-centimeter howitzers in two loads each.[151]

Hitler rode his two political tracks together nonstop to their common terminus. Nothing could sidetrack him, not even another trauma. And he contracted one early along: at midday on 9 November 1923, when he collapsed with his Putsch under fire. The consulting physician at his prison certified that he had suffered "a dislocated left shoulder with the top broken, followed by a very painful traumatic neurosis,"[152] and that "the pain in the injured arm . . . is to be traced back to a traumatic nervous ailment."[153] A trembling of the left arm resulted which subsided over the years. The nervous ailment—he himself called it "my nervous ailment"—resumed when Barbarossa was checked, which he knew meant defeat.[154] The trembling resumed during the Stalingrad disaster, then spread to the leg by association with his 1916 shrapnel wound in the left thigh.[155] It worsened steadily except when the Stauffenberg bomb blast halted it for some weeks.[156] As for the psychological trauma, he had meanwhile purged that through his Blood Purge of 30 June 1934.

The traumatic Pusch was charged with the tension that built up between Bavaria and Berlin when Stresemann, in late September 1923, called off passive resistance to the French occupation of the Ruhr. Bavaria had thereupon appointed a prime minister with dictatorial powers, Gustav von Kahr, to challenge Berlin while restraining the local paramilitary formations, among them

110

Hitler's SA. The chief of the Reichswehr in Bavaria and the chief of the Bavarian police joined Kahr in defying the Reichswehr command in Berlin when it tried to enforce a national state of emergency. Braced for a showdown with Berlin, the three strong men felt out the local political armies for prospective backing. Hitler would provide no support short of full partnership, which threatened to become leadership.[157] When the hesitant triumvirs gathered with Munich's notables in the Bürgerbräu beer hall on the evening of 8 November 1923 to dishonor the fifth anniversary of Eisner's revolution, Hitler burst in upon the scene to proclaim a national revolution—revolver in hand, and with truckloads of elite SA (the "Stosstrupp Hitler") outside. The triumvirs played along after Ludendorff answered Hitler's call to join him; they disavowed the national revolution after Ludendorff let them leave. The next morning Hitler and Ludendorff marched with their adherents to the center of town in faint hopes of sweeping the Reichswehr and Bavarian state troops along. At the Odeonsplatz the procession was dispersed under fire by state troops. "I took them for Reichswehr because of their steel helmets," Hitler testified afterwards.[158] This confusion was general.[159] Hitler's strongest confederate in the Reichswehr had been his *Du*-friend Ernst Röhm. Röhm had seized and held the Reichswehr headquarters just above the Odeonsplatz with an armed following of his own that included flag bearer Heinrich Himmler.[160] The Hitler-Ludendorff columns had been heading for Röhm's besieged stronghold.[161]

The Putsch spirit survived in the SA after 1923 even while Hitler steered his new legal course in perpetual fear of a clash between SA and Reichswehr. Röhm headed the SA during Hitler's imprisonment and again after the Party's electoral upsurge of 1930. After Hitler's takeover of 1933 the SA aspired, Röhm foremost, to a "second revolution" whereby it would supplant the Reichswehr.[162] Hitler let the tension mount between the rival armies. Informed once that Röhm was talking sedition in secret SA councils, he remarked: "We must allow the affair to ripen fully."[163] Then he had top SA leaders convened in Bad Wiessee, in southern Bavaria, to await him at 9 A.M. on 30 June. Röhm supposed that Hitler intended to iron out their differences.[164] Instead Hitler arrived over two hours early with a truckload of Himmler's SS—Hitler from Bonn by way of Munich's Odeonsplatz, the SS from Berlin by way of Landsberg.[165] Revolver in hand, he arrested Röhm, calling him a traitor[166]—the charge he had thrown back at the Bavarian government in his Putsch trial. To the SA in Munich he added afterward that Röhm was in French pay, as had been rumored about Hitler himself in the Putsch days.[167] For forty-eight hours the SS massacred SA by the scores along with a few non-SA, among them old Kahr, dragged out of oblivion to be hacked to bits and thrown into a swamp.[168] Hitler had Röhm incarcerated in Röhm's 1923 prison in Munich-Stadelheim and ordered him shot if he would not shoot himself: he would not. Hitler refused to proceed against Röhm judicially because of his own near acquittal after the Putsch. "I might even have gone scot-free then," he told Hans Frank, Bavarian minister of justice in 1934. "This is a direct threat to the state."[169]

Hitler justified the Röhm purge by the fiction that its victims had been putsching against him.[170] For through it he had relived his own, real Putsch with the pieces rearranged. In the "Röhm Putsch" he took Kahr's 1923 place. Like Kahr before him, he was backed by the local Reichswehr. The SS, an offshoot of the SA, replaced the SA elite that had mounted guard for him at the Bürgerbräu beer hall.[171] Röhm stood in for the putschist that Hitler had been. Afterward Hitler denounced the likes of Röhm as perpetual insurgents,[172] only to remark in 1936 at his annual commemoration of the beer hall Putsch ("the most sacral day on the National Socialist ceremonial calendar"[173]): "I can admit in all candor that from 1919 to 1923 I thought of nothing but a *coup d'État*."[174] Behind Röhm's unused suicide revolver was one that Hitler had surrendered on being apprehended in 1923.[175] The other duplications were graphic: Reichswehr, SA, Odeonsplatz, Landsberg, Stadelheim, traitor, French pay, revolver in hand. The upshot was that the SA did not supplant the Reichswehr. But Hitler later "complained frequently that the army was no militia and in so doing employed almost the same terms as Röhm before him."[176]

Hitler's posture of revolutionary legality toward Röhm, his putschist double, is a reminder that his legal course to power had also been his Putsch relaunched: it reversed the old means to the same end. That is, post-Putsch Hitler used the Weimar system to the avowed end of destroying it. In his oath of legality of September 1930 to the high court in Leipzig he allowed that, though his takeover was to be legal, "heads will roll" afterward.[177] That legal takeover rectified the traumatic Putsch, which he then repeated to a full finish through the "Röhm Putsch."

Hitler answered to Germany for the Röhm purge in terms of abscesses burnt out of the national flesh.[178] Thus he had worked off his Putsch trauma through the Röhm purge[179] only to align the Röhm purge with his Bloch trauma. But through the Putsch itself he had relived his gas trauma. For before the Putsch he had time and again equated his political struggle with his front-line wartime service, and after four years and a few weeks of that struggle he was once again disabled with several of his comrades-in-arms and evacuated under fire even as, in his view of it, the national cause was once again betrayed. In later years, closing the circle, he dated his stomach complaint, based on his mother's agony and his gas trauma combined, from the Röhm purge.[180] Could a psychic economy be tighter?

V

LEADER AND LED

For what is essential will always be the inner accord between leader and multitude.

ADOLF HITLER, 27 October 1928.[1]

Hitler himself, he said, was nothing—nothing but a medium through which the movement operates. But then too he said that only Hitler has a grip on the movement.

HARRY KESSLER, Paris, 6 July 1933, quoting Hermann Keyserlingk.[2]

For Germany traumatized in 1918, Hitler legitimated himself as leader by succeeding, and exceeding, Ludendorff. Here the Putsch was pivotal. Earlier Hitler had bowed to Ludendorff, who towered over Germany's folkic movement.[3] But at the Bürgerbräu beer hall Hitler called the moves; Ludendorff fell in behind him for the "national revolution" as prospective "regent of the Reich" (whatever that meant) and chief of a people's army.[4] Then at their trial Hitler eclipsed Ludendorff by taking full responsibility for their deed; the court bore Hitler out by convicting him and acquitting Ludendorff. He disposed of Ludendorff politically in the spring of 1925 by running him against Hindenburg for president of the Republic: Ludendorff rolled up 1.1 percent of the national vote.[5] Thereafter, the more Hitler superseded Ludendorff, the more hostile Ludendorff grew. With this hostility Ludendorff acquired clairvoyance about his successor's historic role, as can be seen from his private message of 30 January 1933 to Hindenburg, his wartime partner long since estranged from him: "In naming Hitler chancellor you have delivered our holy German fatherland into the hands of one of the greatest demagogues of all time. I solemnly predict to you that this wretched man will hurl our country into the abyss and bring unimaginable misery upon our people."[6] To seal that unholy delivery, Hitler courted reconciliation with Ludendorff. He achieved it in March 1937,[7] and to his telegram on that year's anniversary of their Putsch Ludendorff replied: "Today my thoughts too are more than ever for that joint effort of ours to raise up Germany. My best wishes accompany your effective action for our people's rise."[8] Six weeks later Ludendorff was dead, and Hitler declared in epitaph: "With his name is linked for all time the greatest heroic struggle of the German people."[9] Between telegram and epitaph Hitler had told Party officials in secret sessions that Germany had lacked the "force of leadership" needed to hold Europe in 1918.[10] He completed this thought a year later for a South African interlocutor: "Had an Adolf Hitler stood at the head of Germany during the war, the war would not have been lost."[11]

Hitler's continuity with Ludendorff was clearest in the martial-predatory sphere. He enlarged upon Ludendorff's view of peace-making as imposing one's will on the enemy, Ludendorff's quest for more feeding and breeding ground for future wars, his hard-and-fast operational rule "not to surrender a foot of soil without a tough struggle,"[12] his modus operandi of all or nothing, conquer or perish, even his hope for deliverance from the final bind through a stroke of luck such as had befallen Frederick the Great in the Seven Years War.[13] An overview of Ludendorff as warlord is a preview of Hitler as warlord. "For Ludendorff," runs a recent retrospect, "the First World War neither could nor ought to end with a compromise, but only with victory or defeat." And in his western offensive "Ludendorff staked so much on one card that the high command did not even order a rear line such as Antwerp-Namur-Sedan-Metz built in good time. . . . It is . . . a distinctive mark of Ludendorff's eastern conceptions that no unified plan at all underlay them. . . . Ludendorff's Ukrainian, Crimean, and Caucasian policies in particular were so immoderate that the analogy with 'the National Socialist rampage' is incontestable."[14] Another historian, stressing Ludendorff's idea "that only expansion can bring full security and that without full security Germany would be unable to survive and develop," observes: "But this conception was not gained from a rational analysis of political reality; it was part of a pregiven political outlook, one not rationally grounded, which so absolutized the conflicts of interest between peoples that conquering and surviving became one."[15] This outlook was the typical Wilhelmian one blindingly intensified, the ultimate in proud power politics: pure, and hence unrealistic, realpolitik.[16] "Germany should simply strive for what she needs to live" was Ludendorff's rule covering annexations on all sides.[17] Eschewing mere treaties with future German satellites, he prescribed for Germany in Belgium: "Here too only real power! This we must have. All else is illusion."[18] Hitler preferred to ideologize, yet those same power-political terms of reference for the war he later refought came as if naturally to him after he adopted them on 31 May 1921 to deplore the loss of Ludendorff's eastern conquest.[19]

It was while he was assuming Ludendorff's succession beginning at their Putsch trial that Hitler elaborated his program for German expansion and fitted his anti-Semitism to it for German consumption. To achieve this congruence he generalized his animus against the Jew into an ethnic imperialism continuous with the German supremacism practiced in Eastern Europe in 1917–1918. This supremacism was thereby more radicalized than his other World War I originals except perhaps military aggression. The subjugation of non-Germans in conquered eastern territories under Ludendorff reappeared under Hitler as their spoliation, degradation, extermination. Germany itself was Germanized besides as, with the Polish conquest, Hitler ordered German Jews deported to a "General Government" in Poland (another Ludendorff original[20]) pending worse. The martyrdom of the Jews contributed to validating the moral verdict of 1918 the second time around. And it was central to Hitler's system of false correctives for the 1918 defeat that were suited to fool Germans consciously at most. Once Hitler had subordinated his Jew-baiting to his warmongering, its negative effect on most Germans was blurred or canceled over the years. At length Germany's Jews were lumped together with foreigners in Germany's way. The official euphemisms—"transportation," "special handling," "final solution"—veiled Hitler's Jewish operation only in the sense that they shrouded its starkness.[21] It tried a few private consciences, but no more aroused German opposition to Hitler than did the devastations and depredations inflicted on Poland and Russia.[22] Such organized opposition as did arise in Hitlerized Germany turned on expectations of a German defeat.

The anti-Semitic agitator groomed himself as a drastic latter-day Ludendorff in the mid-1920s by way of gaining the dictatorial power he needed for his traumatic purpose of poisoning Germany's poisoner with Germany succumbing. But the terms of his leadership were a tacit trade-off whereby he would conduct his own traumatic business along with Germany's. He entered into the role of Ludendorff losing World War I the more passionately since it took him back to his own losing struggle of 1914–1918 for mother Germany. His acting for Germany was the central fact of the concurrent German reexperience of 1914–1918. That is, the German nation merely underwent that reexperience, whereas an individual engaged in traumatic reliving will control and even force events. Indeed, to control and thereby detraumatize a traumatic experience is the apparent aim of reliving it. But Hitler controlled events for Germany. For this he was invested by Germans en masse as Ludendorff was not. They deputized him to drive home their 1918 defeat—and then read the signs of a renewal of World War I with submissive foreboding, holding fate to blame.[23] They exalted him personally above both his policy lines like heaven over hell. His atrocities in the ideological line were ascribed to evil henchmen,[24] and when he attacked Russia "a wave of compassion and sympathy welled up" for him as the victim of alleged treachery by the Bolshevik ally.[25] This unreality principle held even high above the popular consciousness. Only two out of seven Reichswehr chiefs' records or recollections of his briefing session of 28 February 1934 mention his representations on living space,[26] and his grim harangue of 30

March 1941 to 200–250 high officers on their duties as ideological gunmen under Barbarossa went practically unheard [27] except, to be sure, by the inner ear.

The hold that Hitler gained over Germany was like a spell that began lifting piecemeal once the tide of conquest turned, then massively in the final debacle. That spell had been prophesied in 1932 as "a reign of the collective beast" [28] and decried as "a mass madness" in 1937 through a tale of Münster possessed by the Anabaptists. [29] Just such a spell was alleged afterward on all sides amid the rubble and ashes—and the exposed horrors—of Hitler's rule. Ribbentrop only went the limit when in captivity he "pleaded with everyone who came within earshot . . . to explain what had happened during the 'mass psychosis' of Hitlerism." [30] The intent of such post-Nazi talk was always at least a little apologetic. [31] Yet the question did repeatedly arise whether that mass phenomenon was Hitler's creation or he its creature, whether it was a mass bewitchment or a mass seizure. In general it came off as a mix of the two in equal overdoses. Thomas Aich's *Massenmensch und Massenwahn* ("Mass Man and Mass Madness") of 1947 argued at once mass hypnosis by Hitler, a "mutual" "frenzy" between Hitler and his public, and a mediumistic pitch of Hitler's voice: "Out of it speaks the collective, the irrational, of the mass soul." [32] "Frenzy" *(Rausch)* was the pat term: reminiscences of the Russian campaign could be marketed in 1948 under the title *Der grosse Rausch* ("The Great Frenzy") without fear that the reference would be missed. (The reference was supplied only incidentally in the work itself: "We were frenzied with the dream of power: the whole world." [33]) The term was all too strong for the surface showing. The frenzy was not demonstrative the year round as if at a permanent Hitler rally. [34] It was rather a diffuse sense of empowerment through Hitler and of powerlessness against him. By the 1950s it was a dead memory. [35] And today's Germans ignore it in retrospect like some fanciful distraction from the objective terms of Hitler's appeal. [36]

That is as if the Thebans of old had unlearned their lesson from Dionysus. In Euripides' awesome masterpiece, *The Bac-*

chae, Dionysus, son of Zeus by a woman of Thebes, proves his divine power to the doubting city by inflicting a ruinous mass enchantment on it. The Theban women in particular succumb, like the maenads who have followed Dionysus from Phrygia. Their enchantment is regressive—a flight from domestic constraint to elemental communion with nature in roving bands. Now quiescent, now frenzied, they suckle beasts only to devour them while chanting and swaying in unison.

Remotely comparable regressive behavior in crowds led Freud to suppose that human consciousness was originally shared within a human horde. In Freud's developed conception, that primal, psychically undifferentiated human mass cohered around an individualized, self-willed tyrant holding it in thrall by his overpowering gaze.[37] Hitler evidently read Freud's *Mass Psychology and Ego Analysis* in prison after the Putsch.[38] His subsequent insistence on "the right of the personality" (that is, of his personality alone) and the "leadership principle,"[39] together with unity of mind and will in his following, suggests a calculated effort to reproduce first in his Party, then in his Reich, the tribal configuration imagined by Freud. But Hitler was less of a terrorizer than his Freudian prototype. In Hans Frank's overstatement of 1946: "One must not say that Hitler *violated* the German people—he *seduced* them! They followed him with a mad jubilation. . . . It was a madness, a drunkenness."[40] Nor was the regressive effect of Hitlerism[41] a trick of psychological manipulation in the manner of Dionysus enticing his antagonist—Pentheus, fledgling tyrant of Thebes—back to babyhood. Even Dionysus only drew on impulses he found latent in Pentheus as in more compliant Thebans. Hitler too, by a sixth sense, caught the mute signals from his constituency: his message of war only verbalized them. Hitlerism harked back to an earlier mass regression contained between the blood lust of 1914 and the shock of defeat in 1918. And Hitlerism tended to become ritualized in its turn, like the celebration of the tempter god.[42]

Hitler's secret intelligence with his public looks like a reversion to a primitive leader's sharing his followers' thoughts. Vestiges of the other side of such thought-sharing are familiar: the child's, the culprit's, or the sinner's fear that his mind is being read by his father, the criminal inspector, or God respectively.[43] The relationship was nonreciprocal in Hitler's practice as in Freud's theory: Hitler's innermost thoughts as leader were sealed off.[44] Yet Hitler was not Freud's self-willed tyrant underneath it all. "The masses must be led," he asserted,[45] and his will was declared law in his Party, then in his Reich. But the theory was that his was the national will. In the juristic diction of the time: "The Leader speaks and acts not merely for the people and in its behalf, but as the people. In him the German people itself shapes its fate."[46] Will-sharing was the *mystique* of his rule, with the hallowed August days of 1914 as its point of reference.[47] It also shaped his politics as he coupled Germany's unconscious purposes with his own and then handled them like his own—programmed them in disguise and, properly enough, called the program his. And in applying that program he turned to Germans regularly even after his national sounding board was reduced to a roomful of generals. As one of these attested: "I have witnessed sessions where he obviously had not yet arrived at a clear decision; he was feeling his way around cautiously in the beginning, slowly convincing himself in a long speech until at the end he pronounced his irrevocable decision."[48]

In *The Bacchae* the sexuality suffusing the divine madness is oral-sadistic. Dionysus the wine-giver, "himself a god, is poured out in offering to the gods."[49] He is symbolized by the beasts that his celebrants both suckle and devour—and at a farther remove by Pentheus, torn limb from limb by his mother in a divine transport. Oral sadism likewise underlay the fierce oratory through which Hitler both fed, and fed off, his audiences.[50] No doubt it also informed the screaming hysteria that his oratory elicited in return. And yet his effect on massed listeners, and on Germany at large, was of a kind with his effect on individuals, which was ascribed more to his eyes than his tongue.[51] Both those effects were attested to time and again in the very same terms. One of his conservative ministers cited "the power of suggestion by which he coerced the individual as well as the masses,"[52] and another declared it "incontestable . . . that something radiated from him which affected individuals and especially the great masses as well."[53] "Especially" here ties in with this observation by one of his generals: "In order to achieve the greatest possible effects of his own suggestive power, and possibly in order to increase his self-confidence, Hitler preferred a not too small audience."[54] This is as far as Hitler's suggestive effect on individuals and groups differed between the two: in degree.[55] A frequent term for that effect was "hypnotic" or "hypnoid," even in the collective case. "Flaming, steel-blue eyes," or again "strangely compelling eyes," dominated Kurt Lüdecke's sense of the "hypnotic spell" that Hitler cast over an entire audience at once: "the whole man," Lüdecke found, "was concentrated in his eyes, his clear, straightforward, domineering, bright blue eyes."[56] Other witnesses attested to his power of "rhetorical hypnosis" or of talking an audience into "a mass psychosis bordering on hypnosis."[57] "The Führer had such a power of hypnotic suggestion that the entire people believed in him," declared his Nuremberg apostle, Julius Streicher, from the prisoners' dock there in 1946.[58] Only the term "hypnotic" is missing from this account of 1934 by a lowly follower: "In 1927 I and my comrades had a chance to look into the eyes of our Führer and to hear from his mouth how Germany could be saved. I shall never forget this, for I think that our Führer radiates a power which makes us all strong."[59] "Mass hypnosis—that hardly explains it," sneered Hans Frank in his death cell,[60] and again: "That so-called fascinating look of his was nothing but the stare of an insensitive psychopath!"[61] But then Frank cited Hitler's "lovely grey eyes" in explaining how Hitler had "lured workers, lawyers, scientists, women and children—everything—to destruction!"[62] Most revealing was the mad "revelation" whereby prisoner Rudolf Hess emerged from amnesia on 4 February 1945: that the atrocities committed by his countrymen were due to world Jewry's hypnotic influence reaching "up to the Führer himself" and evidenced by the glassy, dreamlike eyes of those affected.[63]

Hitler may have practiced deliberate hypnosis at close range, following Freud's theory or Forster's example. "His blue eyes were fascinating," declared his photographer, adding: "they missed their effect on no one."[64] "Now I understand why these people speak of his hypnotic eyes," noted an interviewer in June 1931 with reference to "all the interlocutors he wants to win over."[65] Hitler himself remarked at a military conference of 27 January 1945: "I have another unpleasant job left today. I still must hypnotize Quisling" (his puppet Norwegian ruler).[66] At least Speer's unbreakable fixation on Hitler would seem not to have been visually induced. For Speer claims that Hitler once tried to stare him down and—though the ordeal seemed unending and the strain unendurable—failed.[67]

However induced, the result was similar all around Hitler's circle.[68] Hess's bondage to Hitler was "nearly magical" from its inception in 1920.[69] Goebbels confided to his diary on 19 April 1926: "Adolf Hitler, I love you."[70] "Hitler had a tremendous power of suggestion over Himmler," asserted Himmler's masseur, adding that the mass executioner, when summoned by Hitler, was subject to seizures of panic—"animal, 'baseless,' nervously determined."[71] Hitler drew Ribbentrop to him "magnetically," as Ribbentrop avowed in Nuremberg.[72] "Kaltenbrunner," so recollected an assistant of the Security chief's, "was to the last downright spellbound by Hitler's personality."[73] "An uncanny magic emanated from him," affirmed his sometime Minister of Finance, Schwerin von Krosigk.[74] "Even strong intellects and personalities fell under the spell of his mind and will," observed quondam Labor Service leader Konstantin Hierl.[75] As a non-Nazi visitor to Nazi headquarters put it in 1931, "it is open to no doubt whatsoever that Hitler exerts upon his entourage a power of suggestion the extent of which is difficult to grasp."[76] Throughout his career non-Nazis noted his "altogether fascinating personality"[77] or "very remarkable degree of personal power of fascination."[78] Indeed, German claims to have escaped this fascination in over a brief moment's exposure to him are few enough to look suspicious.[79] Even mixed reactions were rare, or at all odds the negative component winning out was.[80] All his non-Nazi associates in running his Reich, from Hindenburg, Papen, Blomberg, and even Schacht in the first hours[81] to the bunkerful of officers, officials, and staff at the last,[82] came under his "suggestive power" and with it his "laming power." These two effects of his "personal radiation" were distinguished by Otto Dietrich, the second having been felt by would-be contradictors facing him: their resolutely mustered courage would fall away, leaving them "as if in a state of mental narcosis, no longer fit to present their viewpoint."[83] This was the "suggestive power" over "even persons ill-disposed toward him" that Karl Dönitz said held "at all odds when they were in his vicinity and as long as they were."[84] How Stauffenberg finally brought himself to plant that bomb is a puzzle even if he did tell his wife, after his first time in Hitler's vicinity six weeks before, that the notorious eyes did nothing to him—that they were "as if behind veils."[85]

Hitler worked no such magic on anyone before or during World War I. His earlier ascendancy over Kubizek and Bloch was in the same line, yet incommensurable. So were his youthful feats of persuasion, such as getting his medical examiners in the Austrian army to find him "too weak to bear arms"—this just after he was run down in Munich in February 1914 for having evaded conscription, and not long before he joined the Bavarian army for years of tireless front-line service.[86] In his youth he was a loner little noticed amid the groups he passed through—his schools in Linz and Steyr, the men's hostel in Vienna, the List Regiment. His charisma dated from Pasewalk. But it was no part of his trauma specifically, let alone a common traumatic effect: traumas that bad and worse run the streets without anyone following. As political orator he did train himself early to stage his appearances and enhance his delivery.[87] Maybe he even modulated his spoken words to deactivate his listeners' rational, and activate their emotional, brain centers.[88] But such "possibilities of psychoprosodiacal influence,"[89] even maximized, fall short of hypnotic enchantment. And the magic that "his speaker's gift" mediating "the suggestive power of his will" worked on live audiences would not add up to a national enchantment even if he did face a cumulative total of 35 million Germans,[90] for mere suggestive effects hardly last. Dönitz had only to leave Hitler's headquarters in order "to disengage myself from his power of suggestion."[91] Quisling's hypnosis needed periodic renewing. Besides, without such special exertions as on Quisling, and such special susceptibility as Quisling's, Hitler produced "next to no impression" on non-Germans.[92] Keitel's last reckoning mentioned Hitler's "suggestive power of persuasion incomprehensible to outsiders and especially to foreigners."[93] In fact the personal magic went with the national message. "On occasion Hitler simply cried out 'Germany! Germany! Germany!' to his audience and drew enthusiastic acclamation."[94] Who else could ever do that?

To repeat: the magic went with the message. So it was that, as far as the records disclose, Hitler's enthrallments of later co-workers began with him expounding his politics, usually from the rostrum. Speer's devotion was the least political on the surface, yet it started when the then teaching assistant in architecture succumbed to the "suggestive force of conviction" that Hitler conveyed in a speech at the university of Berlin in 1930. "This effect," Speer recollected decades later, "was far deeper than that of the speech itself, not much of which remained in my memory"[95]: the rest had hit home. Hitler's seemingly least charismatized henchman was the deadly cynic Heydrich, yet in 1928 naval careerist Heydrich was enraptured by his first Hitler speech and told his sister: "He alone can save Germany."[96] Hess's infatuation was the most blatant: in one observer's overdrawn image, "Hess hangs with the eyes of a credulous child on the mouth of his deified leader."[97] This idolatry was thoroughly political from the outset, when the war veteran brooding over Germany's fate while studying geopolitics in Munich returned "radiant" from a Hitler meeting to his boardinghouse one evening in 1920. "Only the man, the man! He is all!" Hess explained.[98] That man also overcame Munich law student Hans Frank by "the irresistible power of his oratory" at a public meeting in January 1920: "He spoke everything out of his own soul and out of the soul of us all. . . . From that evening on," Frank related, "I was convinced . . . that Hitler alone, if anyone, could master German fate."[99] Hitler captivated cosmopolitan adventurer Kurt Lüdecke that same way at two successive Nazi rallies on 11 August 1922. "I offered myself to him and to his cause without reservation": such was the sequel as Lüdecke told it.[100] Julius Streicher, master Jew-baiter of Nuremberg, was Hitler's rival until, in the early fall of 1922, he first heard Hitler speak. "When he finished his speech," Streicher proudly recounted, "an inner voice bade me get up. I arose and forced myself through the crowd to the speakers' desk. I went toward him and introduced myself. I spoke to him: 'Heil Hitler! I heard your speech. I only can be the helper but you are the born leader. Here is my movement in Nuremberg.' On that evening I gave the movement which I created in Nuremberg to Adolf Hitler."[101] (This gift doubled Hitler's following.[102]) Swaggering war hero Hermann Göring heard Hitler that same autumn denounce mere verbal protests against Versailles as senseless. "This conviction was spoken word for word as if from my own soul," Göring recollected, adding that he thereupon sought out Hitler in the Party offices: "We spoke at once about the things which were close to our hearts—the defeat of the fatherland, and that one could not let it rest with that. . . . I told him that I myself to the fullest extent, and all I was, and all I possessed, were completely at his disposal."[103] Cultivated, clownish Ernst "Putzi" Hanfstaengl was "captivated" as, in one hour of November 1922, the "up-and-coming virtuoso on the keyboard of the mass soul" turned a seething political assemblage into "a community gripped to the depths" by talk of reviving the German battle spirit.[104] Wellborn Baldur von Schirach's student circle of eighteen joined the Party and SA upon hearing Hitler speak in Weimar in 1925. "He appeared to me to be the man who would pave the way into the future for our generation," Schirach explained at the end of that way.[105] Newspaperman Otto Dietrich yielded in April 1929 only after his second Hitler speech at a year's interval.[106] "Goebbels felt Hitler's tremendous will and magnetic power and succumbed to him from the first moment."[107] Before that first moment the Mephistophelean manipulator had promoted a pro-Soviet policy within the Party, requiring Hitler to call him down from the Ruhr to Munich for a talking-to on living space. The conflict was resolved for all time by the line in Goebbels' diary entry for 13 April 1926: "I love him."[108] Ribbentrop's first, fatal contact was a tête-à-tête in Berchtesgaden. There, on 13 August 1932, Hitler held forth about the national future to the negotiant in foreign liquors and intrigant in foreign policy. "I noticed particularly his blue eyes in his generally dark appearance," Ribbentrop recollected in Nuremberg. ". . . I left that meeting convinced that this man, if anyone, could save Germany."[109] Himmler's fall is not documented except that it was slow. He seems not to have set eyes on Hitler yet—not even in the Putsch—when he recited from Hitler speeches to friends beginning 19 February 1924, apparently to train for his debut in political oratory alongside his job in manure research.[110] Himmler's brother dated it about then that, after long seeking, the disoriented traditionalist "finally found his way in Hitler's mental world."[111] But a vestige of independence shows in Himmler's view of *Mein Kampf* noted three years later, following long months of close work with Hitler: "The first chapters on his youth contain many weaknesses."[112]

Just what, then, was Hitler's "incredible power of suggestion"[113]? It came of his breakdown in 1918, yet that was not a sufficient cause. It was occasionally ascribed to "autosuggestion" on his part,[114] though that was a logical step backward. More often his intense sense of mission and force of conviction were cited,[115] though clearly he could not have put just any mission or conviction across. The reverse explanation was more usual. "He felt just what the masses were longing for and cast it into incandescent phrases," declared his Minister of Finance.[116] He brought the German people's "longings, wishes, and hopes" to expression, deemed an expert on his early career: "he spoke from their hearts."[117] A former SA chief called this the "entire secret" of his success, yet tacked on the rider: "—and from his own heart as well."[118] That "entire secret" makes what Hitler said an index to what his public felt. Yet no one privy to that secret—not even that former SA chief or that expert on his early career—seems also to have caught what he said. As a rule, the auditors most affected by him could least remember his statements afterward. It did not help to call the shared fears and fancies he articulated unconscious[119] if he did articulate them. And it does not suffice to specify that he spoke to a national trauma if he personally came across more strongly than what he said. To be sure, his message also carried in transcription. "In 1928–1929 I read and heard about Adolf Hitler and his words went right to my marrow": this experience by a German farmer can be multiplied by millions.[120] As Hitler liturgically put it to "my columns of flag bearers" in Nuremberg on 11 September 1936 and, by extension, to all Germany lined up behind them: "You once hearkened to a man's voice, and it beat on your hearts, it awakened you, and you followed this voice. You followed it for years without ever having seen the bearer of this voice."[121] Even so, his presence enhanced his message by that "terrific magnetism of his personality."[122] The question is that enhancing.

A single answer remains—the right one. It is that Hitler's uncanny personal power over Germans came from his having coordinated his private traumatic fury with the national traumatic need.

This was a stupendous stunt. It took the devil's own psychological genius. But even with that, it was possible only because of three historic accidents. Hitler was born of a precedent for the German traumatic need, his breakdown coincided with Germany's in time, and his traumatic project complemented Germany's. Otherwise he would have come away from Pasewalk about like the next traumatic casualty before or after him: hellbent on reliving his traumatic experience, but without that imperative engaging anyone else.

An unconscious national regression to time out of mind sounds through the German rhetoric of enslavement and annihilation thrown up by the 1918 defeat. Defeat often carried just such penalties of old, which Hitler went far toward restoring. That does not prevent the apparent logic of traumatic reliving by individuals from fitting the German case. Well may a primitive people that somehow survived a sudden, startling defeat have relived it suicidally in striving to master the attendant fear.

Individuals commonly relive unlivable traumas beyond the point of no return: witness Hitler's mother and Hitler himself. Besides, primitives do not reckon with their own destructibility. No one does deep down, just as no one can conceive of his own end. Hitler's insistence that the German people as such ("an sich") was indestructible rings like an echo from great ages past. If, then, collective is like individual traumatic reliving, the collective form would seem to be the older form of it—as of mental life generally. Yet such reliving looks for all the world as if its prototype were the individual organism inuring itself to irritants by repeated self-exposure. This is troublesome, but happily the trouble lies beyond history, even psychohistory.

Powerful currents of warlike emotion will consolidate nations. National identity within Bismarck's Reich was problematic until 1914. War itself induces a readiness to revert to a state of bondage to an exalted leader. But Germans found no wartime leader they could venerate pro tempore in 1914–1918: the Kaiser was daft, Bethmann Hollweg dull, Hindenburg wooden, Ludendorff metallic. This left the national bonding to be completed by the defeat. The German "community of fate" forged by the lost war was Hitler's province. Its emergence out of the actualities of 1914–1918 raises the question of its psychological continuity with Hohenzollern Prussia and, well before that, the Hohenstaufen Empire, on which Hitler's Reich aligned itself increasingly. Rightly regarded, this question is preliminary to the inquiry that threw it up—a paradox that now brings the inquiry to an illogical halt.

VI

LOOSE ENDS

It would take limitless time and wisdom to grasp the full truth about any piece of reality. Short of that, every insight is tentative and every connection between insights tenuous. An organized presentation of connected historical insights is therefore misleading by its very nature, and the more misleading the more it cuts through complexities and passes over uncertainties. Yet this is just what interpretive histories must do if they are not to be spun out at forbidding length with the threads forever tangling. For the present work, that need to cut through and pass over was the greater since the source materials are so rich and yet so spotty, and because I read them for meanings of the kind that can run on and on behind even the merest fleeting dream.

I left tantalizing questions wide open about Hitler's Pasewalk hallucination, beginning with whether it was spontaneous or induced. The indications one way and then the other are these. Delirium accompanies iodoformism in cases as severe as Klara Hitler's. So does feverish restlessness in all cases. Feverish restlessness was chronic with Hitler after World War I. Presumably his mustard gas poisoning brought it on in lieu of the usual depressive apathy. It is consonant with Forster's false diagnosis of psychopathic hysteria. More, Weiss's novelized Hitler is nervously agitated at Pasewalk, and Weiss was informed by Forster. So Hitler may have appropriated his mother's last symptoms in associating his poisoning with hers. That could account for his hallucinating.[1] But so could Forster's treatment. Forster's regular medicine for war hysterics was, by all accounts including his own, a calling down for shameless shirking. That medicine is indicated in Hitler's case by Forster's transparent reference to Hitler in a 1922 discussion of war hysteria as shameless shirking.[2] A calling down for self-pity instead is suggested by a passage in *Mein Kampf:* "And when in the very last days of the fearful struggle the creeping gas finally attacked me too and began eating into my eyes, and from fear of going blind forever I felt for a moment like despairing, the voice of conscience thundered at me: Miserable wretch, would you cry when thousands are a hundred times worse off than you!"[3] That voice is audibly Forster's. Its having thundered like that would not have prevented Forster, when Hitler relapsed, from using hypnosis as his counterpart in Weiss's novel does on A.H.[4] And the view expressed by Weiss's hero that hypnosis is the patient's achievement was Forster's. By means of hypnosis Forster can have drawn Hitler out of his relapse even without having understood Hitler's complaint any more than did Weiss. Hitler's identification of Forster's voice with his own conscience looks like an aftereffect of just such a treatment. So does the stance as *Willensmensch*—man of will—that Hitler struck after Pasewalk.[5] And so does his perception of Germany's breakdown concurrent with his own as a dysfunction of the national will to be treated by both hortatory and hypnoid devices. His mission would have been recollected from a hypnotic trance with the very uncertainty he did show about how it was conveyed,[6] on top of that deeper uncertainty about it discernible in his order to the Gestapo to destroy all records of his treatment at Pasewalk.[7]

The gas that hit Hitler involves a complication I evaded. It was

not quite gaseous; it was not inhaled; it was a spray that lique-
fied in settling. When it condensed on his skin Hitler associated
it with Bloch's iodoform. But then he expanded it to associate it
with asphyxiating gas as well. The gas chambers resulted. So did
a chimney above the air shaft of his Berlin bunker to keep out
poison gas.[8] Correspondingly, he once held up a military conference to design a tank with an improved exhaust to prevent possible asphyxiation.[9] And when he read one day in 1941 that in
Breslau an elderly Jew named Luftgas ("air gas") had been con-
victed of hoarding 65,000 eggs in a lime pit and sentenced to
two-and-a-half years in prison, he ordered summary execution
instead. The memorandum confirming the execution is headed
like a hate joke: "Subject: Proceeding against the Jew Luftglass
(not Luftgas)."[10]

On to other troubles I skirted. Of Hitler in World War I a trusty
witness related that "the British were for him traitors to the great
cause."[11] That would anticipate a main clause of his program for
refighting that war. At the other chronological end of that program, no proof will avail that he simply could not have conquered Russia when he tried. This is the informed consensus.
Yet it took his mass executions there to stir up effective resistance to his invasion.[12] And if that was decisive, then his expansionist program did not assure its own failure all the way. By
that token, his racial-ideological line would gain new significance for his acceptance as Führer.

The Oedipal-minded will ask where Hitler's father[13] came into
his politics. The answer is: in a bymotive. His pampering at the
breast left him especially vulnerable to the classic moment of
untruth when, in coming to fear castration by the father,[14] a boy
will remember his weaning, construed as a warning. Little Adolf
saw his father, then, as the culprit behind his weaning—as liable
for the mother's breast having been removed. Bloch threw back
to the father once the mother had committed herself to his close
care[15] and to the castrating father when he ordered the mother's
breast removed, especially as the mother too was thereby cas-
trated after a fashion. Hitler's castration complex was implicated
in his blinding because blinding symbolizes castration: witness

Oedipus. His animus against his father revived against the state he set out to supplant.[16] "For it is no wonder," he explained in 1927, "if precisely the best of such a state begin to turn against it; for precisely the best and greatest are more than all others rooted in their people—are not children of the state, but exclusively children of the all-mother, their own nation. It they issue from; it they serve." The state's "loftiest mission," he pursued, was "to shelter and protect the mother of all life."[17] He eroticized that "loftiest mission" ten years later when, after having destroyed the Weimar state, he blustered to Nazi officials in secret: "We alone are entitled to lead the people as such—the individual man, the individual woman. We regulate living relations between the sexes. We form the child!"[18]

Now for the toughest riddle left. Hitler's image of "the Jew" was a self-image over and beyond its distorted reference to Bloch in 1907. More exactly, one part of it was his self-reflection and he aped the other part. Jewish "incest,"[19] "Jewish hate,"[20] Jewish "Old Testament vengefulness,"[21] the Jew "the greatest master of the lie,"[22] the Jew who "turns night into day,"[23] the Jews' "all-or-nothing" war on Nazism,[24] the Jews "who unscrupulously take over every office, who brutally enslave every people"[25]: all this hit home. "The Jewish dream of world dominion," "the goal: world dominion," "his final goal is: world dominion":[26] so did this incessant imputation.[27] Hitler preformulated his eastern policy when, in 1920, he charged the Jew with undertaking "the same predatory campaigns as he undertook of old" and declared: "The Jewish principle is: Divide and rule!"[28] He conceived Nazism as a "substitute" for Marxism, itself Christianity's successor as the Jews' instrument for subjugating "racially conscious Europe."[29] The Nazi mission, he held, was to counterpose to Marxism "a national movement no less philosophical and no less resolved on brute force."[30] After the Putsch he reorganized his Party on the Communist model, calling Munich its Moscow, and adopted the Marxist project of subverting the liberal republic by its own legal devices. Jewry, he insisted, was "never a religious, but only a racial, community,"[31] with racial purity as the secret of its success.[32] "If other peoples debase their worth, taint their blood, then that people must necessarily prevail which keeps itself absolutely pure": this accordingly was his prescription for Germany.[33] He called the Jews a "Satanical power which had taken possession of our whole people" before his own take-over.[34] He cited Jewish scripture and apocrypha to justify his politics toward the Jews. For years he remained a foreigner in Germany and then stateless, as he said the Jews were.[35] He taught himself to speak with his hands as he mocked the Jews for doing.[36] He mimicked Jewish inflections until they brushed off on his own.[37] He styled himself like a Jewish prophet and then a messiah: solitary and uncompromising; his words impassioned, explosive, magical; divinely appointed to deliver his people from bondage and establish their millennial kingdom, or Thousand Year Reich.[38] After establishing his millennial kingdom he remarked that his antagonist had been "that international Jew . . . who believed the time come to establish his millennial kingdom."[39] He identified himself outright with Jesus, a "popular orator of genius" who launched a world-historical movement from humble beginnings and, for bad measure, an Aryan who passed himself off on the Jews as one of themselves only to wield his whip against them.[40]

All this deadly self-projecting would make simple psychological sense if Bloch linked up as "the Jew" with the great rival whom little Adolf had wished to destroy and become—if, that is, Adolf suspected his father of Jewish paternity. This was rumored about his father from the early 1920s on. He must have thought the rumor unfounded when, to quash it, he had Party lawyer Hans Frank check it out in late 1930; otherwise he would hardly have trusted Frank that far. Frank recounted his findings in his death cell in Nuremberg: forty-two-year-old Anna Maria Schicklgruber had conceived Alois while a housemaid for a Jewish merchant, who supported the child afterwards.[41] The occasion alleged by Frank for Hitler's ordering the investigation—a sly letter from, "if memory serves," Hitler's half brother's son mentioning the troublesome rumor—can be verified.[42] This speaks strongly for Frank's account of his findings even if he did misremember the merchant's name and place of residence.[43] More eloquent on the same score are Hitler's instructions for his blood law of 15 September 1935: Jews (and he refused to restrict this to full Jews) were not to marry Aryans or have sexual relations with them or employ German housemaids aged under forty-five.[44] Allowing Frank's account, that undid respectively Alois' marriage to Klara, their premarital relations, and his own procreation. But a Hitler so clearly troubled by Frank's findings was a Hitler that clearly surprised by them.

Hitler's mother relived her maternal trauma in nursing him and then relived that reliving—fatally. Hitler himself relived his iodoform-and-poison-gas trauma in installments—"Operation Reinhard," "Euthanasia," "Final Solution"—climaxed by his suicide and Germany's destruction. (His having contracted that trauma in installments—1907, 1918—may be why he relived it in installments, and even why he programmed Germany's traumatic reliving in installments.) He also relived his gas trauma separately through the Putsch, then relived his Putsch trauma with Röhm as fall guy for him and with the merest guilty souvenir left over, the psychomotor disturbance that recurred after Stalingrad. But what about Germany's 1918 trauma of defeat: was it buried with Hitler's Reich? Hardly. It had been relived with a vengeance, but no tragic awakening ensued amid the wreckage wrought (such as did for Pentheus' mother confronting his bleeding limbs reassembled). Instead Germans afterward popularly bracketed Nazism out of their history even while calling their new defeat and forced retirement from *Weltpolitik* "the catastrophe." At the same time, post-Nazi Germans would seem to have lived politically for years out of Hitler's last hope of averting that "catastrophe." In a traumatic repeat, a failing effort to avert the traumatic outcome accompanies the tendency to carry it to a final extreme. Under Hitler, that effort subserved that tendency down to the last-ditch defense of Germany pending a heralded clash between the eastern and western invaders. German postwar politics began as a failing effort to provoke that clash after all and graduated to mutual provocations between a super-Washingtonian West Germany and a super-Muscovite East Germany. Two countries have since emerged—the two most an-

134

tithetical and antagonistic on opposite sides of that same divide. The political distance between them is like a shared purpose. If it is that, it makes a happier outlet than Hitlerism for the German pathology deriving from 1918.

That pathology was wicked under Hitler, yet not peculiarly so. It accommodated racial discrimination, segregation, and extermination, but these Hitler took from the American heritage—by way of cowboy-and-Indian stories in the first instance.[45] Barbarossa heightened the atrocity level of recent European wars against Europeans only, not against Africans or Asians. Its mass murder toll in the Soviet Union—over a million Jews and five million non-Jews—hardly approached Stalin's own. Except for these so-called excesses, the military operation cost Germans no qualms at the time and no remorse later. For nations are nasty compared with ordinary folk like you, me, and Hitler. This makes national aggression an ideal outlet for the private kind. Here too, in this vicious circle, Hitler and Germany were well met. But they were best met where their meeting ended by preappointment: in Hitler's macabre fulfillment that was Germany's self-chastisement—and that was, like all self-chastisements, unchastening.

APPENDIXES

A. The Pasewalk Hallucination

Hitler's earliest recorded account of his Pasewalk hallucination may be this one of 1921 or 1922, reported by Karl von Wiegand in 1939:

> In simple words he once related to me how [his] divine mandate came to him. It was just at the close of the war in November, 1918, as he lay in the Pasewalk hospital, blinded from a gas attack on the front. *"And as I lay there, it came over me that I would liberate the German people and make Germany great."* That was all. The message, inspiration or whatever you wish to call it did not say he "should" or "must"; it said he "would." That word, to him, contained in it the promise, the assurance that he would succeed in the mission.[1]

A similar version was cited in a *Frankfurter Zeitung* editorial of January 1923:

> About the background of the [Nazi] leader, the scenic painter from Austria Adolf Hitler, the rightist "Politischer Wochenbrief," mailed out confidentially by the Ring-Verlag, related recently that at the time of the revolution Hitler lay in a military hospital as a battle casualty stricken with a sort of blindness from which he was delivered by an inner rapture that set him the task of becoming his people's deliverer.[2]

An unidentified informant of Chancellor Cuno's not personally acquainted with Hitler reported from Munich at the end of 1922:

> By his own account, he thought over all his experiences at the front and in the rear while hospitalized for a severe injury and came to the conclusion that Marxism and Jewry are the German people's worst enemies. From personal experience it has become a certainty for him that wherever misfortune or harm befalls the German nation, a Jew is the culprit behind it.[3]

Here Hitler dated his political anti-Semitism from Pasewalk, but the divine mandate was missing. It was back in his account to Ernst Hanfstaengl, who joined his entourage in November 1922 and who told Franklin Roosevelt in 1942:

> Hitler made it known early that while in the infirmary of Pasewalk he received a command from another world above to save his unhappy country. This vocation reached Hitler in the form of a supernatural vision. He decided to become a politician then and there. He felt that his mission was to free Germany.[4]

This checks with the Office of Strategic Services' "Information Obtained from Ernst Hanfstaengl" in 1943 about Hitler:

> He told Hanfstaengl that while he was in the infirmary in Pasewalk in the fall of 1918 he received a supernatural vision which commanded him to save his unhappy country. As a result of this experience he resolved to become a politician and devote his energies to carrying out the command he received.[5]

Hitler "would not give an interview" to Ludwell Denny, who then "learned something of his story" anyhow for an article of March 1923:

> During the war he was wounded, or through fright or shock became blind. In the hospital he was subject to ecstatic visions of Victorious Germany, and in one of these seizures his eyesight was restored.[6]

For a biographical sketch of himself prefixed to a volume of his speeches issued just before the Putsch, Hitler commissioned and briefed one Viktor-Adolf von Koerber.[7] "In the infirmary of the Pomeranian village of Pasewalk"—thus Koerber's authorized version of the episode—

> a solitary bed stands in a darkened room. A nurse lays cooling bandages on the patient's dead eyes. He starts in fright. Drunken squalling sounds ceaselessly from the barracks where sons of Pomerania once were raised to proud manliness. King's dragoons, victors of Hohenfriedberg, victors of a thousand battles of Prusso-German history, bodyguards of Her Majesty the German Empress!
> The nurse's arms support the tortured one, who sits upright. She wants to push him back down onto the pillows, this uncanny patient brought there

blinded and muted, this—how does his form read?—" . . . private first class, disabled in enemy gas attack. 'Yellow cross gas' poisoning . . . " She knows no more about him. Yet she sees the ineffable suffering of this semicorpse whose facial expressions and whose gestures into the distance indicate more and more distinctly from day to day that he knows that something frightful has broken upon Germany! None of the degrading news from Kiel, Munich, and now from red Berlin has penetrated this solitary ward. And yet—the sister reads it from the martyred countenance: "Not my own suffering, the catastrophe that felled me, not that I am never again to behold the sun or starry heavens or—my homeland, but what is happening out there that I hear, feel— see! *That* is insufferable torment! My Germany!"

The nurse holds the twitching, feverish soldier of the betrayed army in her arms. And a higher constraint brings good words to her lips, words of faith in Germany's resurrection. And a miracle comes to pass. He who was consecrated to eternal night, who had suffered through his Golgotha in this hour, spiritual and bodily crucifixion, pitiless death as on the cross, with senses keen, one of the lowliest out of the mighty host of broken heroes—he becomes *seeing!* The spasms of his features subside. And in an ecstasy peculiar to the dying seer, new light fills his dead eyes, new radiance, new life!

A disarmed warrior was brought, mute and blinded, to the infirmary in the Pomeranian village. An upstanding fighter strides out into the alienized German world. He is armed to the teeth with faith, will, and confidence in victory! Invincible weapons![8]

In a biography of 1935 Rudolf Olden cited the interrogations of Hitler preliminary to the Putsch trial, which are no longer on record, in recounting that in Pasewalk

Hitler certainly seems to have been nervously deranged, disturbed. . . . He heard "voices," and the voices called upon him to become Germany's deliverer.[9]

At the Putsch trial itself, however, Hitler related only that in the night following the revolution in Berlin

my decision emerged. The great vacillation of my life, whether I should enter politics or remain [*sic!*] an architect, came to an end. That night I resolved that, if I recovered my eyesight, I would enter politics.[10]

This time he had censored the miracle for good. But he had not forgotten it, as can be seen from his shouting at Richard Breiting in 1931:

Do you know I was once blind? When the Reds were devastating Germany in November 1918 I lay blind in the infirmary. I became *seeing* then. I go my way to the end.[11]

B. Klara Hitler's Death

The basic document for Klara Hitler's medical treatment of 1907 is the record kept by Dr. Eduard Bloch (see illustration, p. 140). Her first consultation for 1907, on 14 January, looks like a yearly checkup, since Bloch noted above her name and address that she had previously visited him on 3 January 1906. In 1941 he recollected that she came to him in January 1907 complaining of severe pains in her chest and that he traced them to a cancer that was already extensive.[12] In 1943 he added that the operation performed four days later disclosed metastases in the pleura.[13] The surgeon, Karl Urban, told the Nazi Archive only that the "serious operation" lasted "a full hour."[14] The hospital record shows that the patient was discharged eighteen days later.[15] The Linz researcher Franz Jetzinger observed: "Mother Hitler seems to have recovered rather well from her operation, for she was known to at least a few women in Urfahr from marketing."[16] She moved twice in midyear and spent most of the summer at her sister's in their native village with Adolf and Paula.[17] Adolf moved to Vienna between his consultation with Bloch on 27 September and the Academy's entrance test on 1 and 2 October. He was back in Linz by 22 October for the first of two visits to Bloch preceding Klara's iodoform treatment. Kubizek hazily misdated the return "late in November already."[18] Bloch, though, said Adolf was "home again" from Vienna "within a few weeks,"[19] and Paula Hitler in recollecting this period did not even mention Adolf's temporary absence.[20] Apparently he was not away long enough to send Kubizek a postcard,[21] though he seems to have sent Bloch one reading: "From my Vienna trip the most cordial greetings Your ever grateful patient Adolf Hitler!"[22]

For the treatment that followed, Bloch presumably bought the iodoform gauze in five-meter strips as was most economical. Their price in Austria that year was 3.75 crowns for gauze at 10 percent, 4.80 at 20 percent, and 5.80 at 30 percent iodoform.[23] The part of those prices that went for the iodoform content comes to 1.32, 2.64, and 3.96 crowns respectively.[24] That year's price of iodoform powder was 0.90 crowns for ten grams. Therefore each of Bloch's forty-two applications of iodoform gauze to Klara Hitler involved the following average quantities for a total cost of 59 crowns "maximum" or 35 crowns "minimum":

SOLUTION	GRAMS OF IODOFORM		METERS OF GAUZE	
	MAXIMUM	MINIMUM	MAXIMUM	MINIMUM
10%	5.5	3.2	1.9	1.1
20%	8.6	5.1	1.5	0.9
30%	10.5	6.3	1.2	0.7

The "maximum" total cost is the sum of the three "a conto" payments if the one for 3 October is 15 crowns; if it is 18 crowns, then the "maximum" quantities shown above should each be increased by some

The Hitler record in Dr. Eduard Bloch's 1907 case book, from a photostat in the former Hauptarchiv der NSDAP (BAK NS26/65/38). In 1938 Bloch gave an agent of the Hauptarchiv the case book in a sealed envelope for the Führer personally (ibid. 31–33); its fate is unknown. Bloch took a photostat of the record to New York in 1940 (OSS interview of March 1943, "Hitler Source Book" 21); it no longer survives (letter from Dr. Frank Kren, 24 September 1971). The record was evidently prepared from daily notations—down to "Kr. 60.–" at a single sitting, then short of the last two entries at another. It served Bloch as a basis for billing. The underlining of a date designated a house visit. The text reads: "Hitler Humboldstr. 31"; above the line "einen Bs. v. 1906 3/1" (a visit of 3 January 1906); below the line "Urf. Hauptstr. 46, Blütenstr. 9" (the addresses in Urfahr, a suburb of Linz, to which the Hitlers moved in the late spring and late summer of 1907 respectively); "Spit. d. Barmh. währ. d. Op. 1 h." (Sisters of Mercy hospital during the operation one hour); "inc eines Dermoids in Cloräthyl (incision of a dermoid in ethyl chloride); "Pfl. Vb." (treatment, bandage); "Pfl. Vb."; "Pfl."; "Pfl."; "Pfl."; "Bespr." (consultation—obviously with Adolf, as a simple date signified a consultation with Klara); "Rch. betr. Kr. 60.–" (bill comes to 60 crowns); above the line "bz.//neue Rch." (paid; new bill begins); "Bespr. Herr" (consultation with Mr.: cf. previous "Bespr."); "Bespr."; "Rp." (prescription); "Bespr."; "a conto bz." (sums paid in advance for materials: the "2/12" indication above and the "3/10" one below the line were visibly interpolated and bracketed before the next regular line was penned); "M.J." (morphine, iodoform); "M.J."; "J." (iodoform alone) repeatedly; "Jodofgaze, Binde" (iodoform gauze, bandage, nearly spelled out: see "Bespr. Herr" above); "ex. let." (fatal issue); "bz. an Dr. K. f. Vertr. Kr. 4.–" (paid Dr. K. 4 crowns for substitution); "Rechnung beträgt 150 fl" (bill comes to 150 florins, or 300 crowns: unabbreviated notation in another hand); "bz. Kr. 300.–" (paid 300 crowns).

5 percent. The "minimum" cost figure excludes the *a conto* payment for 3 October, the next *a conto* payment having been made before the iodoform treatment began. And it counts only 15 of the 24 crowns paid *a conto* on 2 December, since these 24 crowns may have been meant to last a month, or thirty-one days, whereas the patient lived only nineteen days more. The exclusion is implausible, as it would mean that 15 or 18 crowns were spent on materials not noted that were used in treatments not noted. An unexpended balance of 9 crowns is less implausible: it could have been subtracted from Bloch's final charges for services amounting in that case to some 309 crowns. But the very fact that Bloch noted no balance suggests that the *a conto* payments were expended in full—and indeed, had the first twenty-five applications (through 2 December) cost 15 plus 20 crowns, then 24 crowns would have just covered the last seventeen applications at the same rate. The *a conto* entry for 3 October is especially puzzling in that Bloch inscribed it on his record only after having reached the one for 4 November and having interpolated the one for 2 December (not to mention his changing 18 to 15 crowns or vice versa). An *a conto* payment on 3 October would have been for a treatment previously agreed upon, which would then have been deferred—agreed upon with Adolf present in Linz, that is, and deferred in his absence. As for the figure of forty-two applications, it comprises every date noted from the second 6 November through 20 December even though one "J." and five underlinings are missing. If the iodoform treatment is taken to have begun earlier than Bloch's notations show, the *a conto* payment dated 3 October cannot be left out of account. The "minimum" columns would then fall, while the "maximum" quantities would decrease by some sixteen-and-a-half percent at most for up to seven additional applications.

The "minimum" averages for the entire treatment can be matched for the second *a conto* period alone if the 20 crowns are distributed over twenty-four applications beginning with the first "J." on 6 November:

SOLUTION	GRAMS OF IODOFORM PER APPLICATION	METERS OF GAUZE PER APPLICATION
10%	3.3	1.1
20%	5.1	0.9
30%	6.3	0.7

Only one of the *a conto* sums covers an even amount of medication: 24 crowns bought five five-meter strips of 20 percent gauze. If 20 percent gauze was used, the uneven portion of the earlier *a conto* payment or payments could have gone for the bandage, which I left out of ac-

141

count above because its price was both small and uncertain. The price of the morphine was negligible: one gram in solution, with dropping bottle and all, cost 1.50 crowns and yielded about a hundred injections. The fact that Bloch nonetheless noted his two morphine injections indicates that his record was a complete "case history" (as the Nazi Archive labeled it) and not just a basis for billing.

I can devise only three credible itemizations of Bloch's charges for services:

	A	B	C
Crowns per office visit	2	2.50	2
Crowns per house visit	3	5	4
Crowns per treatment	3	1	2
First bill:			
20 office visits	40	50	40
5 treatments	15	5	10
1 hospital visit, 1 minor surgery, 2 bandages, ethyl chloride	5*	5*	10*
Total	60	60	60
Second bill:			
8 office visits	16	20	16
49 house visits	147	245	196
42 treatments	126	42	84
Prescription; *a conto* debit or credit	7*	-11*	0*
Total	300	300	300

*Plus the amount, if any, by which the bill was rounded down.

All three are on the low side of the range of fees permissible in Germany that same year.[25] Sets B and C are likelier than set A for four reasons: Bloch can hardly have charged as much again for applying iodoform gauze each time as for the house visit itself; the ratio of house to office visit fee for Germany in 1907 was generally 2:1; it would be contradictory for the *a conto* money not to have sufficed; and Bloch was not a man to have rounded a bill up 7 crowns (minus a possible charge for the prescription he noted). Set C in turn improves on set B, since 10 crowns is much more realistic than 5 crowns for the third, composite item of the first bill, and since the 4 crowns that Bloch paid Dr. K. on 21 December would hardly have been less than his own fee for a house visit. And if set C holds, then the *a conto* payments were spent in full.

However it is sliced, the expense of 359 crowns (including the *a conto* payments) for Klara Hitler's final treatment came to a good ten percent of her estate.[26] And by any reckoning consonant with the evidence, the patient cannot have escaped severe, and indeed fatal, poisoning. Officially the cause of her death was cancer, but it was Bloch who prepared the death certificate.[27] The lethal dose of iodoform is given variously as between two and four grams for a single application, four to six grams in one day, and six to twelve grams in a week, absorption through an ulcerating wound being the most toxic and a diseased organism being the most susceptible.[28] On the other hand, in the controversy over iodoform poisoning that broke in the 1880s some doctors reported single postoperative applications of 50, 100, 200, and even 300 grams without deleterious effect.[29] The decisive factor was pinned down only after other antiseptics had largely replaced iodoform in the 1920s: *repeated* use. A few subjects are susceptible at once, but repeated applications will sooner or later sensitize the rest.[30] In no published report I have found of iodoform treatment with or without resultant systemic poisoning did the frequency of application begin to approach that recorded by Bloch. Even so, Klara Hitler was slow to succumb: constitutionally she was strong. In twenty cases of fatality tabulated by one researcher, death came some twenty days on the average after the first application, Klara's forty-six days being exceeded only twice.[31]

The poisoning was not in Bloch's recollections any more than the iodoform itself was. As for Kubizek, he recollected that Hitler deterred him from visiting Klara toward the last (except for a quick leave-taking) because of her "frightful suffering."[32] But Hitler himself supplied Bloch's omission in that he associated the characteristic of iodoformism with dying of cancer. That characteristic is to be tormented by thirst, but unable to drink.[33] And Hitler on 28 December 1944 speculated whether his Ardennes offensive (another desperate remedy in extremis) had not caught the Allies off guard because they were sure he was dead already "or at all odds am down with cancer somewhere and can't live any more or drink any more."[34]

It went with the later Hitler's exceptional interest and learning in medicine that he always wanted "to be informed as exactly as possible about the workings of medications etc."[35] This too points to 1907.[36]

C. The Maternal Trauma

Klara's three missing pregnancies between Adolf and Edmund can be measured from this table with the help of John Knodel's close analysis of data for 1905 on fecundity in three Bavarian villages including Schönberg in the same corner of Upper Bavaria as Simbach, the German side

Children of Alois Hitler born Schicklgruber
(7 VI 37–3 I 03)
by Klara Hitler born Pölzl
(12 VIII 60–21 XII 07)

CHILD	[PRECEDENT INTERPREGNANCY INTERVAL*]	[CONCEPTION*]	BIRTH	EARLY DEATH
Gustav		[23 VIII 84]	17 V 85	8 XI 87 (diphtheria)
Ida	[7 mos. 14 days]	[31 XII 85]	23 IX 86	2 I 88 (diphtheria)
Otto†	[6 mos. ?]	[III 87?]	? ? 87	? ? 87 (diphtheria?)
Adolf	[8 mos. ?]	[27 VII 88]	20 IV 89	
Edmund	[50 mos. 10 days]	[30 VI 93]	24 III 94	2 II 00 (measles)
Paula	[13 mos. 5 days]	[29 IV 95]	21 I 96	

*Assuming a 267-day gestation.

†Otto was born in Vienna in 1887 and died "after a few days" (Paula Hitler)[37] or "three days after birth" (Kubizek).[38] Given a normal gestation, he cannot have been born before late VIII 87 even if Ida was not nursed at all. But he must have been born before 8 XII 87, as by then Klara was back in Braunau, where Gustav and Ida died. This leaves Klara's second interpregnancy interval shorter than her first even at the outside, so the latest dates before 8 XII 87 are the likeliest.

of Adolf's native Braunau.[39] Knodel's data derive from an official Bavarian survey summarily tabulated in a publication of 1910.[40] This provides figures not for Simbach itself, which did not report, but for several localities nearby. The closest, Burghausen (some twelve miles southwest, and washed by the Salzach as is Braunau by the Inn), showed 86.1 percent of newborn children not breastfed in 1905, a figure so close to the corresponding one of 87.2 for Neumarkt,[41] which encompasses Schönberg, that Knodel's computations for Schönberg can be taken as strongly indicative for Simbach-Braunau. The percentages for the localities next closest to Simbach that reported also approximate that for Neumarkt: Altötting[42] 85.5 percent, Pfarrkirchen[43] 90.4 percent, and Eggenfelden 91.9 percent. The infant mortality rates for these localities beside Braunau also cluster around the Schönberg ones. The interval between Klara's first and fourth deliveries would need to have been not the 3.93 years it was, but 4.40, to accord exactly with Knodel's figures for mean intervals between successive legitimate births in Schönberg according to the longevity of the previous child.[44] Klara was running a little short. Had she run just that short again, Edmund would have been born 1.45 rather than Knodel's mean of 1.63 years after Adolf and hence, assuming a 267-day gestation, conceived some eight-and-a-half instead

144

of eleven months after Adolf's birth. In point of fact, Klara's interpregnancy interval following Adolf's birth was over fifty months long, or some nine-and-a-half months longer than her traumatic maternal experience (17 August 1884 to 2 January 1888).[45] Finally, Paula should have been born 1.71 years after Edmund instead of the actual 1.85 for Knodel's mean to have been hit on the nose. To be sure, that mean was unbinding in an individual case, even for Schönberg itself, so that my second decimal places are silly. It remains that Klara's case is decidedly normal throughout if the anomalous interval between Adolf's birth and Edmund's is reduced by the length of her maternal trauma.

If lactation was rare in the vicinity of Braunau, lengthy lactation was practically unknown. No child was still at the breast after twelve months in Neumarkt, Altötting, Pfarrkirchen, or Eggenfelden in 1905 (out of a few hundred infants in each locale); only Burghausen in 1905 reported one child (out of 283) still being breastfed after thirteen months, then two after twelve months in 1906. No figures are available for breastfeeding in Klara's native Waldviertel, a likelier place of reference for her in her maternal trauma than Braunau. But a one-man survey of Austria for the same period concluded: "The least favorable conditions prevail in the Alpine regions and more so in the western regions bordering on Bavaria than in the eastern regions."[46] This slight edge accorded to easterly Alpine nurslings checks with their slightly lower mortality rates.[47] Edge or no, a chronicler of folkways in the Waldviertel lamented in 1926: "The care and feeding of nurslings often leaves much to be desired. The best off are those who are given the breast. But children are often raised only on bottles ('bottle babies') or comforters."[48] Klara herself, it appears, was by far the "best off" of her mother's children (see below). But the chronology rules out her having much breastfed her own children before Adolf. Breastfeeding tends to delay the resumption of fertility after childbirth, only not indefinitely: between two and three years would seem to be the limit as far as physical causality is concerned.[49]

Nearly a third of the children around Braunau died by age ten, but that third as a rule by age one already.[50] A statistical-minded Klara Hitler would have feared for her newborn Otto while counting her Gustav and Ida safe.

D. Johanna Pölzl's Issue

Because successive interpregnancy intervals tend to lengthen, the fact that Johanna Pölzl's fifth and tenth were her shortest suggests possible fetal waste in the others. And, barring fetal waste in the fifth and tenth

Children of Johann Pölzl (24 V 1828–9 I 02)
and Johanna Pölzl born Hüttler (19 I 1830–8 II 06),
wed on 5 IX 1848[51]

CHILD	SEX	BIRTH [Days between Pregnancies*]	EARLY DEATH
1	M	14 X 49 [435]	11 XI 49 (consumption)
2	F	16 IX 51 [518]	10 X 55 (scarlet fever)
3	F	9 XI 53 [355]	7 XI 55† (scarlet fever)
4	M	24 VII 55 [293]	? ? 55 (scarlet fever?)
5	M	3 II 57 [227]	
6	M	12 VI 58 [525]	20 IV 63 (mumps)
Klara		12 VIII 60 [694]	
8	F	31 III 63 [301]	
9	M	19 X 64 [655]	20 I 65 (intestinal grippe)
10	F	29 IV 67 [228]	20 V 67 (smallpox)
11	F	5 IX 68	

*Assuming a 267-day gestation.
†In Vienna.

intervals themselves, the fact that the fifth was as long as the tenth, even though the tenth child died after three weeks, points to probable lactation in the fifth. But the shortness of that fifth interval suggests that Johanna did not normally breastfeed beyond a few months.

Two aspects of this birth record may hold special significance for Klara. The interpregnancy interval following her own birth was by far the longest with the newborn child surviving. And the treble death in late 1855 was a rough precedent for her own maternal tragedy, although it did not affect her mother's subsequent childbearing as far as the mere birth and death dates disclose.

146

NOTES

All source references are in either abbreviated or short form. To identify a source cited, see Sources (pp. 184–99). German symbols are used for German archival references. Expendable punctuation and symbols are omitted. Dates are given the day first, then the month in Roman numerals, then the year (last two digits if since 1876): 14 XI 38 for 14 November 1938. Dates not otherwise identified are for Hitler speeches. Numbers preceded by "p." or "pp." are cross references.

HALF-TITLE PAGE

Epigraph: Domarus 643.

I THE "JEWISH POISON"

1. Klöss 49. ("*Die grösste Gefahr ist und bleibt für uns das fremde Völkergift in unserem Leibe. Alle anderen Gefahren sind zeitlich bedingt. Nur diese eine allein ist in ihrer Folgewirkung ewig für uns vorhanden.*")

2. Hitler *Kampf* 64, 66; Karl Honisch in BAK NS26/17a/XIV; Wiedemann 54; Schaltenbrand 333.
3. BAK NS 26/52/88 (8 XI 30).
4. IfZ Friedrich Krohn ZS89/5. But Krohn added (ibid. 6) that he thereupon arranged for Hitler to attend a meeting of the German Workers Party and meet its chairman, Aton Drexler. In point of fact Hitler did this in September 1919. So Krohn's recollection may have been displaced from a Reichswehr orientation lecture by Hitler. Or it may have been spurious: see Tyrell 'Trommler' 228, 243.
5. Müller *Mars* 388. Further, Deuerlein "Eintritt" 199–201; Benz 86; Müller *Wandel* 144–45.
6. Kempner 74.
7. Ibid. and Wiedemann 26–27. Further, Westenkirchner in HSW: "He never wanted to be anything more than the others." Likewise, Heinrich Lugauer in BAK NS26/47.
8. Wiedemann 54.
9. Further, pp. 121–23. But his eyes were remarkable before: Jetzinger 163; Schaltenbrand 333.
10. Autobiographical letter 29 XI 21 in BAK NS26/17a; typescript of Hitler Putsch trial BAK NS26/1927–1/35; Hitler *Kampf* 54–70.
11. Kubizek 287–90; Hitler *Kampf* 59–70. Further, Jetzinger 207–18; Maser *Hitler* 307–08.
12. Wiedemann 33–34, 209; Schmidt, Westenkirchner in HSW.
13. Karl Honisch in BAK NS26/17a; Hans Raab, Hans Bauer, Heinrich Lugauer in BAK NS26/47.
14. On Dr. Eduard Bloch: below passim. On Lt. Hugo Gutmann: Wiedemann 25–26; Niekisch *Leben* 282–83; Schmidt, Westenkirchner in HSW. Further, memorandum by Renate Bleibtreu 1 XI 38 in BAK NS26/17a; Maser *NSDAP* 69.
15. Mend passim; Mend file in BDC. Further, Maser *Hitler* 138–40.
16. Brandmayer passim.
17. Greiner passim (similarly, interview of Greiner in Daim 27–34, 248–49); Greiner file in BDC. Hanisch 271 ("In those days Hitler was by no means a Jew hater. He became one afterwards") more than cancels Greiner, whose Hitler stories are preposterous, whereas Hanisch only embellished his.
18. Deuerlein "Eintritt" 184–85, 201–05.
19. Ibid. 199.
20. IfZ Friedrich Krohn ZS89/5—but see above n. 4. Further, IfZ Max Amann ZS809/2.
21. Maser *Hitler* 150 and n. 109 (further, n. 106, 153 and n. 131); Hitler *Kampf* 225.
22. *Advance* 282.
23. BAK NS26/12.
24. Hitler to Mayer 4 XI 16, Hitler to Brandmayer 21 and 28 XII 16 in HIS; Brandmayer 71, 88.
25. Wiedemann 29. Further, Westenkirchner in HSW.
26. Schmidt, Westenkirchner in HSW. Further, Hillgruber *Wehrmacht* 1295 (Hitler's order of 8 IX 42): "For every good soldier the regiment or division is his home."
27. BAK NS26/12; Schmidt, Westenkirchner in HSW; three postcards to Max Amann in DLC, Manuscript Division.

28. BAK NS26/12; Westenkirchner in HSW.
29. BAK NS26/12; Schmidt, Westenkirchner in HSW.
30. BAK NS26/1927–1/36; Hitler *Kampf* 210–12.
31. Brandmayer 51.
32. Schmidt in HSW.
33. Westenkirchner in HSW.
34. Letters on Hermann Heer from Stadtverwaltung Rothenburg ob der Tauber 21 XII 70, Krankenbuchlager Berlin 14 I 71, Trudl Schmidt 22 I 71.
35. Ibid.; Hitler's military records in BAK NS26/12/8–18; Hans Raab, Hans Bauer, Heinrich Lugauer in BAK NS26/17a; Hermann Heer's military records in HStA KA 1385 Res. I. R. 16, 5. Kp., Bd. 1, 1–1166, 1 Div. D/23, 9, S. 239.
36. BAK NS26/1927–1/32; *Münchener Neueste Nachrichten* 27 II 24.
37. See Büscher 63–131, esp. 111–13; further references in Ermert 3–4.
38. Hoegner *Republik* 123; letter from Wilhelm Hoegner 5 III 71.
39. Gosset I 71 n. 1; Kersten 209. Further, p. 13 and n. 91.
40. Karl Kroner in DNA Records of the OSS, Navy Intelligence Report 31983 Reykjavik 21 III 43; interview of Balduin Forster 18 VI 73.
41. Büscher 112, 119, 130; cf. Forster "Nervensystem" 303–05 on psychopathy.
42. Hitler *Kampf* 223, 221.
43. Gosset I 71. By Hitler's account at his Putsch trial in BAK NS26/1927–1/36–37 news of the spreading revolution reached Pasewalk on 5–6 XI 18 and his mental crisis ended on 9 XI 18, but in Hitler *Kampf* 222–25 the crisis lasts some days beyond 10 XI 18.
44. See Appendix A.
45. UAG Personal-Akten Nr. 487 Marie Forster to Kurator 10 XI 33 enclosure.
46. Forster "Reaktion" 312–13 and passim.
47. Letter from Jürg Zutt 19 XI 73.
48. Interview of Balduin Forster 18 VI 73.
49. Bonhoeffer 1516.
50. Forster "Nervensystem" 301–03.
51. Ibid. 300.
52. UAG Personal-Akten Nr. 487, 22 XII 24.
53. Ibid. 8 I 25.
54. Letter from Jürg Zutt 19 XI 73; Bonhoeffer 1516.
55. AHU Medizinische Fakultät-Dekanat, Acta . . . betreffend: *Disziplinaria der Universitätslehrer* 1906–1930, Medizin. Fakultät, Nr. 1415/44–45; UAG Personal-Akten Nr. 487/16–43 and passim.
56. Forster "Selbstversuch" 12–14. Further, Forster "Reaktionsformen" 215, "Nervensystem" 308.
57. UAG Medizinische Fakultät Nr. 156.
58. Forster "Suizidneigung" 766.
59. Schwarzschild 273 (with Forster misspelled Förster). Interview of Walter Mehring 10 VIII 75: Forster expressly cautioned against any future report of his suicide. Similarly, Sommer "Gesucht."
60. Mehring 248. Similarly, Sommer "Gesucht" (with "protocol" for "documents").
61. Interview of Walter Mehring 10 VIII 75.
62. Schwarzschild 273.
63. *Braunbuch* 127–29 and facing 57 and 73, 383. Further, Binion "Concept" 205 and nn. 98, 99.

64. UAG Personal-Akten Nr. 487/56–74.
65. Rudolf Nissen in letter from Werner Hügin 27 VI 73.
66. UAG Personal-Akten Nr. 487/75–76, 85.
67. Interview of Balduin Forster 18 VI 73.
68. UAG Personal-Akten Nr. 487/95.
69. Ibid. 64, 75, 85 (verso); interview of Balduin Forster 18 VI 73.
70. UAG Personal-Akten Nr. 487/75–90.
71. Interview of Balduin Forster 18 VI 73.
72. Telephone interview of Dirk Forster 19 VI 73.
73. Interview of Balduin Forster 18 VI 73.
74. Letter from Jürg Zutt 19 XI 73.
75. Interview of Walter Mehring 10 VIII 75 (Weiss being picked over Alfred Döblin). By Mehring's account, Schwarzschild could not publish the Pasewalk material for fear his review would be confiscated.
76. Wollheim 73–74 and telephone interview of Mona Wollheim 14 IX 72; Kesten V, XXII.
77. Weiss 134–51.
78. Ibid. 138; Forster "Nervensystem" 300. Further, Forster "Reaktion" 373–76; Weiss 117–20. Weiss's hero's view is no less Forster's for some mention of the "undersoul."
79. Weiss 151.
80. Ibid. 214.
81. Ibid. 204.
82. Ibid. 222.
83. Ibid. 191, 211.
84. Ibid. 222.
85. Kesten V, XXII. Further, Walter 291; Deutsche Bibliothek, Frankfurt am Main, Abteilung IX Exil-Literatur 1933–1945, Literaturarchiv EB 70/117.
86. Weiss 136–38, 144.
87. Koerber 7 (Appendix A).
88. Interview of Balduin Forster 18 VI 73; Weiss 148–50.
89. Ermert 22.
90. Forster "Reaktion" 381; Weiss 146. Weiss also suggested a sexual disturbance behind A.H.'s hysteria (144, 148)—a mistake about Hitler that, be it Forster's or Weiss's, does not bear on whether Forster used hypnosis or Weiss used Forster's notes. Nor does Weiss's apparent use of additional sources for Hitler's early life (notably *Mein Kampf*) reflect on Forster as his source for the Pasewalk treatment.
91. These latter—the originals of Weiss's hero's unofficial case notes—would seem to be identical with the "case record" (*"Krankenblatt"*) copied for Schwarzschild (see p. 8 and n. 61).
92. Hitler *Kampf* 772.
93. *VB* 2/3 IX 28 in Tyrell *Führer* 208.
94. Koerber 88.
95. Genoud *Le Testament* 148 (2 IV 45), Domarus 2239 (29 IV 45).
96. This account of Klara Hitler's last illness is supplemented in Appendix B.
97. BAK NS26/65/37: "*Sarcoma pectoris. Pector*[um] *minor*" ("Cancer of the breast. Lesser breast"—presumably the left one).
98. Ibid.
99. BAK NS26/65/88, 110.
100. DNA "Book" 21.

101. Ibid. Further, BAK NS26/65/91; Bloch 36; Oplt 4 (Alois Hitler, Jr.: "My stepmother always took his part—she never let him be crossed"); Kubizek 45, 49–50.
102. Dates from Akademie der bildenden Künste, Vienna, letter of 16 IX 71. Vienna was then only five hours from Linz by train at a minimum fare of 5.30 crowns or three hours twenty minutes at 7.40 crowns: letter from Österreichisches Eisenbahnmuseum 12 IX 72. But an entrant to the Akademie would have been busy preparing to start classes in the eight days left after admission: letter from Akademie der bildenden Künste 31 VII 72.
103. Magdalena Hanisch to Frau Motlach 4 II 08 ("fand keine Aufnahme mehr"), cited by Smith Hitler 113 and Maser Hitler 82; Kubizek 153, 188–93.
104. "Adolf Hitler in Urfahr," appended to Bleibtreu report in BAK NS26/17a; Kubizek 157.
105. See p. 140.
106. BAK NS26/65/91 (Bloch's letter of 7 XI 38); Bloch 36; DNA "Book" 21 (interview of 5 III 43).
107. Hitler Kampf 16.
108. BAK NS26/65/90; Delmer 30. He invoked the medical secret, which the Atlantic crossing then washed away.
109. Bloch 37; DNA "Book" 21; (BAK NS26/65/31). On Bloch's faulty memory see further Kurth "Jew" 20 n. 28.
110. Letter from Gertrud Kren 22 XI 71.
111. Kubizek 156; letter from Österreichische Apothekerkammer, Landesgeschäftsstelle Oberösterreich 10 XI 71.
112. Bloch 37.
113. BAK NS26/65/91.
114. Kubizek 157–58.
115. Hitler Buch 75–76. Hitler's term here was "operation," not "remedy," but the referent cannot have been the surgery which Bloch did promptly order and did not himself perform. Compare Hitler Kampf 463.
116. Hitler Buch 74. See also below n. 128, pp. 18–19 and n. 130.
117. Domarus 78 (27 I 32). That "now and again" covered Bloch's minor postoperative surgery of 22 IV 07: see p. 140.
118. See König passim; Ewald passim; Zimmermann 25–29; Bourdette 15–16; Mayer and Gottlieb 468; Lewin 467; Deichmann and Gerarde 331; Oettinger 70; Grossman 772; Hauschild 59; Gleason et al. 82; Braun 179; Moeschlin 219. Germany was "in a fever—a high fever," Hitler declared in IX 30. "That fever is bound to continue. . . . When delirium sets in, it will be too late": Baynes 994 quoting the Sunday Express. See also p. 18.
119. Ewald 129–32, 141–42; also Bourdette 13, 27.
120. Kubizek 159–60.
121. BAK NS26/65/91.
122. Bloch 37. But Kubizek 159: "The mother's bed now stood in the kitchen, as this was heated all day long. . . ."
123. CB Paula 3.
124. Kubizek 163.
125. BAK NS26/65/91, 94 (7 and 16 XI 38).
126. Bloch 37.
127. Krause 52.
128. Meyers 609–10. Further, Hitler Conversations 95; Bein "Parasit" passim,

esp. 145 and n. 84, "Antisemitismus" 360. Hitler once substituted tuberculosis for cancer in a passage like those cited pp. 16–17 and nn. 116, 117, and pp. 18–19 and n. 130, about doctoring around the edges of Germany's mortal ailment: Jochmann 101–02, 104 (28 II 26). And in Viereck 237 he substituted consumption, only to add: "We need violent correctives, strong medicine, maybe amputation," and again: "We must cut out every cancer that corrodes our life." His generic usage is in VB 31 I 23 (29 I 23): "Nationalism is primarily a preventive measure against infectious germs and anti-Semitism the necessary defense against a pestilence that has befallen the world." In standard short form, the Nazi struggle was for "the cure of the German body politic" ("Volkskörper"), "the convalescence of the German people," and the like: Tyrell Führer 318 (letter of 11 V 29), HStA AStA Sonderabgabe I 1480 (18 XI 22).

129. Hitler Conversations 269. Compare Viereck 238 quoting Hitler: "One disease breeds many."

130. Hitler Kampf 164–71. On the Jewish identity of Marxists and Marxism for Hitler, see also ibid. 185, 350–52, 498; Hitler in VB 25 I 23, 3 VIII 29 (1 VIII 29); Viereck 236–37; etc. At his Putsch trial Hitler declared characteristically: "I came to Vienna a cosmopolitan and left an absolute anti-Semite, a mortal enemy of the whole Marxist philosophy": BAK NS26/1927–1/35. Further, Tyrell 'Trommler' 48 and n. 277; Schott 158–87; Thies 29, 42, 45; Treue 204; Grieswelle 99; Adam 23; Schubert 28–29; Calic 107–08.

131. Quoted by Bleibtreu in BAK NS26/17a; cf. Bloch 69–70.

132. BAK NS26/65/44; letters from Frank Kren 24 IX 71 and Gertrude Kren 4 X and 22 XI 71.

133. Dated 14 XI 38: Gertrude Kren in History of Childhood Quarterly II (1974) 267. But the claim that the Führer spoke of Bloch as a noble Jew (Bloch 70) is implausible, as Hitler's position was always the one he took in 1923 (Koerber 109) against Germans who said: " 'But there are so many decent Jews!' . . . To eliminate this sentimentality, the so-called decent . . . Jews are to be fought first, with all severity!"

134. Domarus 421 (13 VII 34).

135. Further, p. 113.

136. Karl Honisch in BAK NS26/17a.

137. Hitler to Ernst Hepp 5 II 15 in Maser Briefe 101: see pp. 20–21.

138. Schmidt in HSW.

139. Westenkirchner in HSW.

140. See e.g. Bein "Parasit" passim, esp. 129–30; Jenks 125–42 and passim; Phelps "Thule" 247. Cohn 262–64: the notion of Jews as poisoners goes back to the twelfth century. A possible additional determinant was the colloquial equivalent "Joden" = "Juden" reported by Arends 186.

141. Above n. 130. Further, BAK NS26/17a Hitler's autobiographical letter of 29 XI 21 (in Vienna he read "the entire anti-Semitic literature then available").

142. Hitler Kampf 54–70.

143. Ibid. 59.

144. See p. 18.

145. Kubizek 160–61.

146. Bloch to Bleibtreu 16 XI 38 in BAK NS26/65/95. Kurth "Jew" 23 n. 35: "The impression of the mutually strong attachment between mother and son was always uppermost in the doctor's memory and was again and again reported spontaneously in conversation with him."

147. BAK NS26/54/178 (9 XI 27): ". . . the source of all life is not the state, but the people in itself. . . . The best and greatest in particular . . . are not children of the state, but children of the all-mother, their own nationhood." *"Mutter"* and *"das deutsche Volk"* are outright synonyms in Preiss 91 (8 XII 28). The German people is termed "the Germanic mother" in Hitler *Kampf* 742.

148. Vondung 173 (2 XI 32). Similarly, *VB* 7 VIII 29 (5 VIII 29: "the people as a body of flesh and blood and bone and spiritual powers").

149. It may also matter that he spent his sixth year with his mother on the German side of the border before they followed his father to Linz.

150. Hitler to Ernst Hepp 5 II 15 in Maser *Briefe* 101.

151. See p. 17.

152. Hitler *Kampf* 220.

153. See pp. 5, 17, and 129–30. The German name for the gas—"yellow cross gas"—may have helped the eruption along by association with the yellowness of iodoform or the yellow star of David.

154. BAK NS26/1927-1/36 (Putsch trial).

155. Hitler *Kampf* 223 re-echoing 221.

156. Ibid. 223.

157. Further, Fest *Hitler* 115 and n. 125.

158. Except that he came away from Pasewalk with bags under the eyes: Wagner 30.

159. See p. 138.

160. Picker 493–94 (30 V 42).

161. His architectural ambitions, now overridden, had previously bound up the destructive energy unloosed by his 1907 trauma. Later he chose architects —Fritz Todt, then Albert Speer—for his ministers of munitions.

162. Kubizek 72–84 and passim.

163. Ibid. 50; Schirach *Hitler* 4; Brandmayer 81–82.

164. DNA "Book" 903. Similarly, Hoffmann *Friend* 141; HSW Hoffmann "Bericht Maraun" 2; Kempner 70 (Walter Buch 16 V 47 quoting Hitler summer 1923: "I can't marry, my wife will be Germania"). Compare Hitler in *VB* 14 III 25 ("I am so wedded to politics that I cannot think of betrothing myself as well").

165. Krause 35.

166. Picker 193. But see also Tyrell *Führer* 59, 'Trommler' 40.

167. Perhaps by hard words: see Heiber *Lagebesprechungen* 124, 130, 134 (130 n. 3 nothwithstanding).

168. Rosalia Hörl in BAK NS26/17a. His father was twenty-three years older than his mother, he nineteen years older than Geli. The blood relationship would have been the same had Johann Nepomuk Hiedler been Alois's natural father as Adolf may have imagined: see pp. 53, 133–34. Hugo Blaschke in DNA "Picture" 3: Hitler's conduct toward Eva Braun was strictly avuncular.

169. HSW Hoffmann. But DNA "Picture" 28 (Hasselbach): she gave up her job after meeting Hitler.

170. HSW Hoffmann. But Hoffmann *Friend* 163: "That Eva became his mistress some time or other before the end is certain."

171. BAK Schramm 65–66 (Karl Brandt); Speer 117–20. But see Müllern-Schönhausen 195.

172. Meyers 609; Schramm *Führer* 109; Speer 117; Deuerlein *Hitler* 130, 163–64.

Hoffmann *Friend* 219: "He suffered from recurrent pains in the stomach, the heritage of gas poisoning during the first war"! The word "gastric" (*"gastrisch"*) can only have eased his choice of the stomach for the compound symptom.

173. Krebs 136–37. Further, Krause 59.
174. JT Giesing 70, 23 VIII 44 ("... *fressen mich täglich mehr auf*").
175. Ibid. 162, 6 X 44. Further, Trevor-Roper 66–67; Röhrs 53–59, 117–24; Kempka 34–38; Krause 57–58; Hoffmann *Friend* 219–20; IfZ Hanskarl von Hasselbach ZS242/1–2; PUL Dethleffsen 18–19.
176. BAK Schramm 65 (Karl Brandt). Similarly, Hitler *Conversations* 161 (9–10 I 42): "I haven't been sick since I was sixteen."
177. Maser *Hitler* 346 quoting Karl von Eicken. For that continual thirst compare p. 143.
178. See p. 3 and n. 18.
179. HStA AStA Sonderabgabe I 1480 (21 IV 22). Similarly, ibid. 1738 (26 II 23); Phelps "Parteiredner" 318 (20 IX 20); Preiss 15 (3 I 23), 74 (24 IV 23); Koerber 73 (1 VIII 23); Kursell 157 ("Aussprüche Adolf Hitlers"); Bonnin 161 (Putsch trial 28 II 24); HIS inscription for Hermann Fobke 11 V 24; BAK NS26/55/48–49 (18 IX 28), 80–81 (18 X 28). But in one such context— ibid. 4 (19 I 28)—his tongue slipped: "We do not believe that a people like us, a people sick as we are, can be delivered through sacrificial courage and virtue." A Nazi archivist noted here: "(?—according to the verbatim record.)"
180. Heiber *Lagebesprechungen* 719 (12 XII 44). Similarly, ibid. 780 (military conference 29 XII 44): "... the war can't last as long again as it has lasted already. That's quite certain. No one could stand that: we couldn't, the others couldn't. The only question is who will stand it longer." Further, IfZ Adolf Heusinger ZS69/59; PUL Dethleffsen 66–67.
181. Domarus 1886 (26 IV 42).
182. Hitler in *VB* 1 XI 22.
183. Phelps "Parteiredner" 322 (22 IX 20). Further, ibid. 298 (17 IV 20); BAK NS26/55/127 (9 XI 28), Jacobsen and Jochmann (25 I 38).
184. Koerber 87 (5 IX 23).
185. Hitler in *VB* 21/22 X 23.
186. Calic 42.
187. Tyrell *Führer* 208 (early VIII 28).
188. BAK NS26/51/7 (31 V 20).
189. HStA AStA Sonderabgabe I 1480 (13 XII 22).
190. Ibid. (11 I 23); ibid. 1755 (27 I 23); Franz-Willing *Krisenjahr* 17; Horn *NSDAP* 101; Müller *Wandel* 143–44. Through his term "November criminals" Hitler struck at Bloch behind the revolutionaries, as by a prank of fate the Kiel mutiny and with it the revolution had begun on 4 November like Bloch's idoform treatment before it. Typically he urged the SA on 7 V 33 to pursue the November criminals "into their last hiding places" and expel "this poison from the body of our people": Wheaton 335. Compare p. 31 and n. 258.
191. Koerber 84 (21 VIII 23).
192. *VB* 24 I 23 (18 I 23).
193. Hitler in *VB* 15 V 21; similarly, ibid. 29 V 21.
194. Ibid. 25 I 22.
195. HStA AStA Sonderabgabe I 1480 (13 XII 22).

196. BAK NS26/55/140–42 (9 XI 28).
197. On 25 IX 30: Tyrell *Führer* 299.
198. Domarus 1829 (30 I 42). Further, BAK NS26/55/140 (9 XI 28: "an eye for an eye"); Calic 28 (" a revenge").
199. Domarus 1316 (1 IX 39). Further, Dawidowicz 110. Compare BAK NS26/53/102 (12 VIII 26: "poison gas against poison gas").
200. HStA AStA Sonderabgabe I 1480 (9 II 22).
201. Jochmann 104 (28 II 26); BAK NS26/55/11 (6 VII 28).
202. It was a variant of extermination in Hitler to Konstantin Hierl 3 VII 20: Erb and Grote 42.
203. *VB* 28 IV 21 (17 IV 21).
204. Phelps "Parteiredner" 302 (11 V 20).
205. Ibid. 300–01 (27 IV 20).
206. Koerber 109 ("Leitworte Adolf Hitlers").
207. *VB* 24 I 23 (18 I 23).
208. Phelps "Parteiredner" 301 (27 IV 20).
209. HStA AStA Sonderabgabe I 1478 (6 IV 20). Likewise, Phelps "Parteiredner" 302 (11 V 20).
210. Koerber 106 (12 IX 23).
211. Phelps "Parteiredner" 319 (20 IX 20).
212. Koerber 88 (5 IX 23).
213. Ibid. 40 (28 VII 22).
214. Hitler in *VB* 30 I 21.
215. *VB* 28 IV 21 (17 IV 21).
216. HStA AStA Sonderabgabe I 1480 (30 X 22).
217. Phelps "Parteiredner" 324 (18 X 20).
218. Kursell 70 (20 IV 23).
219. Hitler in *VB* 8 V 21.
220. HStA AStA Sonderabgabe I 1480 (18 I 23).
221. Ibid. (9 I 22). Similarly, ibid. (20 II 22): "Until the international stock market bandits lie smashed on the ground."
222. Phelps "Parteiredner" 304 (11 VI 20). Further, *Der Kampf* (Munich) 28 VI 20 on an unrecorded talk by Hitler: "Summons followed upon summons to murder the Jews."
223. Kursell 69–70 (20 IV 23).
224. Phelps "Parteiredner" 301 (27 IV 20). Similarly, Deuerlein "Eintritt" 204 (letter of 16 IX 19); HStA AStA Sonderabgabe I 1480 (2 II 22); *VB* 31 I 23 (29 I 23); Koerber 66 (2 IV 23).
225. HStA AStA Sonderabgabe 1478 (24 VI 20).
226. *VB* 17 IV 21 (21 III 21).
227. Phelps "Rede" 417 (13 VIII 20). Further, Hitler in *VB* 29 V 21; ibid. 8 VI 23 (25 V 23).
228. Hitler in *VB* 13 V 21.
229. HStA AStA Sonderabgabe I 1480 (13 XI 22).
230. Ibid. (18 IX 22).
231. IfZ Josef Hell ZS640/6. Ibid. 7: Hitler regained his composure only to pretend—incongruously—that his anti-Semitism was merely opportunistic. Contrast Viereck 237: "What would you do with the Jew?" "We would disfranchise him."
232. BAK NS26/65/34.
233. That remainder was to grow—like Klara's cancer—as the Reich absorbed new territory containing Jews beginning in III 38.

234. Phelps "Parteiredner" 298 (17 IV 20.) Further, Schubert 28–29; Thies 44. Tyrell 'Trommler' 215 adds: "It is already intimated in the expression 'racial tuberculosis of the nations' " in Hitler's letter of 16 IX 19 (Deuerlein "Eintritt" 204). The Jewish peril was international and Bolshevism its acutest form in a pamphlet by Anton Drexler that Hitler read and took to heart in IX 19: Drexler Ch. 8, 9, 12, and passim; Hitler *Kampf* 239.
235. Tyrell *Führer* 209 (early VIII 28).
236. HStA AStA Sonderabgabe I 1482 (8 II 22).
237. See Hitler *Kampf* 185–86: pp. 96–97 and n. 66.
238. BAK NS26/55/130, 133, 127, 137 (9 XI 28). Similarly, *Memminger Zeitung* 20 I 28 (on Hitler's speech of 19 I 28 in Memmingen: "not a single word was uttered against the Jews"); Jochmann 43, 57 (on Hitler's speech of 28 II 26: "In the entire two-and-a-half-hour speech he did not waste a single word on the Jews"). Dissimilarly, BAK NS26/52/38-39 (8 VIII 27). Further, Binion "East" 96–99; Dietrich 36–37; Adam 25–26; Schulz 428; Grieswelle 181, 193; pp. 70–73. Cf. Kele 145.
239. Speer 525.
240. Hale "Taxpayer" 837, 841; Lange *Maximen* 31; Maser *Kampf* 27 n.
241. Kotze and Krausnick 147–48 (29 IV 37). Further, Domarus 299 (3 IX 33), 537 (15 IX 35), 588–89 (interview of 26 XI 35).
242. Thus Adam 207.
243. See pp. 27–28 and n. 230.
244. Schacht 25. Further, Groscurth 167. (Schacht's firing followed, but did not follow from, a Reichsbank memorandum warning Hitler against governmental overspending.)
245. This practice was anticipated in a proposal of 1913 rejected by Bethmann Hollweg as "impractical" and by Wilhelm II as "downright childish": Pogge-von Strandmann 34, 38.
246. *Akten* IV 295. Similarly, BAK Schramm 157.
247. *Akten* IV 293.
248. Ibid. V 784.
249. Ibid. 780–85.
250. Ibid. IV 170.
251. Here Reitlinger 86–89 and passim is conclusive. Similarly, Krausnick "Judenverfolgung" 356; Hillgruber " 'Endlösung' " 138.
252. Domarus 1058 (30 I 39).
253. Genoud *Le Testament* 86; Domarus 2237. Earlier: on 30 I 41, 1 and 30 I 42, 24 II 42, 30 IX 42, 8 XI 42: see Hillgruber " 'Endlösung' " 151 n. 57.
254. Domarus 252 (Hitler to Cabinet 29 III 33). Further, Hanfstaengl *Years* 211.
255. See pp. 27–28 and n. 229.
256. Domarus 1058 (30 I 39).
257. Groscurth 166–67.
258. Genoud *Le Testament* 79–80. The elided clause reads: ". . . *sans quoi nous eussions été asphyxiés et submergés*" (". . . except for which we would have been asphyxiated and overwhelmed"), which mixes the metaphor too oddly to be trusted.
259. Adam 130; IfZ "Ärzte-Prozess" 2498–99; Kaul 30; Gruchmann 258.
260. On the moment before or after, see Krausnick 325 and n. 36.
261. IfZ "Ärzte-Prozess" 2410, 2508; Kaul 24.
262. Kaul 52, 57–58 (another sign—if one were needed—that he meant war then, at least on this gut level of decision).

263. IfZ "Ärzte-Prozess" 2407; IMT(G) XVIII 207.

264. IfZ "Ärzte-Prozess" 2486 ff. and passim; DNA "Vernehmung des Viktor Brack 4 IX 46" 8.

265. Kaul 58; IfZ "Ärzte-Prozess" 2687–88.

266. IfZ "Ärzte-Prozess" 2513, 7758, 7770, 7866.

267. Kaul 65; IMT(G) XX 540, XLII 563–64.

268. IfZ "Ärzte-Prozess" passim, esp. 2420, 2491, 2502, 2506–07; DNA "Vernehmung des Viktor Brack 4 IX 46" 11.

269. IfZ "Ärzte-Prozess" 7753–54; Kaul 64, 67, 77–78; DNA "Testimony of Karl Brandt 1 X 45" 7.

270. IfZ "Ärzte-Prozess" 2431–32, 7422, DNA "Vernehmung des Viktor Brack 4 IX 46" 8.

271. Kaul 97, 99–101, 109–10.

272. Ibid. 102–04; Gruchmann 278; Krausnick "Judenverfolgung" 409–10.

273. Hillgruber Strategie 523–24 and " 'Endlösung' " 137–38, 140, 144–45; Jacobsen "Kommissarbefehl" 167.

274. Gruchmann 278.

275. IMT(G) XLII 55–67, 563–65; Gruchmann 278; Kaul 146–48, 151–54, 159; Krausnick "Judenverfolgung" 407–10; Reitlinger 150–52; IfZ "Eichmann" Sitzung 11 and Urteil § 141, 166.

276. Adam 248–49, 314 n. 51; DNA "Nuremberg EC–307–1 (also PS-3363)" 1 and "Vernehmung des Viktor Brack 13 IX 46" 8; Höhne 368–69; Broszat Polenpolitik 19, 66.

277. Genoud Le Testament 86 (13 II 45).

278. Ibid. 143 (2 IV 45).

279. The infant was also lame on one side, corresponding to Hitler's first war wound.

280. See pp. 16–17.

281. Hillgruber Strategie 545–46, 575, Rolle 122; Dallin 73–74 and passim; Ulam 549 ff. and passim; Hesse 40, 47–48, 99–100; Jacobsen "Kommissarbefehl" 196.

282. Hillgruber " 'Endlösung' " 151, Strategie 392–93; Hildebrand Aussenpolitik 112–13, 115, 118–20, 129; Deuerlein Hitler 154; Jäckel 79–80; Krausnick "Judenverfolgung" 370, 425–30, 434, 441; Nolte 399–400.

283. Hillgruber Strategie 553–54, " 'Endlösung' " 150; Schramm Führer 67. Further, Milward 64 ff., 102; p. 47.

284. Hillgruber " 'Endlösung' " 138: in 1941 the German army advancing in Russia already constituted, "objectively seen, . . . a shield" for Hitler's extermination program. Similarly, Hillgruber Strategie 523–25, 531. Further, pp. 94–95.

285. Hillgruber Staatsmänner I 22–23, Strategie 556; IMT(G) XVI 539, 542; Dietrich 125; Picker 202; Heiber Lagebesprechungen 738, 739, 741, 780; PUL Dethleffsen 29; Besymenski Tod 47–48. Perhaps he began in VIII 39: see Speer 181 and Halder Feldherr 62.

286. Schellenberg 199.

287. Greiner and Schramm IV 1580–81; Hubatsch 348–49; Schwerin von Krosigk 223; Milward 184–89.

288. See p. xii.

289. See p. 31 and n. 258. Further, Irving II 3 quoting Hitler to Giesing: "You know, doctor, when I was young I always wanted to be a doctor too. Then my other career came along, and I recognized what my mission really was."

II TOMORROW THE WORLD

1. *Ursachen* V 324.
2. Phelps "Parteiredner" 298 (17 IV 20). Similarly, *VB* 3 VIII 29 (1 VIII 29 on "the poison of those foreigners . . . disguised as Germans"). Further, BAK NS26/55/50 (18 IX 28), 106 *verso* −107 (27 X 28).
3. Phelps "Parteiredner" 300 (27 IV 20).
4. Hiller 132; Kaehler 305; Thimme 68–69. Further, Rudin 384.
5. *Ursachen* I 141–42, 358, IV 160, 167–68, V 46–50, 323, VII 196–99, 367–68, 371, 381, X 295, 301; VdR CDXXII No. 4124 5, 8; Rudin 201 and passim; Ritter 48, 49–50; Krausnick "Weg" 233; Kielmansegg 670–71.
6. Rudin 12–23, 35–36, 206, 218.
7. Koerber 98 (12 IX 23).
8. *Ursachen* I 141–42, IV 160, 260; Ritter 50–53, 58.
9. *Ursachen* IV 82–83, 91–117, V 46, 50, VII–2 352; VdR CCCXI 4544B.
10. *Ursachen* IV 228 and passim, V 1–3, 50–54, 96–97; VdR CDXXII No. 4124 8; Schmolze 3; Kolb *Arbeiterräte* 56–60, "Rätewirklichkeit" 169 and n. 8; Mitchell 139, 141–42, 151, and passim; Carsten *Reichswehr* 10–11 and *Revolution* 323; Ryder 266; Kielmansegg 682–84.
11. Schulze 55–57; Waite 42–44.
12. Rudin 131 ff., 172–73, 193 ff., 204, 222 ff.; Sauer "Scheitern" 78 and n. 4; Fischer *Griff* 558–59.
13. Schmolze 76–77.
14. Ibid. 158–59; Mitchell 105–06, 127, 161; Abel 17–18, quoting Max Weber in *Frankfurter Zeitung* 22 XI 18; Troeltsch 1, 16–18; Eyck I 138; Nicholls 53–54; Heiber *Weimar* 64. Further, Schwabe 202–03 n. 31; Krüger 212.
15. Kotowski 764.
16. Schubert 128.
17. Ibid. 134; Angress *Revolution* 281.
18. Fries-Thiessenhusen 349–52; Hiller 122–34; Kaehler 314–16; Thimme 78–80; Krausnick "Weg" 233; Fischer *Griff* 557.
19. Ritter 59; Matthias and Morsey 62 and passim; Kielmansegg 664, 670; Krausnick "Weg" 233; Nicholls 1, 5. Further, Dorpalen *Hindenburg* 52 and n. 14.
20. *This* was not wholly groundless: see Rudin 320–21, 324 n. 8, 257 n. 29.
21. Warweariness to the rear did hurt fighting morale, but not enough for any revolutionary soldiers' councils to form on the front in XI 18: see Rudin 207, 218; Schulze 2 and nn. 6, 7.
22. Krausnick "Weg" 234; Thimme 74–75; Dehio 24; Troeltsch 317. For the germ of the legend see Rudin 376 (Solf to Lansing 10 XI 18).
23. Hitler *Kampf* 225; Domarus 648 (17 IX 36).
24. BAK NS26/55/134 (9 XI 28).
25. BAK NS26/53/205 (9 XI 27). Further, Hitler in *VB* 25 I 23; BAK NS26/54/189 (9 XI 27: "a coalition of pimps, thieves, deserters, burglars, and racketeers, headed by the organizer of this genial mode, the international Hebrew, the Jew"); Calic 103–04; Picker 348; Hitler *Conversations* 392. Also, on 9 XII 32 an anguished Hitler called Gregor Strasser's break with him a stab in the back "five minutes before victory": Meissner and Wilde 142.
26. HStA AStA Sonderabgabe I 1478 (5 XI 20); Phelps "Parteiredner" 329 (24 VII 20).

27. HStA AStA Sonderabgabe I 1478 (4 III 20). Further, Phelps "Parteiredner" 305 (6 VII 20), 315–16 (5 IX 20); Deuerlein "Eintritt" 225 (29 X 20); Hitler in VB 28 IV 21; HIS speech outline of 24 V 21; Preiss 148 (24 VII 30); Domarus 1802 (11 XII 41).

28. Phelps "Parteiredner" 315–16 (5 IX 20).

29. HStA AStA Sonderabgabe I 1480 (26 II 23). Further, Picker 348.

30. HStA AStA Sonderabgabe I 1478 (4 III 20). Further, ibid. (24 XI 20); Preiss II (1 VIII 20).

31. HStA AStA Sonderabgabe I 1480 (24 X 22).

32. Deuerlein "Eintritt" 207 (13 XI 19).

33. BAK R431/2681/83; Schmolze 17–19, 126, 181–82, 228, 268–69, 293, 349, 395; Denny 297.

34. Deuerlein "Eintritt" 214 (11 VI 20). Further, HStA AStA Sonderabgabe I 1480 (2 XI 22); Domarus 729–30 (13 IX 37)—and for that "smashing" p. 39 and n. 31.

35. Angress "Juden" 242 and n. 437; Schmolze 17–19, 126, 181–82, 228, 268–69, 293, 327, 349, 395; Horn NSDAP 30–31; Nicholls 93; Maser NSDAP 18, 153.

36. Frankfurter Zeitung 27 I 23; Moser von Filseck 86. Further, ibid. 174, 226; Lurker 9–11.

37. Hitler Kampf 736, Buch 113–14, 163.

38. Hillgruber Strategie 36 n. 39, 565–66, Rolle 68–74, "Place" 8–12; Thies 9–17 and passim; Herwig 651–52; Hildebrand Reich 77–83, Aussenpolitik 89, 93, 95, 97; Dülffer 207–08, 210–16; Henke 20–27, 203–04; Wollstein 5–13; Leach 13, 49, 228; Moltmann passim. Further, Speer 184–85, 524–25.

39. Further, Carr 15–16.

40. Maser Briefe 101 (Hitler to Ernst Hepp 5 II 15); Westenkirchner in HSW; Hitler in VB 6 III 21, Buch 87–89.

41. Ursachen I 154–55; Hillgruber Rolle 17–23, 34–57; Herwig 664.

42. Preiss 165, 171–72 (13 XI 30). Further, pp. 69–70; Thies 23, 55–56 on this Erlangen speech, 182–86 on growing British recognition in 1933–1939 of Hitler's ultimate goal as expounded in Mein Kampf and elsewhere. When Arnold J. Toynbee told him in II 36 that a German takeover of the Ukraine and the Urals would put the western nations at his mercy, Hitler denied harboring any such eastern aims: Toynbee Acquaintances 282–83. With that he implicitly acknowledged the flaw in his program.

43. Henke Kalkül 72–73; Hildebrand Aussenpolitik 76.

44. See Hildebrand Aussenpolitik 92.

45. Henke 287. But Hitler hinted at such an enlarged offer as early as 1930: Aigner 36. And Göring imparted it to a journalist in 1937: Henke 75. "We were . . . ready to throw our force into the balance to keep the British Empire going," Hitler lamented when that force was spent: Genoud Le Testament 61.

46. Henke Kalkül passim; Hillgruber "Place" 12–16. Further, IfZ Fritz Wiedemann ZS191/I/4.

47. Hillgruber Rolle 48, "Lage" 283; Groscurth 167; Bullock "Origins" 281–85; Hildebrand Aussenpolitik 58; Speer 181.

48. Speer 179.

49. Schmidt 473.

50. Hitler in VB 28 IV 21. Further, Hitler Buch 183; BAK NS26/55/120 (9 XI 28: "of 4 August"); Domarus 1333–34, 1340 (3 IX 39), 1468 (24 II 40).

51. Martin *Friedensinitiativen* 448. Similarly, Toynbee *Experiences* 224.
52. IfZ Adolf Heusinger ZS69/3.
53. Hillgruber *Strategie* 391–93 and passim; Leach 66–78.
54. Hillgruber *Strategie* 219. Further, ibid. 174, 365 and n. 68, 373–74; Leach 63–86, 100, 132, 229–31.
55. Hillgruber *Strategie* 392 and n. 5, 553, " 'Endlösung' " 150 n. 56; Schramm *Führer* 67. As early as 19 XI 41 Hitler said he expected "that the recognition that the two sides could not destroy each other will lead to a negotiated peace": Halder *Kriegstagebuch* III 295.
56. Hillgruber *Staatsmänner* I 686–87; Bracher *Diktatur* 441. Further, Speer 181.
57. Hillgruber *Strategie* 554, *Rolle* 126 ("turn fate" was General Alfred Jodl's phrase). Further, Gehlen 18; pp. 108–10.
58. Max von Baden 242. Further, *Ursachen* I 158; Kielmansegg 630; Martin *Friedensinitiativen* 504, 506.
59. Vogelsang "Dokumente" 435 (4 II 33).
60. Jäckel *Weltanschauung* 135, 142, 149, and passim.
61. Further, Wollstein 12.
62. Hillgruber *Strategie* 157–62, 167–69, and passim.
63. Ibid. 560, 562 and nn. 125–26; Seaton 217–23, 587, and passim; Leach 168, 224, 238–41; Laqueur 263. Further, Besymenski *Sonderakte* 298–301.
64. Hillgruber *Strategie* 165, 192–94, 352–62, and passim; Seaton 33; Leach 172–74, 229–30; Domarus 1424 and Jacobsen and Jochmann (23 IX 39: "Time is working for the enemy"); IMT(E) XXXVII 466–86 (Document 052–L: memorandum of 9 X 39); Genoud *Le Testament* 95 ("Time was working against us on both fronts").
65. Domarus 681 (20 II 33).
66. Hillgruber *Strategie* 371 and n. 105, 397, *Rolle* 74–75; Leach 157, 228–29, 241; IfZ Adolf Heusinger ZS69/75.
67. Mann 64. Similarly, Toynbee *Acquaintances* 291 on "the doom toward which Hitler was leading Germany—'with the unfalteringness of a sleepwalker,' as Hitler himself once put it in an illuminating flash of self-analysis."
68. *Ursachen* I 61, 342, 454–55, IV 132, 153, V 221. Further, Calic 94; Baumgart 372, 376; Hillgruber *Strategie* 71, *Rolle* 70–73, *Kontinuität* 13–14, 25; Hildebrand *Aussenpolitik* 15, 89, 97; Farrar 89–90.
69. *Ursachen* I 454. On 12 IV 43 Hitler remarked to Antonescu that in 1918 Germany "could have got by with political skill and diplomatic wiles, as no opponent was left to the east": Hillgruber *Staatsmänner* II 215.
70. Hillgruber *Rolle* 70–71, *Kontinuität* 15, 23; Hildebrand *Aussenpolitik* 15, 89; Fabry *Sowjetunion* 34; Binion "East" 85–87.
71. Baumgart 204, 247–50; Volkmann 233; Ritter 50; *Ursachen* I 392–401. For Hitler's repeated, telltale insistence on the differentness of Barbarossa see Hillgruber *Staatsmänner* II 19–20 and further, pp. 107–08.
72. *Ursachen* VII-2 306 (letter of 19 V 27)—which checks with *VdR* CCCXI 4462B, 4466A-B, and passim. Further, *Ursachen* I 119, 384, IV 132–33, V 184, 277, 282–83, X 280; *VdR* CCCXIII 5642D, 5648B; Thimme 82 quoting *Kreuz-Zeitung* 31 XII 18; Fischer *Griff* 610; Kohn 311; Hillgruber *Rolle* 65–66; Hildebrand *Aussenpolitik* 16; Breitling 74; HIS speech outline of 4 I 21; Hitler *Kampf* 214–17; BAK NS26/55/129 (9 XI 28); p. 80. Müller *Mars* 239 claims to have felt an inner foreboding at the height of German power in early 1918.

73. Hillgruber *Rolle* 105, *Strategie* 219; Seaton 51–52. Further, Leach 99–118, 219–20; IfZ Adolf Heusinger ZS69/4. Hitler went the limit when he told the Japanese ambassador on 14 VII 41 that "he would chase Stalin wherever the latter fled": Hillgruber *Staatsmänner* II 545. With Antonescu on 11 II 42 he was back to years-long anti-"partisan" warfare beyond the Urals: ibid. 47.

74. Zechlin "1915" 352 (Ludendorff to Hans Delbrück 29 XII 15). Further, pp. 115–16.

75. *Ursachen* VII 152–53, 171, and passim, VII–2 320–22; Baumgart passim; Geiss passim; Hildebrand *Aussenpolitik* 118–19 and nn. 55a, 56.

76. Dallin 409–27; Jacobsen "Kommissarbefehl" 185–93; Leach 213–14.

77. VdR CCCXI 4479C–D. Further, ibid. 4545A–B, 4553C.

78. Ibid. 4553D.

79. Schramm *Führer* 67.

80. Hillgruber *Strategie* 392 and n. 5.

81. IMT(E) XLII 328–30 (PL-49: Party circular 9 X 42); DNA RFSS T–175/94/2615097 (Himmler "Vortrag beim Führer am 19.6.1943"); Adam 306; Rich II 11; Dietrich 82; Ribbentrop 240; Schellenberg 179–80; Hillgruber *Strategie* 371–72 n. 105.

82. Schramm *Führer* 154.

83. Genoud *Le Testament* 93. Further, Hillgruber *Staatsmänner* II 544, 552; Schellenberg 179–80, 223; Dietrich 82; Ribbentrop 240.

84. Phelps "Parteiredner" 289 (10 XII 19). Further, Thies 41–45.

85. *VB* 10 III 21 (6 III 21).

86. *VB* 3 III 21.

87. See e.g. Deuerlein "Eintritt" 209 (10 XII 19); Phelps "Parteiredner" 298 (17 IV 20). Further, BAK NS26/55/3 (19 I 28), etc.

88. Hitler *Kampf* 524. Further, ibid. 518–19, 525, 527. He had treated the theme at least on 11, 12, 13 XI 19 and 4 III, 7 V, 19 VI, 1 VIII, 22 IX 20: BAK NS26/51/4–5, 8; Deuerlein "Eintritt" 206; Phelps "Parteiredner" 320; HStA AStA Sonderabgabe I 1478; Preiss 9.

89. *VB* 5 VI 21 (31 V 21), stress added. Further, Binion "East" 85–87.

90. Speech outline from BAK NS26/49 in Maser *Briefe* 268, 270, 276, 278, 280, 282, 284; my quotation on 276. Also congruent is ibid. 266: "Increase of population equal to increase of land No. Is a perpetual increase of soil yield possible? No. Options. Colonization or world trade. Emigration or world trade."

91. Hitler *Kampf* 143–56, *Buch* 99–103; BAK NS26/52, 53, 55 (6, 26 III and 8 VIII 27, 19 I, 5 III, 18, 30 IX, 18, 23, 27 X 28); Preiss 39–40 (23 III 27), 77–79 (21 VIII 27), 95–98, 101–04 (8 XII 28), 122–46 (30 XI 29); *VB* 7 VIII 29 (5 VIII 29); Treue 206–07 (memorandum of VIII 36); Domarus 1422 (23 XI 39); Kotze and Krausnick 312–16 (15 II 42); Picker 497–99 (30 XI 42).

92. Maser *Briefe* 268.

93. BAK R431/2681/88 (Scharrer to Cuno 30 XII 22). Further, Hanfstaengl *Haus* 78; Viereck 236.

94. Hitler *Kampf* 741–42. Comparably, ibid. 152–58, 753. Further, Rauschning 43; Jäckel *Weltanschauung* 40, 42.

95. Hitler *Kampf* 518–20, 523–27.

96. Koerber 56 (13 IV 23).

97. Domarus 70 (27 I 32).

98. Tyrell *Führer* 319–20 from BAK Sammlung Schumacher 373 (Hitler to Stahlhelm leaders 11 V 29). Similarly, BAK NS26/55/2 (19 I 28), 52 (18 IX

28: "*der urgewaltige Wille*"), 59–64 (18 X 28). Further, Heiden *Fuehrer* 139–40; Horn *NSDAP* 424.

99. See esp. Kotze and Krausnick 268–86 (10 XI 38).
100. Domarus 609 (20 III 36), 612 (24 III 36). Similarly, ibid. 570 (30 I 36: see p. 57), 643 (13 IX 36), etc.
101. See esp. Krebs 138–40; also Lüdecke 22–23; Rauschning 127–28; Speer 32–33; Baeyer-Katte 134; Merkl 105–06.
102. Heiden *Fuehrer* 140.
103. *Basler Nachrichten* 5 V 45. Similarly, Franz-Willing 6: "The medium of a conquered . . . people."
104. Above II n. 3.
105. Heiber *Lagebesprechungen* 106–07; Hillgruber *Wehrmacht* 1292–97; Gehlen 18.
106. This emerged with lurid intensity at the last: see esp. PUL Dethleffsen passim.
107. Müller *Mars* 14. Merkl 168 speaks comparably of "the legacy of an 'unfinished war' that led to the Third Reich and on to World War Two."
108. Hiller 143–44.
109. Rudin 131–32, 173. Further, Luckau 411–19 (Allied reply to the German counterproposals 16 VI 19); Kaehler 309–14; BAK NS26/55/70 (18 X 28). Appropriately, Hitler justified diplomatic deceit as a revenge for the "Wilson swindle": IfZ Fritz Wiedemann ZS191/I/23–24.
110. See pp. 101–07.
111. See Hillgruber "Place" 20–21.
112. See Hillgruber *Strategie* 394 on fateful Barbarossa.
113. Burckhardt 269–70.
114. Domarus 1459, 1460 (30 I 40).

III   THE LOUD-SPEAKER

1. Knickerbocker 46.
2. Heiden *Fuehrer* 140.
3. Jetzinger 48; Harry Schulze-Wilde in *Der Spiegel* XXI (1967) No. 33 8, 10.
4. Rosalia Hörl in BAK NS26/17a.
5. Eastman and Hallman 221–22; Marshall 357; Harrison 19.
6. Further, Binion "Concept" 206 and n. 112.
7. For this and what follows see Appendix C.
8. CB Paula 1.
9. Kubizek 42, 43, 50; similarly, 46, 49.
10. Ibid. 50. Further, Oplt 4; NYPL Brigid 8; DNA "Book" 2 (William Patrick Hitler), 21 (Bloch); BAK NS26/65/91 (Bloch); Bloch 37; Maser *Hitler* 52–53.
11. Further, Kurth "Comment" 237–38.
12. See Appendix C.
13. See Appendix D.
14. See Moll *Säuglingssterblichkeit* 17.
15. Muslin and Pieper 232, 235. Further, Muslin et al. 805, 806; Katz et al. 514, 515; Aimez passim.
16. Again to the day (meaninglessly) if her first conception fell six days later than my estimate of 23 VIII 84, which was 7,796 days after her first sibling loss and 7,808 days before her father's death.

17. Groth and Hahn 125 (enumerator for Altötting and Burghausen).
18. BAK NS26/52/101 (8 XI 30). (Hitler here claimed to be that latter "someone"!)
19. DNA "Book" 21 (Bloch).
20. These were eschewed as poisonous: Müller *Wandel* 132; Krause 17, 31; DNA "Koeppen" 37 (evening meal 5 XI 41); DNA "Picture" 36–37; JT Giesing 63–64, 71–72; BAK Schramm 149.
21. Domarus 140 (25 X 32).
22. Tyrell *Führer* 320 (Hitler to Stahlhelm leaders 11 V 29).
23. Domarus 135 (7 IX 32). Further, ibid. 1810 (11 XII 41); Stein 109; JT Giesing 131, 134, 176; BAK Schramm 86–88 (Karl Brandt).
24. Hitler *Kampf* 116.
25. Domarus 570 (30 I 36).
26. Moser von Filseck 179 (29 IX 25).
27. Rich 210; Hanfstaengl *Years* 69 and passim; Grieswelle 124–27. In the 1920s he sported a whip for phallic effect: see Moser von Filseck 203–04.
28. Lurker 11 (report dated 8 I 24); similarly, StAfO Staatsanwaltschaft No. 3099:69 (report dated 19 XII 23: "a traumatic nervous injury").
29. Moser von Filseck 146 (23 XI 23).
30. Deuerlein *Hitler* 66; DNA "Book" 893 (Hanfstaengl), 935 (Friedelind Wagner); Hanfstaengl *Years* 114, *Haus* 154, 157; Röhm 272; Schlabrendorff 345–46; Lurker 68 (medical report dated 2 IV 24); Wagner 30; Picker 193; BAK NS26/114/7; IfZ Mathilde von Scheubner-Richter ZS292/3. But see AA 291/183744–46 (24 XI 23) on the hunger strike as Hitler's protest against the refusal to let him consult his defense lawyer without witnesses.
31. Kuhn 99–104.
32. See p. 49 and Hitler *Kampf* 741–42. Further, pp. 61–63.
33. Preiss 40 (23 III 27).
34. Jäckel *Weltanschauung* 123; p. 90.
35. See pp. 47–49.
36. See above I nn. 130, 234.
37. Koerber 29 (12 IV 22), stress added.
38. Tyrell *Führer* 49. Further, Koerber 83 (21 VIII 23: "the final, decisive struggle: swastika or Soviet star!"), 105 (12 IX 23: "swastika or Soviet star"); Jochmann 103 (28 II 26: "Either Marxism exterminates us, or we exterminate it to the last traces"); *VB* 26 V 26 (23 V 26: "We are convinced that the struggle against Marxism shall and must come to a final decision, because two world views are fighting each other with only one possible outcome: *One stays and the other goes*"); etc.
39. See p. 26 and n. 209.
40. Such was, at all odds, the expository sequence in BAK R431/2681/88 (Scharrer to Cuno 30 XII 22).
41. Vogelsang "Dokumente" 435 and below IV n. 37. "As far as schemes for war were concerned, none was mentioned, and all present were uncommonly pleased with this speech": thus naval chief Erich Raeder in *IMT*(E) XIV 21.
42. Sauer "Gewalt" 749–50 and at greater length O'Neill 40–41.
43. Jacobsen and Jochmann; Jäckel *Frankreich* 27–28. Further, Henrikson passim.
44. Jacobsen and Jochmann.
45. Hitler *Kampf* 750–52.

46. Hitler *Buch* 128.
47. *Treue* 204, 206.
48. Jacobsen *Aussenpolitik* 427, 821 and *Weltkrieg* 26; Henke 95–96; Laqueur 170, 176–95; Kuhn 196–98; Fabry *Sowjetunion* 58–59. Further, Carr 57.
49. Sommer *Japan* 31, 34 (9 VI and 22 VII 36). Thus Hitler told the Reichstag on 30 I 37 that the point was "to immunize the German people as well as possible" against Bolshevism. This followed an assurance that, coming from him, was ominous: "I could never be absolved by my people's history if, for whatever reasons, I should neglect anything necessary for that people's survival." It also echoed his earlier assurance that "a prodigious immunization of the German people has been attained" against Jewry. Domarus 671, 670, 666. Further, Jacobsen *Aussenpolitik* 460 and n. 22; also Greiner 272 and Buchheit 167 (quoting Heydrich in 1938: "It is the Führer's will to liberate Russia from the Communist yoke! The war with Soviet Russia is a settled matter").
50. Quoted by Hillgruber *Strategie* 145 and *Rolle* 105.
51. Halder II 336–37. Further, Greiner and Schramm I 341, 346; Warlimont 175–77; Hillgruber *Strategie* 526, 530 n. 62, " 'Endlösung' " 144; Jacobsen "Kommissarbefehl" 165–67; IfZ Adolf Heusinger ZS69/8; Heusinger 125.
52. DNA Nuremberg NO–4145/2 (deposition of Walter Blume 29 VI 47).
53. Jacobsen *Aussenpolitik* 459 n. 21. Further, Steinert 205.
54. *Ursachen* I 456, VII–2 348.
55. Burckhardt 348 (Hitler told Burckhardt in VIII 39: "I need the Ukraine so that we won't be starved out again as in the last war"). Similarly, Tyrell *Führer* 191 (17 VI 29: ". . . so that we never again get into a situation such as the World War and even the prewar period put us in").
56. Dallin 406–07; Wright 118–19, 122–23, 137.
57. Format, pagination, and handwriting suggest this, though the page headings are different (Maser *Briefe* 272, 274) and despite some congruence with Phelps "Rede" 412 (13 VIII 20). Further, HIS speech outline of 31 VIII 21: "Racial suicide Precondition for this is <u>mass madness</u> Can be induced through mass need—<u>hunger.</u> Hunger as weapon in all periods. Hunger in the Jew's service. Destroys bodily strength and health disturbs the understanding. Planned starvation by price rises. 1.) In Germany before the war. 2.) During the war. 3.) After the war."
58. Ludendorff 160–61; *Ursachen* VII–2 225 n. 19 and Hahlweg *Friede* 118 ("Richtlinien an Oberost für die Friedensbesprechungen" 16 XII 17). Similarly, ibid. 38 ("Leitsätze für einen Separatfriedensvertrag mit Russland" 3 XII 17). Further, Hahlweg *Diktatfrieden* 43–46.
59. Koerber 106 (12 IX 23). Similarly, *VB* 22 II 23 (20 II 23): "Here there is only a life-and-death struggle. Either Jewish-international Marxism holds the battlefield, or—Germany does."
60. HStA AStA Sonderabgabe I 1480 (21 IV 22).
61. *VB* 25 II 26 (14 II 26), Party meeting at Bamberg. Similarly, *VB* 26 V 26 (23 V 26), postmortem on the Bamberg meeting: "the final reckoning" with the "Jewish international bloodsuckers" *within* Germany. On this Bamberg confrontation, see Schüddekopf 174–84; Reimann 63–67; Schildt 155–65, esp. 159–60; Wörtz 97–107, esp. 101; Schulz 426. Further, Horn *NSDAP* 269–70. Goebbels' sarcastic résumé of Hitler's Bamberg speech is misleading: "Our task is to smash Bolshevism. Bolshevism is Jewish handiwork! We must inherit Russia!" Goebbels *Tagebuch* 59–60. So, doubtless, is Goebbels' diary

version of Hitler's private explanation of 1 III 26: "Italy and England our allies. Russia wants to devour us. It is all in his pamphlet and in the second volume of his *Kampf* soon to appear." Ibid. 72. The pamphlet was also Chapter 13 of that second volume, which nowhere argued from smashing Bolshevism, or from a Russian threat, to a war on Russia. Further, Kuhn 124–31, esp. 127, and 273–74.

62. He anticipated that grounding as early as the spring of 1919 if IfZ Friedrich Krohn ZS89/5 is accurate: "he designated . . . the fight against Communism and Bolshevism as the primary domestic and foreign aim."

63. Jäckel *Weltanschauung* 135–41. Further, pp. 90–91.

64. Hitler *Buch* 220–24 and pp. 87–90. For an earlier, arrested development of another such link out of the concept "hunger" see p. 61 and n. 57.

65. Jacobsen *Weltkrieg* 180–81. Further, Goebbels *Tagebücher* 326–27 (8 V 43: Hitler saying the same thing).

66. Lange "Terminus" 426–27, 432–33.

67. Horn "Aufsatz" 280–84 and passim; Kuhn 99–104. The first term alone of Hitler's later argument for the British alliance against Russia came into HStA AStA Sonderabgabe I 1755 (10 IV 23): "In 1899 we might have been able to conclude a treaty with England to bring down Russia or a treaty with Russia against England." But in a speech outline of shortly before the Putsch—HIS "Germany at the Crossroads"—Hitler gave Germany's first "political task" as the "creation of a continental power position" and the "overall aim" as "land and soil for the nation." And at about this time he told the German-American publicist George Sylvester Viereck that "we must expand eastward" and that "we can stretch our cramped limbs only towards the East"—this after expounding the need to restore the "body politic" beforehand by ridding it of Bolshevism alias Jewry: Viereck 236.

68. Grieswelle 146.

69. Horn *NSDAP* 264; Hildebrand *Aussenpolitik* 19–25.

70. Merkl 313–445; Wheaton 125; Bracher *Diktatur* 163; Canetti 204–05.

71. BAK NS26/54/5 (12 VI 25). Further, Grieswelle 74–79; Orlow I 7.

72. BAK NS26/54/6 (12 VI 25). Similarly, Koerber 78–79 (21 VIII 23); BAK NS26/52/31; Domarus 85 (27 I 32).

73. Grunberger 18. Further, ibid. 31.

74. Horn *NSDAP* 27. Further, Bracher *Diktatur* 370; Vondung 198.

75. Broszat *Staat* 380–81. Further, Schoenbaum 285–87.

76. Fabry *Mutmassungen* 17–170; Lange *Maximen* 30–74. But compare Thies 23–25. IfZ Paul Schmidt ZS1433: Hitler's interpreter held that Hitler's program of revision first, then eastward expansion, was surely clear "to all sensible people."

77. *Dingolfinger Anzeiger* 2 X 28.

78. *Deutscher Michl* 2 XI 28. Further, Thies 45–57.

79. See p. 60 and nn. 41–42.

80. On the problems raised by the documentation for this conference, see Henrikson passim.

81. Hildebrand *Aussenpolitik* 61, 74, 76; Hillgruber "Lage" 289–91; Henke 308.

82. Hildebrand *Aussenpolitik* 52–54; Henke 308–10.

83. See above n. 61; Heiber in Goebbels *Tagebuch* 11.

84. Höhne 273; Hildebrand *Reich* 475 n.; p. 99.

85. Hildebrand *Aussenpolitik* 28.

86. IfZ Hjalmar Schacht ZS135/II/40–41, 48–49.
87. Speer 189–91; Hillgruber *Strategie* 156–57, 174–75, 513–16; Gilbert *Dictatorship* 124; Martin *Friedensinitiativen* 425–27; IfZ Karl Bodenschatz ZS 10/32–33. Further, Thies 53, 177.
88. On this language, see Fischer "Weltpolitik" passim; Hildebrand *Aussenpolitik* 58.
89. Dickmann 920. Further, Thies 192–93.
90. Binion "East" 96–99; Grieswelle 181, 193; Jacobsen *Aussenpolitik* 13; Thies 55.
91. Gamm 43.
92. BAK NS26/52/90 (8 XI 30). Similarly, ibid. 76 (7 XI 30). Further, Jacobsen *Aussenpolitik* 14 n. 8.
93. Preiss 165, 171 (13 XI 30): see pp. 41–42 and n. 42.
94. Domarus 85 (27 I 32). Further, ibid. 90.
95. Ibid. 173 (3 I 33).
96. Ibid. 760 (21 XI 37).
97. Ibid. 761 (23 XI 37). Further, Carr 75; above II n. 69.
98. Hitler *Buch* 28 (18 VIII 28). This too was continuous with his prior usage: thus Deuerlein "Eintritt" 207 (15 XI 19): "we want to be a free people and not a 'free state' "). But it was inconsistent: thus Tyrell *Führer* 191 (17 VI 29): ". . . *two aims*. The first is to win freedom, the second to win land and soil." Further, Thies 59, 107 n. 9, 108, and passim (on Hitler's post-1930 "suggestion" of his expansionist goal).
99. See BAK NS26/55 (30 IX, 18 and 27 X 28); also (protoschematic) BAK NS26/54 (6 III and 9 XI 27), Preiss (23 and 26 III, 9 VI, 21 VIII 27), BAK NS26/52 (8 VIII 27), VB 23 VIII 27 (21 VIII 27), BAK NS26/55 (18 I, 18 IX 28)—and (less schematic again) Preiss (8 XII 28, 30 IX 29, 13 XI 30), BAK NS26/55 (23 X 28), VB 7 VIII 29 (5 VIII 29); BAK NS26/52 (7, 8 XI 30). Further, Binion "East" 92–99.
100. HStA AStA Sonderabgabe I 1478/68–69 (4 III 20).
101. Ibid. 94 (9 IV 20).
102. Kursell 67 (20 IV 23).
103. Deuerlein *Aufstieg* 267–69.
104. BAK NS26/54/162, 145, 163. Similarly, ibid. (9 XI 27) and 55 (18 I 28).
105. BAK NS26/55/44 (18 IX 28).
106. Domarus 117 (15 VII 32).
107. Quoted by Grieswelle 135.
108. Domarus 183. Further, ibid. 115 (10 VII 32); Grieswelle Ch. 7; Binion "East" 97–99.
109. From his first day in office: Deuerlein *Kanzler* 485.
110. To judge from Abel 204–301 and Merkl 468–77, 689–90, and passim (esp. the statements quoted 469–73, 540, 663, and passim), the national aspirations expressed by hundreds of Nazi militants in an autobiography contest of 1934 appear to match up in each case with at least one of the three associated terms of Hitler's formula of de-Judaization to restore national oneness for the expansionist war ahead—mostly with the unhushed middle term, but often with all three through vague allusions to Hitler's "idea" or "mission." Evidently the autobiographers did not associate the 1918 defeat with that program or, in many cases, with their adherence to Nazism: this parallels the individual traumatic tendency (Hitler did not consciously motivate his Jewish policies with reference to 1907).

111. He may well have won out within a stable total of non-Marxist, non-Centrist votes (McKibbin 27–28; Shively 1220–22), but neither the Centrist nor even the Marxist vote was class-specific. Although class distribution does not vary significantly with sex, in Cologne in 1928 "45.5 per cent of the men voted for a Marxist party, compared with 32.0 per cent of the women" (Shively 1219). Further, Merkl 711 and passim.

112. Above I n. 130. "I have the impression that he doesn't fear the Communists at all," Richard Breiting noted after his interview of VI 31: Calic 115.

113. Kele 203. Further, ibid. 210–11, 215–16; Schulz 721.

114. Bahne 662.

115. Angress *Stillborn* 475; Abshagen 120; Viereck 235; Epstein 74; Merkl 375–77 and passim. Bahne 661: turnover in Communist membership was largely a changeover to the SA in the early 1930s and ran between 80 and 100 percent annually.

116. Bahne 722; Diels 153.

117. Moser von Filseck 229.

118. *VB* 20 IX 22 (18 IX 22). Similarly, *VB* 7 VIII 29 (5 VIII 29). Further, IfZ Fritz Wiedemann ZS191/II/1.

119. IfZ Horst von Mellenthin ZS105/4, 3 II 33.

120. Carr 21–23; Kele 177; Grieswelle 55.

121. Schwerin von Krosigk 195.

122. See, for example, Preiss 199 (13 X 32) and further, Deuerlein *Kanzler* 483; Greiswelle 55; Bracher *Diktatur* 178–79; Orlow I 180 and passim.

123. IfZ Otto Dietrich ZS874/107–08. Further, Merkl 699.

124. Horn *NSDAP* 254, 256; Holzer 180–83; Schulz 479; Bracher *Diktatur* 183; Wheaton 100.

125. Orlow I 286–89. Further, McKibbin 30, 33.

126. Epstein passim, esp. 75.

127. Deuerlein "Eintritt" 214 (11 VI 20).

128. Heiber *Hitler* 85. Similarly, Heiber *Weimar* 275–76; Hellpach 233; Deuerlein *Hitler* 123; IfZ Werner Best ZS207/II/9.

129. Mommsen 199. Further, ibid. 164–201. Similarly, Papen 296.

130. Quoted by Bracher "Stufen" 166.

131. See pp. 49–50 and n. 98.

132. Similarly, Hillgruber "Quellen" 115 (the Germans gave Hitler his way "for whatever reasons and with whatever reservations").

133. Wheaton 247.

134. Dietrich 125–36.

135. See Bollmus 241–42, 247–49; Adam 360 and passim; Jacobsen *Aussenpolitik* 613–19; Milward 145–46, 188, and passim; Höhne 15–16 and passim.

136. See p. 33.

137. Thimme 65; Deuerlein *Putsch* 11. Further, Monaco 141, 149.

138. *Ursachen* IV 20–21, 39, 239; VdR CCCLXXXVIII 4723A; Rudin 354, 357, 363; Kolb "Vorwort" 10.

139. Domarus 88–89 (27 I 32). Similarly, HStA AStA Sonderabgabe I 1480/53 (25 X 22); Preiss 20 (6 VIII 23). Further, Röhm 164.

140. BAK NS26/1927–1/36.

141. And by captured German gas, as he claimed until 1933: ibid. 32; Foulkes 327.

142. Rudin 349 ff., esp. 353; Thimme 81 quoting *Kreuz-Zeitung* 31 XII 18.

143. Carsten *Reichswehr* 6–7, 38; Schulze 1.

144. Schieder 53–54 and passim.
145. The common, ambiguous use of the term is illustrated by such titles as *Die Ursachen des deutschen Zusammenbruchs* (the Reichstag inquiry: see pp. 82–83) and Philipp Scheidemann's *Der Zusammenbruch.* Further, Thimme 64–65.
146. Dehio 19. Further, *Ursachen* IV 160; Hitler in *VB* 26 V 21; IfZ Franz von Pfeffer ZS177/33–34; Ringer 181, 189, and passim.
147. See esp. IfZ Franz von Pfeffer ZS177/33–34.
148. *Münchener Post* 22–23 XII 23; Fischman passim; Hitler *Kampf* 771–73; Gordon *Putsch* 352; Nicholls 111; Zimmermann *Bayern* 138–40, 187–88. Further, Mitchell 138 and passim; Schmolze 158, 214, 339, and passim; Bonnin 24 quoting Haniel von Haimhausen.
149. See, for example, Fischer *Griff* 44, 82–85, and passim; Zechlin "1914" 174–81; Troeltsch 7. Further, BAK NS26/54/185–86 (9 XI 27), NS26/55/118–19 (9 XI 28).
150. See *Ursachen* I 424, 430, 445–52; Fischer passim, esp. Ch. 14.
151. Genoud *Le Testament* 63.
152. See p. 94 and n. 50.
153. Steinert 207. Further, ibid. 86–87, 91 (on Polish war), etc.; Speer 162, 173, 178, 181–84; Höhne II 442. Franz Seldte, Minister of Labor, afterward maintained he required hospitalization for his shock: IfZ Franz Seldte ZS1495/15.
154. Hoffmann *Widerstand* 459–61 and nn. 378, 379; Bracher *Diktatur* 489–91.
155. BAK NS26/55/135 (9 XI 28). Further, Merkl 716.
156. Kohn 311.
157. Dehio 24–25. Further, Eyck I 138–39; Thimme 77–78, 146; Heiber *Weimar* 66. But the complementary unconscious motive behind that brooding found some expression, as in Hermann Hagedorn, Sr., to Irma Hagedorn Bensen 12 VII 19, quoted by Hagedorn 257: "We have been weighed in the balance and found wanting. We must have erred greatly, sinned greatly...."
158. *Ursachen* IV 111: point made by Arthur Rosenberg and ignored.
159. Ibid. V 225.
160. Rudin 393.
161. Krüger 211; Hildebrand *Aussenpolitik* 16; Waite 41. Further, Thimme 64–64; Kimmich 32–33; Kohn 311; Schulze 1–2; Fraser 64–65.
162. *Ursachen* I 141, IV 82, 160, VII 371.
163. Ibid. X 295.
164. Schauwecker 9.
165. Jünger 271–72. Further, Niekisch *Verhängnis* 20.
166. Evans 61 (Jung's English).
167. VdR CDXXII No. 4124 3. Further, Farrar 89–90.
168. *Ursachen* I 392 (1 IV 25). Brest-Litovsk was investigated by the second subcommittee in 1923–1924 with respect to missed opportunities for peace: Hahlweg *Diktatfrieden* 6. The documentation was first published in Hahlweg *Friede.* On the blurred view of Brest-Litovsk after 1918 see further, Hahlweg *Diktatfrieden* 10.
169. "Mündlicher Bericht des 20. (Untersuchungs-)Ausschusses (für Kriegsschuldfragen)" VdR CDXXII No. 4124 3, 5–7, 12. Further, Hahlweg *Diktatfrieden* 7–10.
170. VdR CDXXII No. 4124 14; also *Ursachen* IX–1 xxiv. ("Nur *im wechselsei-*

*tigen Zusammenwirken zahlreicher Ursachen, von denen der Ausschuss
die hauptsächlichen hervorgehoben hat, kann die Schuld am Zusammenbruch gefunden werden."*)

171. Further, VdR CCCLXXXVI 3273B–C.

172. The ambiguity was actually double in that the concluding paragraph, containing the line quoted, is situated in the document as if it applied to the
revolution alone. But it was intended to apply to the "collapse" as a whole,
since it follows a paragraph on the subjects the subcommittee had no time
to investigate and since its first sentence, rejecting "monocausal explana-
tions of the collapse," refers back to the dagger legend mentioned in the
general introduction (page two) and propounded by Hindenburg and Ludendorff at a notorious early session of the committee. See Verfassung-
gebende Deutsche Nationalversammlung, 15. Ausschuss Stenographischer
Bericht über die öffentlichen Verhandlugen des Untersuchungsausschusses
fourteenth session (18 XI 19) 731; VdR CCCXCV 13619D, 13622A–B; Ursachen V 246–47.

173. Ibid. V 234. Similarly, Troeltsch 21.

174. See p. 45. Further, Hillgruber Kontinuität 15, 23.

IV THE DOUBLE TRACK

1. Quoted by Hanser 300.

2. It was also as when he had gone on having his way with his mother later—
when, in his half brother's words, "he had the craziest notions and put
them across" (Oplt 4).

3. Unless her not having her three lost children in succession while nursing
him came through to him as her undoing and reversing her loss.

4. Koerber 6–7; Appendix A; p. 21 and n. 159.

5. A possible partial exception was his occasional reference to his politics in
general as a desperate, painful effort to rescue Germany from slow decline,
as when he declared at his Putsch trial: "We are convinced that the great
crime the German people committed against itself in 1918 can be expiated
only by prodigious efforts, perhaps by very great and cruel sufferings," and
even if the chance of success is only one in a hundred "then better die, die
at once" (quoted by Bonnin 153–54). For the Jewish side, see p. 64.

6. Hitler Kampf 742. Compare HStA AStA Sonderabgabe I 1480 (2 XI 22):
"Hitler sharply abjures all compromising and exhorts Germany to become
strong and mighty so as either to conquer or—perish."

7. See pp. 48–49 and n. 93, pp. 59–60 and n. 40, p. 61 and n. 57, p. 63 and
n. 64.

8. To be exact, two fragmentary alternative outlines: reproduced in Maser
Briefe 291, 292, 295. Maser's transcription—ibid. 293–94, 296–97—is defective and faulty.

9. Hitler Kampf 551–57; Franz-Willing 122–26; Phelps "Parteiredner" 309,
"Rede" 402 (13 VIII 20). Further, Hitler in VB 20 II 21: "A black swastika
in a white disk on a red field: that must be the right flag!"

10. Phelps "Rede" 402.

11. Ibid. 402–05, 411. Compare Deuerlein "Eintritt" 203 (Hitler to Gemlich 16
IX 19); BAK NS26/51/6 (31 V 20).

12. Similarly BAK NS26/52/38 (8 VIII 27: "the eternal antipode of our own nature").
13. Hitler *Kampf* 333–34. Further, BAK NS26/52/38 (8 VIII 27: "We see in them not, as do others, nomads, but we see in them parasites").
14. Compare Preiss 113 (4 VIII 29: "Peoples were never yet ruined by wars so long as they were inwardly healthy").
15. Compare Hitler *Kampf* 316.
16. Phelps "Parteiredner" 289–90 (10 XII 19), 297 (17 IV 20), 318–19 and Deuerlein "Eintritt" 215–17 (20 IX 20).
17. Deuerlein "Eintritt" 218 (24 IX 20).
18. Phelps "Rede" 409 (13 VIII 20).
19. Phelps "Parteiredner" 305 (6 VII 20).
20. Maser *Briefe* 270.
21. Compare Preiss 168 (13 XI 30): "In economic life as a whole, in life itself as a whole, the idea will have to be done away with that the individual's interest is fundamental and that the general interest is built upon the interest of the individual—that therefore the individual's interest is the source of the general interest. The opposite is true."
22. Preiss 16 (3 I 23). Similarly, *VB* 12 IV 23 (10 IV 23): "the banner with the white field and black swastika" would float over all Germany.
23. Koerber 57 (13 IV 23).
24. Ibid. 62.
25. Hitler in *VB* 3 V 23; above I n. 234. Similarly, Hitler in *VB* 25 I 22: "... the race in which we see the world enemy of the freedom of all the peoples of the earth."
26. Hitler *Buch* 225. On the synthesis see Jäckel *Weltanschauung* 139–41 and passim.
27. BAK NS26/55/83 (18 X 28). Further, Thies 32 and n. 5, 48 and n. 12, 186, and passim.
28. Jäckel *Weltanschauung* 86, 98–101; BAK NS26/55/2 (18 I 28); Domarus 70 (27 I 32); Treue 204 (memorandum of VIII 36).
29. BAK NS26/54/178 (9 XI 27).
30. Hitler *Buch* 64–68; Jäckel *Weltanschauung* 126–35.
31. See above III n. 99. It did not matter that Jewish divisiveness, on which the means-end formula turned, was no part of the antithesis.
32. This substitution was prepared earlier. Thus Kursell 57 (13 IV 23: "the democratic-Marxist-Jewish world press"), 62 (13 IV 23: "the democratic-Marxist Jew"), 69 (20 IV 23: the Jew propagates democracy and Marxism to gain power over peoples); Jochmann 101 (28 II 26: "The question of Germany's rising again is a question of destroying the Marxist world view in Germany"), 102–03, 114, etc. Further, Binion "East" 96–98.
33. BAK NS26/55/43 (18 IX 28: "Why must precisely these three [Aryan qualitie] be of overwhelming importance for our German people? For the sole reason that today more than ever the German people needs strength for its existence"—from "want of space and soil").
34. Hillgruber *Grossmachtpolitik* 44–45 and n. 15; Sontheimer 118–21.
35. Domarus 68–90, quotations 88, 86, 84 (27 I 32). Re-echoed DNA "Koeppen" 7 (evening meal 18 IX 41).
36. Vogelsang "Brief" 437. Further, Hillgruber *Grossmachtpolitik* 47–49.
37. Vogelsang "Dokumente" 434–35. According to these notes Hitler held out the possibility of economic in lieu of military expansion. This would contra-

dict his stock argument that the German economy required expansion by military means: see p. 60 and n. 47, also pp. 69–70 nn. 92–94. So the version in IfZ Horst von Mellenthin ZS105/5 looks more accurate here: "Two possibilities remain for resolving our dilemma: 1. forcibly acquiring outlets for our production 2. acquiring new living space for our human surplus." See also ibid. 6: "Decisive above all else is defense policy, as it is certain that the final conflicts will be fought out by force."

38. Hillgruber *Grossmachtpolitik* 49. Similarly, Hildebrand *Aussenpolitik* 107–08.
39. Felice 150 quoting Vittorio Cerruti's notes.
40. Hess's mad visions of 1945–1946 are instructive here: see p. 121. Compare Himmler: p. 99.
41. Binion "East" 96–99.
42. Domarus 117 (15 VII 32—Hitler's first speech released on phonograph records).
43. Hillgruber *Rolle* 115, " 'Endlösung' " 138–43; Jäckel 79, 83; Aleff 213; Krausnick "Judenverfolgung" 360–61; Hildebrand *Aussenpolitik* 111–12, 114–15; Adam 333.
44. See p. 32 and Hillgruber *Strategie* 519 n. 11.
45. See p. 30 and n. 253; Domarus 1312; Jäckel *Weltanschauung* 81–83; Hillgruber " 'Endlösung' " 151 n. 57; Dawidowicz 110–11.
46. Adam 257–58—and for emigration Reitlinger 33–34 (cf. Himmler 138–39).
47. See p. 33.
48. Hillgruber *Strategie* 517 n. 4; Krausnick "Judenverfolgung" 348–50; Höhne 316–19; Adam 247–51; Broszat *Polenpolitik* 28–31. Aronson 192 views this "division of labor" between army and SS as a legacy of the Röhm affair—on which see pp. 110–13.
49. Greiner and Schramm I 341; Warlimont 170, 172.
50. Philippi and Heim 50–51; Hillgruber *Strategie* 523–28, " 'Endlösung' " 143–50, *Grossmachtpolitik* 49–50; Halder *Kriegstagebuch* 336–37; Krausnick "Judenverfolgung" 361–63; Jacobsen "Kommissarbefehl" 170–82; Warlimont 173–85; Höhne 371–73; Leach 153–55.
51. JT Giesing 122a, 17 XI 44. Hitler continued, echoing Hitler *Kampf* 225 (p. 3 and n. 21): "Providence showed me the way: that there is no dealing with Bolshevism. And I shall never hold my hand out to Russia." Also DNA "Picture" 18 (poor translation). Similarly, BAK Schramm 86 (Karl Brandt).
52. Quoted by Hillgruber *Strategie* 528 n. 52.
53. See p. 34 and n. 284.
54. Goebbels *Reden* II 178.
55. Dallin 75; Steinert 251; Hillgruber " 'Endlösung' " 145–49; Krausnick "Judenverfolgung" 368–69. Hitler therefore welcomed Stalin's call of 3 VII 41 for partisan warfare.
56. DNA "Koeppen" 20, 7 X 41.
57. Himmler 162–83, 200–05. Further, Krausnick "Judenverfolgung" 387, 446–47. Bormann was nearly that explicit to Party officials in X 42: Steinert 252–53.
58. Goldhagen 47 and n. 19; Himmler 170.
59. See p. 34 and nn. 282, 283.
60. Hildebrand *Aussenpolitik* 109, 112–13.
61. See p. 30.

62. Groscurth 166–67; p. 31 and n. 257.
63. Hillgruber *Strategie* 111 and n. 35; Hildebrand *Aussenpolitik* 120 and passim.
64. Hillgruber *Strategie* 111, 392–93, 518, 520–23; Hildebrand *Aussenpolitik* 114–15.
65. Kotze and Krausnick 148, tape in BAK.
66. Hitler *Kampf* 185–86. Compare p. 27 and n. 219.
67. Adam 359–60; Hildebrand *Aussenpolitk* 113; Broszat *Staat* 379–82 and passim; Buchheim 13–30 and passim.
68. See p. 32. Further, Broszat *Staat* 398–401.
69. Greiner and Schramm I 341; Hillgruber *Strategie* 523 n. 33; Warlimont 168.
70. Hillgruber *Strategie* 524 n. 34.
71. Steinert 251–52; Hillgruber " 'Endlösung' " 146–48; Jacobsen "Kommissarbefehl" 187–97.
72. Hildebrand *Aussenpolitik* 114, 120; Hillgruber *Staatsmänner* II 553–54 and 557 respectively.
73. Heiber *Lagebesprechungen* 258, 8 VI 43.
74. Ibid. 259. Similarly, ibid. 256 (Hitler describing Bethmann Hollweg, his ideological whipping boy since the 1920s, as the only level-headed German in 1916).
75. DNA "Koeppen" 24 (dinner at headquarters with Constantin von Neurath, Hans Frank, Herbert Backe). Compare ibid. 38 (5 XI 41 dinner with SS medico Plaschke): "The Führer denied the Jews any capacity in any realm whatsoever" and Picker 465 (21 VII 42): ". . . behind Stalin stands the Jew."
76. Hillgruber *Strategie* 524 nn. 34 and 37, 531–32; Kater 359; Hildebrand *Aussenpolitik* 126–27, 129; Bracher *Diktatur* 387–88, 450–57, 502; Broszat "Konzentrationslager" 10, 97–98; Höhne 419–503; Buchheim 29–30; Bollmus 245–46 and passim; Jung 11–13. IfZ Fritz Wiedemann ZS191/II/2: the SS already began supplanting the army in Hitler's secret plans as war approached.
77. Bollmus 245; IfZ Rudolf Diels ZS537/II/21; Milward 145–46; p. 76 and nn. 134–35.
78. See p. 32 and n. 265.
79. Krausnick "Judenverfolgung" 298–99, 302–04; Kater 359 and passim; Höhne 132–59 and passim; Buchheim 98, 246, and passim; Aronson 30.
80. Hillgruber " 'Endlösung' " 152. Further, Krausnick "Judenverfolgung" 369–70.
81. Biss 37, 156–57, and passim; Höhne 582. Further, Jung 92–93.
82. Höhne 586.
83. Kersten 286; Besgen 52.
84. Jäckel *Weltanschauung* 84.
85. Picker 497, 30 V 42. Similarly, through late 1944: Domarus 2161–64 (12 XI 44); Heiber *Lagebesprechungen* 714–15 (11 and 12 XII 44).
86. Ibid. 739.
87. Ibid. 738–39.
88. Genoud *Le Testament* 78–86 (13 II 45).
89. Ibid. 93–96 (15 II 45).
90. Ibid. 80 (13 II 45).
91. Ibid. 143.
92. Domarus 2237, 2239.

93. Ibid. 2242.
94. Ibid. 933 (26 XII 38).
95. Shirer 142.
96. Domarus 1315, 1316.
97. Ibid. 1340–41.
98. Broszat "Konzentrationslager" 104–05; Aipfel 205–06; Bracher *Diktatur* 452–53.
99. Domarus 1427 (23 XI 39).
100. Kotze and Krausnick 328 (15 II 42). Further, Domarus 1342 (3 IX 39: twice again), 1363 and 1364 (19 IX 39), 1393 (6 X 39), 1396–98 (10 X 39), 1405–14 passim (8 XI 39), 1460 (30 I 40), etc. Also Baeyer-Katte 147.
101. Kotze and Krausnick 367–68 (26 VI or 4 VII 44).
102. Domarus 2128.
103. Heiber *Lagebesprechungen* 587–88.
104. Ibid. 617.
105. Domarus 2165.
106. Heiber *Lagebesprechungen* 741 (28 XII 44).
107. Domarus 2179–80, 2186.
108. Speer 433.
109. Domarus 2212. Similarly, ibid. 2205–06 (24 II 45).
110. Hubatsch 348–49; pp. 34–35 and n. 287.
111. Domarus 2237 (29 IV 45).
112. Ibid. 2242 (29 IV 45). On Hitler's delusions of treachery toward the end see further, PUL Dethleffsen 22–24.
113. Kotze and Krausnick 319–20. Similarly, Domarus 1460 (30 I 40).
114. Kotze and Krausnick 250 (8 XI 38).
115. Buchheit 426. He also worsened his chances the more drastically he ideologized the war, after the precedent of 1914–1918: Hildebrand *Aussenpolitik* 175 n. 40.
116. Rudin 173.
117. Domarus 1442.
118. Hillgruber *Staatsmänner* II 233 (13 IV 43).
119. Ibid. 377.
120. Kotze and Krausnick 351. Further, Hillgruber *Staatsmänner* II 302.
121. Heiber *Lagebesprechungen* 616 (31 VIII 44). Further, ibid. 612.
122. Schmidt 587. Further, BAK Schramm 127 (Hans Kehrl to Schramm 5 VI 63); Jung 95–96; Martin *Friedensinitiativen* 448–504.
123. PUL Dethleffsen 28 ("*Ich mache keine Politik mehr*").
124. DNA "Hitler's Last Session in the Reichs Chancellory, 24 Feb 45" 2.
125. See pp. 110–13 for a notable exception.
126. Hillgruber *Rolle* 24–25, 105–07; Leach 87–158, 231–38.
127. Hildebrand *Aussenpolitik* 75–76.
128. Leach 95 and n. 3; Milward 7–8; Hillgruber *Strategie* 593.
129. See pp. 23–24 and n. 180.
130. Heiber *Lagebesprechungen* 71, 106, 107. On the Italian liability to Germany, see Leach 176–78.
131. Heiber *Lagebesprechungen* 369 and n. 3; Hillgruber *Staatsmänner* II 303–04, 315–19, 336–37.
132. Hillgruber *Strategie* 206, 414–19, 485–88; Sommer *Japan* 455.
133. Domarus 1466 (24 II 40). Further, Speer 179, 184–85.

134. Kotze and Krausnick 323 (15 II 42). Compare Leach 191: "Thus Hitler led Germany into the very revival of the great coalition struggle of the First World War which he had always sought to avoid."

135. Treue 197; Carr 49, 58; Weinberg 353. IMT(E) XXXVI 490, 491, and Weinberg 355: Göring, in presenting it to the cabinet, declared: "Its basic premise is that the showdown with Russia is inevitable" and "All measures are to be taken as if we were at the stage of imminent threat of war"—the very term that had prefaced the 1914 mobilization. (Hitler's phrasing was similar: Treue 204.) Further, Leach 150–51.

136. Milward 7–8, 12–13, and passim; Carr 61–62 and passim; Carroll 100–01 and passim; Weinberg 353; Treue 197–98, 202–03, 207–08.

137. Treue 207. Further, ibid. 198.

138. Milward 64–66 and passim; Carroll 29–30; Speer 198, 223, 225, and passim.

139. Order of 16 XII 41. He gave no such orders outside Russia: see, for example, Heiber Lagebesprechungen 313 and n. 2, 327 (on Sicily). Further, Jung 19.

140. Heiber Lagebesprechungen 106–07 (12 XII 42). Further, Hillgruber Wehrmacht 1293, 1297 (Hitler's order of 8 IX 42): "With this conception I am consciously returning to the style of defense that was successfully employed in the heavy defensive battles of the World War, especially until the end of 1916. . . . Hence the watchword for the defensive front is: Dig in and again dig in."

141. Maser Briefe 65 (Hitler to Josef Popp 4 XII 14), 97 (Hitler to Ernst Hepp 5 II 15).

142. But Fromelles is west-southwest of Lille. And Hitler's letters of the time (below) were from Messines northwest of Lille.

143. Wiedemann 103–04. Further, ibid. 104 on Hitler in 1914–1918 and the future West Wall.

144. Maser Briefe 71–72, 75 (Hitler to Josef Popp 26 I 15).

145. Heiber Lagebesprechungen 84 (12 XII 42).

146. Picker 493 (30 V 42). Similarly, Kotze and Krausnick 323 (15 II 42); Heiber Lagebesprechungen 777 (29 XII 44: "I was through it before, I was a runner . . ."').

147. Ibid. 742 n. 3; Jung 3, 101, 103, 200–01, 203.

148. Heiber Lagebesprechungen 751 (28 XII 44).

149. Ibid.

150. Ibid. 766 (29 XII 44).

151. Ibid. 777 (29 XII 44), 859 (27 I 45), 917 (2 III 45); also 31. Further, HSW Hoffmann on Hitler retracing his steps of 1914–1918 just before and after the western offensive of V–VI 40.

152. Lurker 10–11 (report of 8 I 24 signed Brinsteiner).

153. StAfO Staatsanwaltschaft No. 3099:69 (report of 19 XII 23 signed Brinsteiner).

154. Heiber Lagebesprechungen 609 and n. 1.

155. The shoulder injury brought this association with it: "I had the feeling it was a shot in my left arm because my first wound in the war gave me more the feeling of a blow than of a cut": BAK NS26/1927–1/115.

156. Heiber Lagebesprechungen 609 (31 VII 44); BAK Schramm 66 (Karl Brandt); DNA "Picture" 6–7 (Karl Brandt). Erwin Giesing, who treated Hitler from 22 VII to 6 X 44, first observed it when he encountered Hitler in mid-II 45: JT Giesing 175.

157. Deuerlein *Hitler-Putsch* 77–80, 87–90; Carsten *Reichswehr* 177–80; Gordon 234–37 and passim.
158. BAK NS26/1927–1/114.
159. Gordon 362.
160. HStA AStA Sonderabgabe I 1494/332–34. Further, Franz "Munich" 331–32.
161. Gordon 352; Smith *Himmler* 136.
162. Bennecke 216; Broszat *Staat* 257; Wheaton 480, 483; Schoenbaum 194. Further, IfZ Gotthard Heinrici ZS66/II/180.
163. O'Neill 42.
164. Höhne 109, 112; Bloch *SA* 95, 102; IfZ Franz von Gaertner ZS44/18–24, Franz von Pfeffer ZS177/9.
165. Höhne 106, 112, 114; Gallo 208–09; IfZ Sepp Dietrich ZS450/5–6 (who, however, claims that his commandos routed through Landsberg were not those that did Hitler's dirty work), Erich Kempka ZS253/1.
166. Höhne 115; DNA "Picture" 7 (Wilhelm Brückner).
167. Ibid. 117; Bullock *Hitler* 84; Schubert 210–11; Maser *NSDAP* 371 and n. 29; Bonnin 195–220.
168. Höhne 116; Bullock *Hitler* 305; Wheaton 488.
169. Frank 153. Further, Gilbert *Dictatorship* 75–76.
170. Domarus 413–24 (13 VII 34).
171. Höhne 25–26. Further, IfZ Fritz Wiedemann ZS191/II/2: "The SS had in 1934 inherited the position of the SA."
172. Domarus 411–12 (13 VII 34).
173. Vondung 83. Further, Grunberger 75.
174. Quoted by Deuerlein *Hitler* 73 (8 XI 36).
175. Frankel memorandum (undated) BAK NS26/115; Helene Niemeyer "notes" in Egon Hanfstaengl collection.
176. Aronson 192.
177. Tyrell *Führer* 299. Compare p. 27 and n. 220.
178. See p. 19 and n. 134.Similarly, BAK Schramm 150: Hitler privately related that he had never visited Röhm "for fear of poisoning."
179. Or almost. His failed Putsch showed faintly in his pitch for world power programmed just afterward. Thus he told the high court in Leipzig that after his legal takeover "we shall fight the [peace] treaties with any and every—in the sight of the world even illegal—means": Deuerlein *Aufstieg* 331. In his world Putsch, the British government replaced the Bavarian and Moscow replaced Berlin. In the thick of this armed struggle abroad, he called it a repetition of the Nazi struggle for power at home: Picker 187 (22 VII 42) and Goebbels *Tagebücher* 326–27 (entry 8 V 43).
180. Irving 10 quoting Karl von Eicken. So too his insomnia here—which he elsewhere dated from his dispatch bearing in the List Regiment: BAK Schramm 147.

V LEADER AND LED

1. BAK NS26/55/111.
2. Kessler 727. On Hitler as medium, see also Hanfstaengl *Years* 265–66.
3. Franz "München" 4; IfZ Franz von Pfeffer ZS177/5, 21, 22.
4. Further, Horn *NSDAP 160*; Tyrell 'Trommler' 163–65.
5. Further, Horn *NSDAP* 166–67, 216–17, 229.

6. Deuerlein *Aufstieg* 418.
7. Domarus 499–500, 683–85; Hossbach 50–51.
8. Domarus 758 (Ludendorff to Hitler 9 XI 37).
9. Ibid. 767 (20 XII 37).
10. Ibid. 761 (23 XI 37): see p. 70 and n. 97.
11. *Akten* IV 295. Further, Calic 104.
12. *Ursachen* I 171.
13. Ibid. IV 45.
14. Baumgart 371, 372, 375, 376; subquotation from Herzfeld 243.
15. Kielmansegg 630.
16. Dehio 96; Hildebrand *Aussenpolitik* 138–39 and n. 26.
17. Zechlin "1915" 352 (Ludendorff to Hans Delbrück 29 XII 15).
18. Ibid. 353.
19. See p. 60.
20. Domarus 1399.
21. See Gamm 110–11; Grunberger 466.
22. See Steinert 243–44, 261–63; Grunberger 464.
23. Steinert 86–87, 91; Speer 162, 173, 178, 181–82, 184.
24. Grunberger 85, 89; Krause 71–72; FH Paula 2.
25. Steinert 207; Boberach 151.
26. Sauer "Gewalt" 749 n. 14.
27. Warlimont 175–78; Hillgruber " 'Endlösung' " 149–50. Compare p. 50 and n. 101.
28. Wheaton 124 quoting Friedrich Wilhelm Foerster.
29. Reck-Malleczewen. Similarly, Broch 77–236 on "mass theory" (1939, 1941).
30. Gilbert *Dictatorship* 193.
31. Thus Ribbentrop facing the evidence of Nazi atrocities: "He offered to be cut to pieces or thrown over a cliff if he had really had any responsibility for those things": ibid.
32. Aich 210 and passim. Further, Weber 205–06; Pribilla 77; Grau 82–85.
33. Kern 187.
34. Hellpach 138–39.
35. It left some last traces in Baeyer-Katte passim; IfZ Friedrich Krohn ZS89/17.
36. A parallel development is discernible in German studies of mass phenomena generally. Where Revers (1947) argued for a distinct collective consciousness, Hagemann and Pöll (both 1951) recognized only group situations or contexts intensifying suggestive effects on individuals.
37. Freud XIII 136–43. Further, ibid. IX 189–91, XV 74. Freud tended to equate the "primary process" governing individual unconscious thinking with the dynamics of that original shared consciousness.
38. Woerden 115; Binion "Foam" 523–24.
39. Subleaders had personality rights beneath themselves, but none toward Hitler: see Tyrell "Führergedanke" 545–46 and passim.
40. Quoted by Gilbert *Dictatorship* 148.
41. On this see esp. Baeyer-Katte 146–48, 166–67.
42. Vondung 47 and passim.
43. Further, Freud XV 59–60.
44. Schramm *Führer* 155.
45. Calic 47. Similarly, Hitler *Kampf* 83.
46. Bracher *Diktatur* 371 quoting Gottfried Neesse *Führergewalt* (Tübingen 1940) 54. Further, Halder *Feldherr* 62.

47. He even meant for Germany to recover that will-sharing definitively (Grieswelle 135 quoting 31 VII 32: "*endgültig wieder zu einer Willensbildung zusammengerissen werden*"). Freud also ascribed will-sharing to the primal horde, presumably apart from its leader (Freud XIII 137 n.: "there was only a common, no singular, will").
48. DNA "Picture" 31 (Adolf Heusinger). Further, p. 49 and n. 95.
49. Euripides 190.
50. See pp. 57–58.
51. Schramm "Anatomie" No. 5: 40.
52. Schwerin von Krosigk 196.
53. Papen 293. Similarly, Hierl 159–60; IfZ Werner Best ZS207/II/6; DNA "Picture" 30–31 (Adolf Heusinger).
54. DNA "Picture" 31 (Adolf Heusinger).
55. Hierl 159–60: the collective was continuous with the individual effect. Further examples in Stein 94–113; Friedländer 162–65; Lambertson 123–27; Lange-Eichbaum and Kurth 385–86; Fest *Gesicht* 349 and n. 24; Dietrich 30–31; IfZ Adolf Heusinger ZS69/77.
56. Lüdecke 13, 17, 13, 16. Compare the 1934 autobiographer in Merkl 540: "How his blue eyes sparkled. . . ."
57. *Basler Nachrichten* 5 V 45; IfZ Josef Hell ZS640/8.
58. IMT(E) XII 322.
59. Merkl 540. Similarly, ibid. 539 (a public employee's first Hitler speech: "The personality of the Führer had me totally in its spell"); Abel 153 ("Hitler looks every man in the eye"; "he emanates a power that draws everybody to him"; "his eyes became like hands that gripped men"), 182; HStA AStA Sonderabgabe I 1838 (police report of a Nazi section meeting of 28 IV 25 in Munich: "Hitler thereupon made his usual round of the hall, shaking hands with everyone individually while looking him straight in the eyes"); *VB* 18 IV 25, 22 IV 25, etc.
60. Gilbert *Diary* 83.
61. Gilbert *Dictatorship* 147.
62. Ibid. 152.
63. IMT(E) XXII 368–73; Rees 126–27, 210–11; Manville and Fraenkel *Hess* 176–77; Gilbert *Dictatorship* 124, 126, 130–31; Fest *Gesicht* 231 and n. 45.
64. HSW Hoffman 46/2.
65. Calic 116. Similarly, ibid. 55; Hanser 299 quoting Truman Smith.
66. Heiber *Lagebesprechungen* 862 (editor's quotation marks around "hypnotize" deleted).
67. Speer 114. Another case in point was Gerhard von Schwerin, who at his first encounter with Hitler, in V 43, was overcome as Hitler approached him. Then "with deep amazement I looked into his dull, tired eyes of an unnatural faded blue. No doubt they were sick eyes": DNA "Picture" 39.
68. Fest *Gesicht* 349 n. 24. (Fest excepts Heydrich, but see p. 124 and n. 96.)
69. Hess 43–44. Further, Krebs 170.
70. Goebbels *Tagebücher* 64.
71. Besgen 72.
72. IfZ Joachim von Ribbentrop ZS1357/34. Further, Gilbert *Dictatorship* 199.
73. Hoettl 83–84.
74. Schwerin von Krosigk 222.
75. Hierl 159. Compare DNA "Picture " 30 (Adolf Heusinger): "especially weak characters succumbed very quickly."
76. Calic 54 (4 V 31).

77. Moser von Filseck 108. Similarly, Lurker 10 quoting Brinsteiner report of 8 I 24.
78. BAK R431/2681/82 (Scharrer to Cuno 30 XII 22, enclosure). Similarly, Viereck 235: "he fascinates his audiences," and 238: "He carries his hearers with him, often against their will, by the sheer force of his personality."
79. IfZ Josef Hell ZS640/7–8; Pechel 277–80; Brüning 195–96; Deuerlein Aufstieg 305; IfZ Franz Seldte ZS1495/10; DNA "Picture" 10 (Erwin Giesing).
80 Some cases in point: Friedrich Krohn (IfZ Friedrich Krohn ZS89/2–5), Josef Hell (IfZ Josef Hell ZS640), Heinrich Class (Schlabrendorff 341–43, 352), Richard Breiting, Hermann Rauschning, Paul von Eltz-Rübenach.
81. Fest Gesicht 349 n. 24; Papen 67; Schwerin von Krosigk 201 ("his suggestive influence, which even I could not escape").
82. Schramm "Anatomie" No. 10: 59; Schwerin von Krosigk 221; PUL Dethleffsen 16.
83. Dietrich 30–31. Similarly, IfZ Joachim von Ribbentrop ZS1357/34 and Stein Hitler 111–12 quoting Ribbentrop; Schwerin von Krosigk 201; Papen 293; DNA "Picture" 30–31 (Adolf Heusinger), 41 (Lutz Schwerin von Krosigk); Reimann 53 ("even Gregor Strasser lost his power in Hitler's presence").
84. Dönitz 477. Similarly, Dönitz in IMT(E) XIII 301.
85. Hoffmann Widerstand 450. Further, p. 79 and n. 154.
86. Jetzinger 265.
87. Deuerlein Hitler-Putsch 57; Vondung 33–36; Schnauber 113–15; Grieswelle 124–29.
88. Schnauber 52, 83, 86–88, 112. Compare Rosenberg Aufzeichnungen 320: Hitler claimed that his rapport with the national psyche was musical.
89. Schnauber 112.
90. Dietrich 30.
91. Dönitz in IMT(E) XIII 301. Similarly, Dönitz 477. But Dönitz's characterization of Hitler for the IMT leaves some doubt about that disengagement: "In Hitler I saw a powerful personality who had extraordinary intelligence and a practically universal knowledge, from whom power seemed to emanate and who was possessed of a remarkable power of suggestion": IMT(E) XIII 301.
92. Knickerbocker 46. See Stein 114–33; Olden 225–26. Cf. Schwerin von Krosigk 201–02; DNA "Picture" 30 (Adolf Heusinger), 37–38 (Paul Schmidt), 41 (Lutz Schwerin von Krosigk).
93. Keitel 393 (with specific reference to Barbarossa).
94. Grieswelle 126.
95. Speer 33.
96. Aronson 34.
97. Calic 54.
98. Hess 23, 25. Hess's future wife followed suit. Ibid. 26: "We fell under a spell. . . . Did not this spell grip millions?" The story that Hess had passed through the List Regiment and encountered Hitler there (ibid. 32–33) is baseless: see Hess's file in HStA KA.
99. Frank 40, 42.
100. Lüdecke 16.
101. IMT(E) XII 309 (first sentence) and DNA Nuremberg pretrial interrogation 1 IX 45 8 (interpreter's English): 1921 corrected to 1922. Further, Tyrell 'Trommler' 40, 103; Horn NSDAP 86–87.
102. Deuerlein Aufstieg157, Hitler 59.

103. IMT(E) IX 237–38. Similarly, Gilbert *Dictatorship* 92 quoting Göring.
104. Hanfstaengl *Haus* 42, 41, 39, 37–38.
105. IMT(E) XIV 369.
106. IfZ Otto Dietrich ZS874/3, 107.
107. Reimann 50.
108. Goebbels *Tagebücher* 72; Reimann 68 and, more generally, 54–72; above III n. 61, V n. 70.
109. IMT(E) X 227–28.
110. Smith *Himmler* 137, 146; Ackermann 28; Manvell and Fraenkel *Himmler* 14; HStA AStA Sonderabgabe I 1494/332 –34.
111. Quoted by Ackermann 9.
112. Quoted ibid. 30 n. 71b.
113. IfZ Friedrich Krohn ZS89/16.
114. Lurker 10 quoting Brinsteiner report of 8 I 24; Schwerin von Krosigk 193 and DNA "Picture"41 (Lutz Schwerin von Krosigk).
115. IfZ Werner Best ZS207/II/5 ("infectious possession"); Papen 293; Baeyer-Katte 134–35.
116. Schwerin von Krosigk 194.
117. Franz-Willing *Ursprung* 368. Similarly, Viereck 236 quoting Munich's satirical journal *Simplicissimus:* "He hears the people's voice—what ears he must have!"
118. IfZ Franz von Pfeffer ZS177/I/47.
119. Schwerin von Krosigk 194.
120. Merkl 89. Similarly, ibid. 387, 396, 643.
121. Domarus 640–41 (11 IX 36). Further, Merkl 89.
122. Gilbert *Dictatorship* 196 quoting Ribbentrop. Similarly, Lüdecke 14.

VI LOOSE ENDS

1. And for his choice of mental incurables as his Euthanasia victims: pp. 33–34.
2. See p. 7 and n. 51.
3. Hitler *Kampf* 223, quoted by Ermert 27.
4. Forster "Reaktion" 370 is relevant here: "If I use suggestive methods, then as far as the patients know I apply them not as methods for curing a sickness, but I tell them the methods only prove they are not sick, as they would do no good otherwise."
5. Schott 73–81. On this stance as consciously struck: DNA "Picture" 31 (Adolf Heusinger).
6. See Appendix A.
7. See p. 5.
8. IMT(E) XVI 494–95; Speer 437–38. Further, on his fear of gas warfare: Heiber *Lagebesprechungen* 566–67.
9. Ibid. 417–18.
10. DNA NG–287 (29 X 41).
11. Westenkirchner in HSW. Compare BAK Schramm 87 (Karl Brandt): Hitler saw Germany as "betrayed" by England and France in 1939.
12. See above I n. 281—but also Leach 201, Wright 137.
13. Cutely, Alois is an anagram of Laios, the German spelling for Oedipus' father.

14. Hitler's fear of castration would have been the more marked if he had only one testicle as the Russian autopsy says, but the evidence to the contrary is at least as strong: Besymenski *Tod* 69; DNA "Picture" 11, "Hitler As Seen By His Doctors" 10; JT Giesing 151; Irving I 4 (Morell).
15. Kurth "Jew" 30. Further, Cohn 262–64.
16. That animus was offset by grudging deference to Hindenburg, who was the image of Alois: Dorpalen *Hindenburg* 199 and "Twelve" 493–94, 498.
17. BAK NS26/54/178 (9 XI 27).
18. Domarus 762 (23 XI 37). Further, Gilbert *Dictatorship* 75–76. Klara Hitler, by calling Alois "Uncle," had in effect condoned incest for child Adolf while denying Alois as her husband and Adolf's father—a threefold Oedipal encouragement.
19. Phelps "Rede" 404 (13 VIII 20).
20. Hillgruber *Staatsmänner* II 233: above IV n. 118.
21. Domarus 1058 (30 I 39).
22. Kursell 153 ("Aussprüche Adolf Hitlers"); DNA "Koeppen" 38 (5 XI 41).
23. Phelps "Rede" 404 (13 VIII 20). Compare DNA "Picture" 14 (Erwin Giesing): "He completely reversed day and night."
24. Genoud *Le Testament* 80 (13 II 45): p. 31 and n. 258.
25. Koerber 64 (13 IV 23).
26. Ibid. 47 (28 VII 22), 64 (13 IV 23); Kursell 72 (24 IV 23). Further, Thies 31, 33–35, 43–45.
27. Further, BAK NS26/51/7 (31 V 20), 15 (26 X 20), 37 (Hitler in *VB* 30 I 21), etc.; also p. 100 and n. 90.
28. Phelps "Rede" 405 (13 VIII 20); Phelps "Parteiredner" 300 (27 IV 20).
29. Hitler *Kampf* 191–92; DNA "Koeppen" 29 (21 X 41).
30. *VB* 26 V 26 (23 V 26). Further, p. 26 and n. 200.
31. DNA "Koeppen" 29 (21 X 41). Similarly, ibid. 38 (5 XI 41); Deuerlein "Eintritt" 203 (Hitler to Gemlich 16 IX 19); etc.
32. See p. 88.
33. BAK NS26/52/98–99 (8 XI 30). Further, Rauschning 139.
34. Quoted by Hilberg 12 from a German press report of 10–11 XI 40 on a Hitler speech.
35. See pp. ix–x and, for example, Viereck 237: "They are an alien people in our midst."
36. Grieswelle 126; HStA AStA Sonderabgabe I 1480/57 (21 XI 22).
37. Phelps "Rede" 413 (13 VIII 20); Müller *Wandel* 147; Heiden *Geschichte* 51–52.
38. Further, IfZ Werner Best ZS207/II/5–7; Schulz 224.
39. Picker 497 (30 V 42): "*tausendjähriges Reich*" both times.
40. Hitler *Conversations* 63, 586; BAK Schramm 157; DNA "Picture" 23 (Hanskarl von Hasselbach); HIS speech outline for 21 IV 21; BAK NS26/95 (Party information sheet 26 IV 22); HStA AStA Sonderabgabe I 1480 (12 IV 22, 2 XI 22); *VB* 22 XII 22 (17 XII 22); Tyrell '*Trommler*' 397; Klöss 52 (27 II 25); Deuerlein *Aufstieg* 266 (18 XII 26); Horn *NSDAP* 221 and n. 41; Grieswelle Ch. IV passim and 56, 175; DNA "Koeppen" 29 (21 X 41). Compare above III n. 27.
41. Frank 330–31; Gilbert *Dictatorship* 17.
42. Frank 330. As that half brother's son told it in DNA "Book" 926–27 (OSS interview of William Patrick Hitler, 10 IX 43), he wrote to his father from England in the fall of 1930 requesting background information on the

180

family for a lucrative press interview, whereupon the father extorted two thousand dollars from Hitler in return for the son's agreement to deny being related to the homonymous Nazi leader. That is verification even if it was the father who contacted Hitler about the son's letter. Further, NYPL Brigid 54–71—a much garbled version.

43. The fact that the name Frank gave, Frankenberger, contains his own name suggests a trick of memory: compare Harry Schulze-Wilde in *Der Spiegel* XXI (1967) No. 33: 8.
44. Schleunes 122–25. Compare HStA AStA Sonderabgabe I 1480/12 (2 II 22: death to Jews caught with blondes).
45. Heer 293, 573, 651, 704. Further, Hitler *Buch* 125.

APPENDIXES

1. Wiegand 152.
2. *Frankfurter Zeitung* 27 I 23. I could not trace that confidential newsletter. Mohler 294, 417 cites only a *Politische Wochenschrift* published by the Ring-Verlag beginning in 1924 or 1925. The Ring-Verlag was the organ of the "Ring" or Juni-Klub, a rightist political circle around Moeller van den Bruck, which Hitler addressed once in late 1922. After this address, which fell flat, Moeller "took Hitler by the soul, so to speak, and tried by stiff-necked, superior questioning to lay his spirit bare": Pechel 278.
3. BAK R431/2681/81 (Scharrer to Cuno 30 XII 22, enclosure).
4. Hyde Park "Adolf Hitler" (3 XII 42) 40.
5. DNA "Book" 901.
6. Denny 295.
7. Heiden *Hitler* I 65 and *Fuehrer* 138. On Koerber further, BDC Koerber file.
8. Koerber 6–7.
9. Olden 62.
10. BAK NS26/1927–1/37 (26 II 24).
11. Calic 46 (4 V 31).
12. Bloch 36.
13. DNA "Book" 21.
14. BAK NS26/65/43.
15. BAK NS26/65/35.
16. Jetzinger 172.
17. Johann Schmidt, Maria Koppensteiner in BAK NS26/17a.
18. Kubizek 156; also 158.
19. Bloch 36. Bloch even thought this was before Klara's operation, so he may have remembered only the 1906 trip. He also misdated Klara's fatal illness as 1908, presumably after *Mein Kampf*: his photostat of his medical record did not show the year (see p. 140).
20. CB Paula 3–4.
21. Kubizek thought he had lost Adolf's correspondence for this period (though he preserved it intact for every other period): Kubizek 150.
22. Quoted in Bleibtreu report BAK NS26/17a with a second, New Year's card. Adolf took an earlier "Vienna trip" in 1906, but was not Bloch's patient

before 1907 or Bloch would have displayed the records along with the 1907 one.

23. Official prices for 1907 from Österreichische Apothekerkammer, letters of 16 IV and 16 IX 71; related pharmaceutical information from Vester's Archiv für Geschichte der Pharmazie, letter of 20 III 71.

24. But the charge for idoform content was slightly regressive: for regularity, 5.80 should have been 5.85.

25. See Moll Ethik 177 ff. in the Countway Library's copy annotated in 1907.

26. Jetzinger 180–81, assuming that the medical expenses hardly added up, estimated the estate "at least 3000 crowns." Further, Smith Hitler 111; Maser Hitler 80.

27. BAK NS26/65/85; Bloch 37.

28. See, for example, Lewin 464–65; König 125–26; Bourdette 23; Deichmann and Gerarde 331; Osol et al. 617; Grossman 772; Gleason et al. 82; Todd 682; Oettingen 69; Dreisbach 273; Møller 759.

29. See Fürst 5; Zimmermann Psychosen 10.

30. Bizzozero and Ferrari passim. But earlier warnings were rife, as in Bum 240: "To avoid a cumulative effect, the idoform pack is to be changed as infrequently as possible" (similarly, ibid. 239). Further, Hauschild 59.

31. König passim. But averages ran higher in smaller sets of cases reported. Bum 202 estimated some four weeks as typical. Further, Bourdette 30 ff.; Zimmermann Psychosen 11–17.

32. Kubizek 162.

33. See p. 17 and n. 119.

34. Heiber Lagebesprechungen 746–47.

35. BAK Schramm 10 (Hanskarl von Hasselbach). Further, DNA "Picture" 15, 21 (Erwin Giesing).

36. Compare p. 31 and n. 258 with Hitler's boast in Calic 111: "We know all the prescriptions of the poison mixers."

37. Quoted by Jetzinger 56. Similarly, CB Paula I.

38. Kubizek 48.

39. Knodel passim.

40. Groth and Hahn passim.

41. That is, for the Mühldorf district, of which only the subdistrict Neumarkt reported: ibid. 109.

42. The subdistrict is meant (the district of the same name takes in Burghausen as well).

43. The subdistrict Pfarrkirchen alone reported in the district of this same name, which includes Simbach: ibid. 115.

44. Knodel 310 Table 7.

45. Or 305 days longer, as between 338 for Knodel's mean and 262 for Klara's adjusted mean. But it is an open question whether she unconsciously timed her childbearing cycles in days, months—or menstrual cycles.

46. Moll Säuglingssterblichkeit 13. On the force of regional tradition in breast-feeding: ibid. 14.

47. Ibid. 16, 60. Specifically, Gmünd and Zwettl (near Klara's native Weitra) are slightly lower than Braunau.

48. Rauscher 44.

49. This is indicated by the data tabulated in Cantrelle and Leridon 526 and Potter et al. 1130–32. Anent Klara's shorter interpregnancy intervals before Adolf's birth, see Perez et al. passim and Leridon passim.

50. Knodel 305, 313 Table 11; Moll *Säuglingssterblichkeit* 53, 60.
51. Adapted from Koppensteiner 40 (and, for child 4's death in infancy, Maser *Hitler* 50n.).

SOURCES

Abbreviations of frequently cited archives and—in **boldface type**—holdings:

AA   Auswärtiges Amt, Bonn

AHU   Archiv der Humboldt-Universität, Berlin (East)

BAK   Bundesarchiv, Koblenz: Kl. Erw. Nr. 441-3 (notes by Percy Ernst **Schramm** on interviews 1945–1946)

BDC   Berlin Document Center

CB   Carlisle Barracks, Pennsylvania, U.S. Army Military History Research Collection: "Personality Report. Berchtesgaden, June 5, 1946. Mrs. **Paula** Wolf (Paula Hitler, sister of the late Adolf Hitler)"

DLC   Library of Congress, Washington, D.C.

DNA   National Archives, Washington, D.C.: "Hitler Source **Book**"; "Berichte Dr Werner **Koeppen** (No 27-55) (6. Sept bis 7. November 1941)"; "Adolf Hitler: A Composite **Picture**"

HIS   Jäckel-Kuhn collection, Historisches Institut, Stuttgart

HStA AStA   Bayerisches Hauptstaatsarchiv, Allgemeines Staatsarchiv, Munich

HStA KA   Bayerisches Hauptstaatsarchiv, Kriegsarchiv, Munich

HSW   Harry Schulze-Wilde collection, Ottobrunn bei München: interviews of Heinrich **Hoffman** fall 1952; interviews by Julius Hagemann of Ernst **Schmidt** and Ignaz **Westenkirchner** [1950s]

IfZ	Institut für Zeitgeschichte, Munich: **"Ärzte-Prozess"** (Amtliche Niederschrift des Militärgerichtshofes in Sache Vereinigten Staaten von Amerika gegen K. Brandt u. Genossen); **"Eichmann-Prozess"** (Bezirksgericht Jerusalem, Strafakt 40/61)
JT	John Toland collection, Danbury, Connecticut: Erwin **Giesing,** "Bericht über meine Behandlung bei Hitler"
NYPL	New York Public Library, Manuscripts Division: **Brigid** Hitler, "My Brother-in-Law Adolf"
PUL	Princeton University Library, Manuscripts Division, Alan W. Dulles papers: Erich **Dethleffsen**, "Notizen"
StAfO	Staatsarchiv für Oberbayern, Munich
UAG	Universitäts-Archiv Greifswald

Other archives and holdings are spelled out in the Notes. I held those interviews and received those letters cited without archival reference.

Abbreviations of some printed sources:

Advance	Committee of Imperial Defense, Historical Section. *History of the Great War, based on official documents. Military Operations France and Belgium 1918.* Vol. V: *26th September – 11th November. The Advance to Victory.* London 1947.
Akten	*Akten zur deutschen auswärtigen Politik 1918–1945.* Series D, Vols. IV, V. Baden-Baden 1951, 1953.
Braunbuch	World Committee for the Victims of German Fascism. *Braunbuch über Reichstagsbrand und Hitler-Terror.* Basel 1933.
IMT(E)	*Trial of the Major War Criminals before the International Military Tribunal Nuremberg 14 November 1945 – 1 October 1946.* 42 vols. Nuremberg 1947–1949.
IMT(G)	*Der Prozess gegen die Hauptkriegsverbrecher vor dem Internationalen Militärgerichtshof Nürnberg.* 42 vols. Nuremberg 1947–1949.
Meyers	*Meyers grosses Konversations-Lexikon.* Vol. X. Leipzig 1908.
Ursachen	*Die Ursachen des deutschen Zusammenbruchs im Jahre 1918. Vierte Reihe im Werke des Untersuchungsausschusses.* 12 vols. Berlin 1925–1929.
VB	*Völkischer Beobachter.* Munich.
VdR	*Verhandlungen des Reichstags.* Berlin.
VfZ	*Vierteljahrshefte für Zeitgeschichte.* Munich.

Other printed sources are cited throughout the Notes by author's name and, where necessary, by a short title as well. For the reader's convenience, they are here alphabetized by author's surname without topical or other subdivisions and by short title, shown in **boldface type**. German editions of German and even English works were generally preferred because of the importance of the original wording of quoted matter.

Abel, Theodore. *Why Hitler Came Into Power. An Answer Based on the Original Life Stories of Six Hundred of His Followers.* New York 1938.

Abshagen, Karl Heinz. *Schuld und Verhängnis. Ein Vierteljahrhundert deutscher Geschichte in Augenzeugenberichten.* Stuttgart 1961.

Ackermann, Josef. *Heinrich Himmler als Ideologe.* Göttingen 1970.

Adam, Uwe Dietrich. *Judenpolitik im Dritten Reich.* Düsseldorf 1972.

Aich, Thomas. *Massenmensch und Massenwahn. Zur Psychologie des Kollektivismus.* Munich 1947.

Aigner, Dietrich. *Das Ringen um England. Das deutsch-britische Verhältnis. Die öffentliche Meinung 1933–1939. Tragödie zweier Völker.* Munich 1969.

Aimez, P. "Psychophysiologie du cancer. Existe-t-il un terrain psychologique prédisposant? Influence des facteurs psychiques sur la relation hôte-tumeur." *Revue de médecine psychosomatique,* XIV (1972), 371–81.

Aleff, Eberhard. "Mobilmachung." *Das Dritte Reich.* Edited by Eberhard Aleff. Hannover 1963.

Allen, William Sheridan. *The Nazi Seizure of Power. The Experience of a Single German Town.* Chicago 1965.

Andernach, Andreas. *Hitler ohne Maske.* Munich 1932.

Angress, Werner T. "**Juden** im politischen Leben der Revolutionszeit." *Deutsches Judentum in Krieg und Revolution 1916–1923. Ein Sammelband.* Edited by Werner E. Mosse. Tübingen 1971. *Stillborn* **Revolution.** *The Communist Bid for Power in Germany, 1921–1923.* Princeton 1963.

Arends, Johannes. *Volkstümliche Namen der Arzneimittel, Drogen, Heilkräuter und Chemikalien. Eine Sammlung der im Volksmund gebräuchlichen Benennungen und Handelsbezeichnungen.* Berlin 1961.

Aronson, Shlomo. *Reinhard Heydrich und die Frühgeschichte von Gestapo und SD.* Stuttgart 1971.

Baeyer-Katte, Wanda von. *Das Zerstörende in der Politik. Eine Psychologie der politischen Grundeinstellung.* Heidelberg 1958.

Bahne, Siegfried. "Die Kommunistische Partei Deutschlands." *Das Ende der Parteien 1933.* Edited by Erich Matthias and Rudolf Morsey. Düsseldorf 1960.

Baumgart, Winfried. *Deutsche Ostpolitik 1918. Von Brest-Litowsk bis zum Ende des Ersten Weltkrieges.* Vienna 1966.

Baynes, Norman H., editor. *The Speeches of Adolf Hitler April 1922 – August 1939.* Vol. II. New York 1969.

Bein, Alexander. "Der moderne **Antisemitismus** und seine Bedeutung für die Judenfrage." *VfZ,* VI (1958), 340–60. " 'Der jüdische **Parasit**'. Bemerkungen zur Semantik der Judenfrage." *VfZ,* XIII (1965), 121–49.

Bennecke, Heinrich. *Hitler und die SA.* Munich 1962.

Besgen, Achim. *Der stille Befehl. Medizinalrat Kersten, Himmler und das Dritte Reich.* Munich 1960.

Besymenski, Lew. *Sonderakte* **Barbarossa.** *Dokumente, Darstellung, Deutung.* Stuttgart 1968. *Der* **Tod** *des Adolf Hitler. Unbekannte Dokumente aus Moskauer Archiven.* Hamburg 1968.

Binion, Rudolph. "Hitler's **Concept** of Lebensraum: The Psychological Basis." *History of Childhood Quarterly,* I (1973), 187–215, 249–58. "Hitler Looks **East.**" *History of Childhood Quarterly,* III (1975), 85–102. "**Foam** on the Hitler Wave." *Journal of Modern History,* XLVI (1974), 521–28.

Biss, Andreas. *Der Stopp der Endlösung. Kampf gegen Himmler und Eichmann in Budapest.* Stuttgart 1966.

Bizzozero, Enzo, and A. V. Ferrari. "Sull'idiosincrasia all'iodoformio." *Giornale italiano di dermatologia e sifilologia,* IX (1931), 3–23.

186

Bloch, Charles. *Die SA und die Krise des NS-Regimes 1934*. Frankfurt/Main 1970.

Bloch, Eduard. "My Patient, Hitler. By Dr. Eduard Bloch as told to J. D. Ratcliff." *Collier's*, CVII (15 March 1941), 11, 35–37, (22 March 1941), 69–73.

Boberach, Heinz, editor. *Meldungen aus dem Reich. Auswahl aus den geheimen Lageberichten des Sicherheitsdienstes der SS 1939–1944*. Munich 1968.

Boepple, Ernst, editor. *Adolf Hitlers Reden*. Munich 1933.

Bollmus, Reinhard. *Das Amt Rosenberg und seine Gegner. Zum Machtkampf im nationalsozialistischen Herrschaftssystem*. Stuttgart 1970.

Bonhoeffer, Karl. "Edmund Forster." *Deutsche medizinische Wochenschrift*, LIX (1933), 1516.

Bonnin, Georges. *Le Putsch de Hitler à Munich en 1923*. Les Sables-d'Olonne 1966.

Bouhler, Philipp. *Kampf um Deutschland. Ein Lesebuch für die deutsche Jugend*. Berlin 1938.

Bourdette, Albert. *De l'iodoforme et de l'iodoformisme*. Paris 1893.

Bracher, Karl Dietrich. *Die deutsche **Diktatur**. Entstehung, Struktur, Folgen des Nationalsozialismus*. Cologne 1969. "**Stufen** der Machtergreifung." In Karl Dietrich Bracher, Wolfgang Sauer, and Gerhard Schulz, *Die nationalsozialistische Machtergreifung. Studien zur Errichtung des totalitären Herrschaftssystems in Deutschland 1933/34*. Cologne 1962.

Brandmayer, Balthasar. *Meldegänger Hitler, erlebt und erzählt von Balthasar Brandmayer, mitgeteilt von Hans Bayer*. Überlingen 1933.

Braun, Hans. *Pharmakologie des deutschen Arzneibuchs*. Sixth edition. Stuttgart 1949.

Breitling, Rupert. *Die nationalsozialistische Rassenlehre. Entstehung, Ausbreitung, Nutzen und Schaden einer politischen Ideologie*. Meisenheim am Glan 1971.

Broch, Hermann. *Massenpsychologie. Schriften aus dem Nachlass*. Zurich 1959.

Broszat, Martin. "**Konzentrationslager**." In Martin Broszat, Hans-Adolf Jacobsen, and Helmut Krausnick, *Konzentrationslager, Kommissarbefehl, Judenverfolgung*. Olten 1965. *Nationalsozialistische **Polenpolitik** 1939–1945*. Stuttgart 1961. *Der **Staat** Hitlers. Grundlegung und Entwicklung seiner inneren Verfassung*. Munich 1969.

Brüning, Heinrich. *Memoiren 1918–1934*. Stuttgart 1970.

Buchheim, Hans. *Die SS—Das Herrschaftsinstrument. Befehl und Gehorsam*. Olten 1965.

Buchheit, Gert. *Hitler der Feldherr. Die Zerstörung einer Legende*. Rastatt 1958.

Büscher, Hermann. *Grün- und Gelbkreuz. Spezielle Pathologie und Therapie der Körperschädigungen durch die chemischen Kampfstoffe*. Leipzig 1932.

Bullock, Alan. **Hitler**. *A Study in Tyranny*. Revised edition. New York 1962. "Hitler and the **Origins** of the Second World War." *Proceedings of the British Academy*, LIII (1967), 259–87.

Bum, Anton. "Zur Frage der Jodoform-Intoxikation." *Wiener Medizinische Presse*, XXIII (1882), 201–04, 238–40.

Burckhardt, Carl J. *Meine Danziger Mission 1937–1939*. Munich 1960.

Calic, Edouard. *Ohne Maske. Hitler-Breiting Geheimgespräche 1931*. Frankfurt/Main 1968.

Canetti, Elias. *Masse und Macht*. Hamburg 1960.

Cantrelle, P., and H. Leridon. "Breast Feeding, Mortality in Childhood and Fertility in a Rural Zone of Senegal." *Population Studies*, XVIII (1965), 505–33.

Carr, William. *Arms, Autarky and Aggression. A Study in German Foreign*

187

Policy, 1933–1939. New York 1972.

Carroll, Berenice. *Design for Total War. Arms and Economics in the Third Reich.* The Hague 1968.

Carsten, F. L. *The Reichswehr and Politics 1918 to 1933.* Oxford 1966. *Revolution in Central Europe 1918–1919.* Berkeley 1972.

Cohn, Norman. *Warrant for Genocide. The Myth of the Jewish World Conspiracy and the Protocols of the Elders of Zion.* New York 1967.

Daim, Wilfried. *Der Mann, der Hitler die Ideen gab.* Munich 1958.

Dallin, Alexander. *German Rule in Russia 1941–1945. A Study of Occupation Policies.* London 1957.

Dawidowicz, Lucy S. *The War against the Jews 1933–1945.* New York 1975.

Dehio, Ludwig. *Germany and World Politics in the Twentieth Century.* Translated by Dieter Pevsner. New York 1967.

Deichmann, William B., and Horace W. Gerarde. *Toxicology of Drugs and Chemicals.* New York 1969.

Delmer, Sefton. *Black Boomerang.* London 1962.

Denny, Ludwell. "France and the German Counterrevolution." *The Nation,* CXVI (1923), 295–97.

Deuerlein, Ernst, editor. *Der **Aufstieg** der NSDAP 1919–1933 in Augenzeugenberichten.* Düsseldorf 1968. "Hitlers **Eintritt** in die Politik und die Reichswehr." *VfZ,* VII (1959), 177–227. **Hitler.** *Eine politische Biographie.* Munich 1969. *Deutsche **Kanzler** von Bismarck bis Hitler.* Munich 1968. *Der Hitler-**Putsch.** Bayerische Dokumente zum 8./9. November 1923.* Stuttgart 1962.

Dickmann, Fritz. "Machtwille und Ideologie in Hitlers aussenpolitischen Zielsetzungen vor 1933." In *Spiegel der Geschichte. Festgabe für Max Braubach zum 10. April 1964.* Edited by Konrad Repgen and Stephan Skalweit. Münster 1964.

Diels, Rudolf. *Lucifer ante Portas.* Zurich 1949.

Dietrich, Otto. *12 Jahre mit Hitler.* Munich 1955.

Dönitz, Karl. *Zehn Jahre und zwanzig Tage.* Bonn 1958.

Domarus, Max, editor. *Hitler. Reden und Proklamationen 1932–1945. 4 half-volumes paginated consecutively.* Munich 1965.

Dorpalen, Andreas. **Hindenburg** *and the Weimar Republic.* Princeton 1964. "Hitler—**Twelve** Years After." *Review of Politics,* XIX (1957), 486–506.

Dreisbach, Robert H. *Handbook of Poisoning: Diagnosis and Treatment.* Los Altos 1969.

Drexler, Anton. *Mein politisches Erwachen. Aus dem Tagebuch eines deutschen sozialistischen Arbeiters.* Munich 1923.

Dülffer, Jost. *Weimar, Hitler und die Marine. Reichspolitik und Flottenbau 1920 bis 1939.* Düsseldorf 1973.

Eastman, Nicholson J., and Louis M. Hellman. *Williams Obstetrics.* New York 1961.

Epstein, Klaus. "The End of the German Parties in 1933." *Journal of Central European Affairs,* XXIII (1963), 52–76.

Erb, Herbert, and Hans Henning Grote. *Konstantin Hierl. Der Mann und sein Werk.* Munich 1939.

Ermert, Ekkehard. "Hitlers Erlebnis in Pasewalk im Herbst 1918." Unpublished.

Ernst, Fritz. "Zum Ende des ersten Weltkrieges." *Die Welt als Geschichte,* XVII (1957), 55–67.

Euripides. "The Bacchae." In *The Bacchae and Other Plays.* Translated by Philip Vellacott. London 1954.

Evans, Richard I. *Conversations with Carl Jung and Reactions from Ernest Jones.* New York 1964.

Ewald, Gottfried. "Die Jodoform und ihre Stellung innerhalb der exogenen Prädilektionstypen." *Monatsschrift für Psychiatrie und Neurologie*, XLVII (1920), 125–48.

Eyck, Erich. *A History of the Weimar Republic.* Translated by Harlan P. Hanson and Robert G. L. Waite. 2 vols. New York 1970.

Fabry, Philipp. **Mutmassungen** *über Hitler. Urteile von Zeitgenossen.* Düsseldorf 1969. *Die* **Sowjetunion** *und das Dritte Reich. Eine dokumentierte Geschichte der deutsch-sowjetischen Beziehungen von 1933 bis 1941.* Stuttgart 1971.

Farrar, Lancelot L., Jr. "Opening to the West. German Efforts to Conclude a Separate Peace with England, July 1917–March 1918." *Canadian Journal of History*, X (1975), 73–90.

Felice, Renzo De. *Storia degli ebrei italiani sotto il fascismo.* Turin 1962.

Fest, Joachim C. *Das* **Gesicht** *des Dritten Reiches. Profil einer totalitären Herrschaft.* Frankfurt/Main 1969. **Hitler.** *Eine Biographie.* Frankfurt/Main 1973.

Fischer, Fritz. **Griff** *nach der Weltmacht. Die Kriegszielpolitik des kaiserlichen Deutschland 1914/18.* Düsseldorf 1967. "**Weltpolitik,** Weltmachtstreben und deutsche Kriegsziele." *Historische Zeitschrift*, CIC (1964), 265–346.

Fischman, Sterling. "The Rise of Hitler as a Beer Hall Orator." *Review of Politics*, XXVI (1964), 244–56.

Forster, Edmund. "Das **Nervensystem**." In *Lehrbuch der pathologischen Physiologie.* Edited by H. Lüdke and C. R. Schlayer. Leipzig 1922. "Hysterische **Reaktion** und Simulation." *Monatsschrift für Psychiatrie und Neurologie*, XLII (1917), 298–324, 370–81. "Über normale und pathologische **Reaktionsformen** (Halluzinationen)." *Ibid.*, LXVIII (1928), 201–16. "**Selbstversuch** mit Meskalin." *Zeitschrift für die gesamte Neurologie und Psychiatrie*, CXXVII (1930), 1–14. "Wann muss der praktische Arzt **Suizidneigung** vermuten und wie verhält er sich dann." *Münchener medizinische Wochenschrift*, XX (19 May 1933), 766–69.

Foulkes, C. H. *"Gas!" The Story of the Special Brigade.* London 1934.

Frank, Hans. *Im Angesicht des Galgens. Deutung Hitlers und seiner Zeit auf Grund eigener Erlebnisse und Erkenntnisse.* Munich-Gräfelfing 1953.

Franz, Georg. "**München:** 8. November 1923. Voraussetzungen und Hintergründe des Hitler-Putsches." *Die österreichische Furche*, IX (1953), No. 45 (7 November), 3–5. "**Munich:** Birthplace and Center of the National Socialist German Workers' Party." *Journal of Modern History*, XXIX (1957), 319–34.

Franz-Willing, Georg. **Krisenjahr** *der Hitler-Bewegung 1923.* Oldendorf 1975. **Ursprung** *der Hitler-Bewegung 1919–1922.* Oldendorf 1974.

Fraser, Lindley. *Germany between Two Wars. A Study of Propaganda and War-Guilt.* London 1944.

Freud, Sigmund, *Gesammelte Werke.* 18 vols. London 1952–1968.

Friedländer, Saul. *L'antisémitisme nazi. Histoire d'une psychose collective.* Paris 1971.

Fries-Thiessenhusen, Karen. "Politische Kommentare deutscher Historiker 1918/19 zu Niederlage und Staatsumsturz." In *Vom Kaiserreich zur Weimarer Republik*, edited by Eberhard Kolb. Cologne 1972.

Fürst, Ferdinand. *Klinische Untersuchungen über die Jodoformgazetamponade.* Marburg 1889.

Gallo, Max. *Der schwarze Freitag der SA. Die Vernichtung des revolutionären Flügels der NSDAP durch Hitlers SS im Juni 1934.* Vienna 1970.

Gamm, Hans-Jochen. *Der Flüsterwitz im Dritten Reich.* Munich 1963.

Gehlen, Reinhard. *Der Dienst. Erinnerungen 1942–1971.* Mainz 1971.

Geiss, Imanuel. *Der polnische Grenzstreifen 1914–1916. Ein Beitrag zur deutschen Kriegszielpolitik im Ersten Weltkrieg.* Lübeck 1960.

Genoud, François, editor. **Le Testament** *politique de Hitler. Notes recueillies par Martin Bormann.* Translated by François Genoud. Paris 1959. *The* **Testament** *of Adolf Hitler. The Hitler-Bormann Documents February-April 1945.* Translated by R. H. Stevens. London 1961.*

Gilbert, G. M. *Nuremberg* **Diary**. New York 1947. *The Psychology of* **Dictatorship**. New York 1950.

Gleason, Marion N., Robert E. Gosselin, Harold C. Hodge, and Roger P. Smith. *Clinical Toxicology of Commercial Products. Acute Poisoning.* Baltimore 1969.

Goebbels, Joseph. **Reden.** Edited by Helmut Heiber. 2 vols. Düsseldorf 1971, 1972. *Das* **Tagebuch** *von Joseph Goebbels.* Edited by Helmut Heiber. Stuttgart 1960. **Tagebücher** *aus den Jahren 1942–43 mit anderen Dokumenten.* Edited by Louis P. Lochner. Zurich 1948.

Goldhagen, Erich. "Albert Speer, Himmler and the Secrecy of the Final Solution." *Midstream,* XVII (1971), 43–50.

Gordon, Harold J., Jr. *Hitler and the Beer Hall Putsch.* Princeton 1972.

Gosset, Pierre and Renée. *Adolf Hitler.* 2 vols. Paris 1961, 1962.

Grau, Rudolf. *Gehört er ins Pantheon der Weltgeschichte? Versuch einer kritischen psychologischen Analyse Adolf Hitlers.* Weisbaden 1947.

Greiner, Helmuth, and Percy Ernst Schramm. *Kriegstagebuch des Oberkommandos der Wehrmacht.* Edited by Percy Ernst Schramm in collaboration with Hans-Adolf Jacobsen, Andreas Hillgruber, and Walther Hubatsch. 4 vols. Frankfurt/Main 1961–1965.

Greiner, Josef. *Das Ende des Hitler-Mythos.* Zurich 1947.

Grieswelle, Detlef. *Propaganda der Friedlosigkeit. Eine Studie zu Hitlers Rhetorik 1920–1933.* Stuttgart 1972.

Groscurth, Helmuth. *Tagebücher eines Abwehroffiziers 1938–1940. Mit weiteren Dokumenten zur Militäropposition gegen Hitler.* Edited by Helmut Krausnick and Harold C. Deutsch. Stuttgart 1970.

Grossman, Morris. "Iodoform Poisoning." *Medical Record,* XCVIII (1920), 772–74.

Groth, Alfred, and Martin Hahn. "Säuglingsverhältnisse in Bayern." *Zeitschrift des bayerischen Landesamtes* 1910, 78–164.

Gruchmann, Lothar. *Der zweite Weltkrieg. Kriegführung und Politik.* Munich 1967.

Grunberger, Richard. *The 12-Year Reich. A Social History of Nazi Germany 1933–1945.* New York 1971.

Hagedorn, Hermann. *The Hyphenated Family.* New York 1960.

Hagemann, Walter. *Vom Mythos der Masse. Ein Beitrag zur Psychologie der Öffentlichkeit.* Heidelberg 1951.

Hahlweg, Werner. *Der* **Diktatfrieden** *von Brest-Litowsk 1918 und die bolschewistische Weltrevolution.* Münster 1960. Editor, *Der* **Friede** *von Brest-Litowsk.* Düsseldorf 1971.

Halder, Franz. *Hitler als* **Feldherr.** Munich 1949. **Kriegstagebuch.** *Tägliche Aufzeichnungen des Chefs des Generalstabes des Heeres, 1939–1942.* Edited by Hans-Adolf Jacobsen. 3 vols. Stuttgart 1962.

Hale, Oron James. "Gottfried **Feder** Calls Hitler to Order: An Unpublished Letter on Nazi Party Affairs." *Journal of Modern History,* XXX (1958), 358–62. "Adolf Hitler: **Taxpayer.**" *American Historical Review,* LX (1955), 830–42.

---

* I used both versions together. The English one contains some evident misreadings where the two differ. Genoud owns and is withholding the original.

Hanfstaengl, Ernst. *Zwischen Weissem und Braunem* **Haus**. Munich 1970. *Hitler. The Missing* **Years**. London 1957.

Hanisch, Reinhold. "I Was Hitler's Buddy." *New Republic*, XCVIII (1939), 270–72, 297–300.

Hanser, Richard. *Putsch! How Hitler Made Revolution*. New York 1970.

Harrison, Richard J. *Reproduction and Man*. New York 1967.

Hauschild, Fritz. *Pharmakologie und Grundlagen der Toxikologie*. Leipzig 1961.

Heiber, Helmut. *Adolf* **Hitler**. *Eine Biographie*. Berlin 1960. Editor, *Hitlers* **Lagebesprechungen**. *Die Protokollfragmente seiner militärischen Konferenzen 1942–1945*. Stuttgart 1962. *Die Republik von* **Weimar**. Munich 1966.

Heiden, Konrad. *Der* **Fuehrer**. *Hitler's Rise To Power*. Translated by Ralph Manheim. London 1945. **Geschichte** *des Nationalsozialismus. Die Karriere einer Idee*. Berlin 1932. *Adolf* **Hitler**. *Eine Biographie*. 2 vols. Zurich 1936, 1937.

Hellpach, Willy. *Der deutsche Charakter*. Bonn 1954.

Henke, Josef. "Hitler und **England** Mitte August 1939." *VfZ*, XXI (1973), 231–42. *England in Hitlers politischem* **Kalkül** *1935–1939*. Boppard am Rhein 1973.

Henrikson, Göran. "Das Nürnberger Dokument 386-PS (das 'Hossbach-Protokol'). Eine Untersuchung seines Wertes als Quelle." *Probleme deutscher Zeitgeschichte*, Lund Studies in International History 2, 151–94. Stockholm 1971.

Herwig, Holger H. "Prelude to *Weltblitzkrieg*: Germany's Naval Policy toward the United States of America, 1939–41." *Journal of Modern History*, XLIII (1971), 649–68.

Herzfeld, Hans. "Die deutsche Kriegspolitik im Ersten Weltkrieg." *VfZ*, XI (1963), 224–45.

Hess, Ilse. *Ein Schicksal in Briefen. England—Nürnberg—Spandau. Gefangener des Friedens. Antwort aus Zelle Sieben*. Leoni 1971.

Hesse, Erich. *Der sowjetische Partisanenkrieg 1941–1944 im Spiegel deutscher Kampfanweisungen und Befehle*. Göttingen 1969.

Heusinger, Adolf. *Befehl im Widerstreit. Schicksalsstunden der deutschen Armee 1923–1945*. Tübingen 1950.

Hierl, Konstantin. *Im Dienst für Deutschland 1918–1945*. Heidelberg 1954.

Hilberg, Raul. *The Destruction of the European Jews*. Chicago 1961.

Hildebrand, Klaus. *Deutsche* **Aussenpolitik** *1933–1945. Kalkül oder Dogma?* Stuttgart 1971. *Vom* **Reich** *zum Weltreich. Hitler, NSDAP und koloniale Frage 1919–1945*. Munich 1969.

Hiller von Gaertringen, Friedrich Freiherr. " 'Dolchstoss'-Diskussion und 'Dolchstosslegende' im Wandel von vier Jahrzehnten." In *Geschichte und Gegenwartsbewusstsein. Historische Betrachtungen und Untersuchungen*, edited by Waldemar Besson and Friedrich Freiherr Hiller von Gaertringen. Göttingen 1963.

Hillgruber, Andreas. "Die **'Endlösung'** und das deutsche Ostimperium als Kernstück des rassenideologischen Programms des Nationalsozialismus." *VfZ*, XX (1972), 133–53. **Grossmachtpolitik** *und Militarismus im 20. Jahrhundert. 3 Beiträge zum Kontinuitätsproblem*. Düsseldorf 1974. **Kontinuität** *und Diskontinuität in der deutschen Aussenpolitik von Bismarck bis Hitler*. Düsseldorf 1969. "Die weltpolitische **Lage** 1936–1939: Deutschland." In *Weltpolitik 1933–1939. 13 Vorträge*, edited by Oswald Hauser. Göttingen 1973. "England's **Place** in Hitler's Plans for World Dominion." *Journal of Contemporary History*, IX (1974), 5–22. "**Quellen** und Quellenkritik zur Vorgeschichte des Zweiten Weltkrieges." *Wehr-Wissenschaftliche Rundschau*, XIV (1964), 109–26. *Deutschlands* **Rolle** *in der Vorgeschichte der beiden Weltkriege*. Göttingen 1967. Editor, **Staatsmänner** *und Diplomaten bei Hitler. Vertrauliche Aufzeich-*

nungen über Unterredungen mit Vertretern des Auslandes 1939–1941. 2 parts. Frankfurt/Main 1967, 1970. Hitlers **Strategie**. Politik und Kriegführung 1940–1941. Frankfurt/Main 1965. Editor, Kriegstagebuch des Oberkommandos der **Wehrmacht** (Wehrmachtführungsstab), Vol. II. Frankfurt/Main 1963.

Himmler, Heinrich. Geheimreden 1933 bis 1945 und andere Ansprachen. Edited by Bradley F. Smith and Agnes F. Peterson. Frankfurt/Main 1974.

Hitler, Adolf. Hitlers zweites **Buch**. Ein Dokument aus dem Jahr 1928. Edited by Gerhard L. Weinberg. Stuttgart 1961. Hitler's Secret **Conversations** 1941–1944. Translated by R. H. Stevens and Norman Cameron. New York 1953. Mein **Kampf**. Munich 1935.

Hoegner, Wilhelm. Die verratene Republik. Munich 1958.

Höhne, Heinz. Der Orden unter dem Totenkopf. Die Geschichte der SS. 2 vols. Frankfurt/Main 1969.

Hoettl, Wilhelm. Die geheime Front. Linz 1950.

Hoffmann, Heinrich. Hitler Was My **Friend**. Translated by R. H. Stevens. London 1955.

Hoffmann, Peter. **Widerstand**, Staatsstreich, Attentat. Der Kampf der Opposition gegen Hitler. Munich 1969.

Holzer, Jerzy. Kryzys Polityczny w Niemczech 1928–1930. Partie i Masy. Warsaw 1970.

Horn, Wolfgang. "Ein unbekannter **Aufsatz** Hitlers aus dem Frühjahr 1924." VfZ, XVI (1968), 280–94. Führerideologie und Parteiorganisation in der **NSDAP** 1919–1933. Düsseldorf 1972.

Hossbach, Friedrich. Zwischen Wehrmacht und Hitler 1934–1938. Göttingen 1965.

Hubatsch, Walther, editor. Hitlers Weisungen für die Kriegführung 1939–1945. Dokumente des Oberkommandos der Wehrmacht. Munich 1965.

Irving, David. "Hitler and his Medicine Men." Unpublished.

Jacobsen, Hans-Adolf. Nationalsozialistische **Aussenpolitik** 1933–1938. Frankfurt/Main 1968. **"Kommissarbefehl."** In Martin Broszat, Hans-Adolf Jacobsen, and Helmut Krausnick, Konzentrationslager, Kommissarbefehl, Judenverfolgung. Olten 1965. Der zweite **Weltkrieg**. Grundzüge der Politik und Strategie in Dokumenten. Frankfurt/Main 1965.

Jacobsen, Hans-Adolf, and Werner Jochmann, editors. Ausgewählte Dokumente zur Geschichte des Nationalsozialismus 1933–1945. Bielefeld 1966. [Unpaginated.]

Jäckel, Eberhard. **Frankreich** in Hitlers Europa. Die deutsche Frankreichpolitik im Zweiten Weltkrieg. Stuttgart 1966. Hitlers **Weltanschauung**. Entwurf einer Herrschaft. Tübingen 1969.

Jenks, William A. Vienna and the Young Hitler. New York 1960.

Jetzinger, Franz. Hitlers Jugend. Phantasien, Lügen—und die Wahrheit. Vienna 1956.

Jochmann, Werner. Im Kampf um die Macht. Hitlers Rede vor dem Hamburger Nationalklub von 1919. Frankfurt/Main 1960.

Jünger, Ernst. Annäherungen. Drogen und Rausch. Stuttgart 1970.

Jung, Hermann. Die Ardennen-Offensive 1944/45. Ein Beispiel für die Kriegführung Hitlers. Göttingen 1971.

Kaehler, Siegfried A. Studien zur deutschen Geschichte des 19. und 20. Jahrhunderts. Aufsätze und Vorträge. Edited by Walter Bussmann. Göttingen 1961.

Kater, Michael H. Das "Ahnenerbe" der SS 1935–1945. Ein Beitrag zur Kulturpolitik des Dritten Reiches. Stuttgart 1974.

Katz, Jack, Thomas Gallagher, Leon Hellman, Edward Sachar, and Herbert Weiner. "Psychoendocrine Considerations in Cancer of the Breast." *Annals of the New York Academy of Sciences*, CLXIV (1969), 509–16.

Kaul, Friedrich Karl. *Nazimordaktion T4. Ein Bericht über die erste industriemässig durchgeführte Mordaktion des Naziregimes.* Berlin 1973.

Keitel, Wilhelm. *Generalfeldmarschall Keitel. Verbrecher oder Offizier?* Edited by Walter Görlitz. Göttingen 1961.

Kele, Max H. *Nazis and Workers. National Socialist Appeals to German Labor, 1919–1933.* Chapel Hill 1972.

Kempka, Erich. *Ich habe Adolf Hitler verbrannt.* Munich 1950.

Kempner, Robert. *Das Dritte Reich im Kreuzverhör. Aus den unveröffentlichten Vernehmungsprotokollen des Anklägers.* Munich 1969.

Kern, Erich. *Der grosse Rausch. Russlandfeldzug 1941–1945.* Zurich 1948.

Kersten, Felix. *Totenkopf und Treue. Heinrich Himmler ohne Uniform. Aus den Tagebuchblättern des finnischen Medizinalrats Felix Kersten.* Hamburg [1952].

Kessler, Harry Graf. *Tagebücher 1918–1937.* Edited by Wolfgang Pfeiffer-Belli. Frankfurt/Main 1961.

Kesten, Hermann. "Vorwort." In Weiss (below).

Kielmansegg, Peter Graf. *Deutschland und der Erste Weltkrieg.* Frankfurt/Main 1968.

Kimmich, Christoph M. *The Free City. Danzig and German Foreign Policy, 1919–1934.* New Haven 1968.

Klöss, Erhard, editor. *Reden des Führers. Politik und Propaganda Adolf Hitlers 1922–1945.* Munich 1967.

Knickerbocker, H. R. *Is Tomorrow Hitler's? 200 Questions on the Battle of Mankind.* New York 1941.

Knodel, John. "Infant Mortality and Fertility in Three Bavarian Villages." *Population Studies*, XXII (1968), 297–318.

König, F. "Die giftigen Wirkungen des Jodoform, als Folge der Anwendung desselben an Wunden." *Centralblatt für Chirurgie*, IX (1882), 101–11, 117–27, 273–78.

Koerber, Adolf-Viktor von, editor. *Adolf Hitler. Sein Leben und seine Reden.* Munich [1923].

Kohn, Hans. *The Mind of Germany. The Education of a Nation.* New York 1960.

Kolb, Eberhard. *Die **Arbeiterräte** in der deutschen Innenpolitik 1918–1919.* Düsseldorf 1962. "**Rätewirklichkeit** und Räte-Ideologie in der deutschen Revolution von 1918/19." In *Vom Kaiserreich zur Weimarer Republik*, edited by Eberhard Kolb. Cologne 1972. "**Vorwort.**" In Schmolze (below).

Koppensteiner, Rudolf. *Die Ahnentafel des Führers.* Leipzig 1937.

Kotowski, Georg. "Die deutsche Novemberrevolution." *Aus Politik und Zeitgeschichte*, B 49/60 (1960), 763–70.

Kotze, Hildegard von, and Helmut Krausnick, editors. "*Es spricht der Führer*": *7 exemplarische Hitler-Reden.* Gütersloh 1966.

Krause, Karl Wilhelm. *Zehn Jahre Kammerdiener bei Hitler.* Hamburg 1949.

Krausnick, Helmut. "**Judenverfolgung.**" In Martin Broszat, Hans-Adolf Jacobsen, and Helmut Krausnick, *Konzentrationslager, Kommissarbefehl, Judenverfolgung.* Olten 1965. "Unser **Weg** in die Katastrophe von 1945. Rechenschaft und Besinnung heute." *Aus Politik und Zeitgeschichte*, B 19/62 (1962), 229–40.

Krebs, Albert. *Tendenzen und Gestalten der NSDAP. Erinnerungen an die Frühzeit der Partei.* Stuttgart 1959.

Krüger, Peter. *Deutschland und die Reparationen 1918/19. Die Genesis des Reparationsproblems in Deutschland zwischen Waffenstillstand und Versailler Friedensschluss.* Stuttgart 1973.

Kubizek, August. *Adolf Hitler, mein Jugendfreund.* Graz 1953.

Kuhn, Axel. *Hitlers aussenpolitisches Programm. Entstehung und Entwicklung 1919–1939.* Stuttgart 1970.

Kursell, Otto von, editor. *Adolf Hitlers Reden.* Munich 1925.

Kurth, Gertrud M. **"Comment."** *History of Childhood Quarterly,* I (1973), 236–38. "The **Jew** and Adolf Hitler." *Psychoanalytical Quarterly,* XVI (1947), 11–32.

Lambertson, F. W. "Hitler, the Orator. A Study in Mob Psychology." *Quarterly Journal of Speech,* XXVIII (1942), 123–31.

Lange, Karl. *Hitlers unbeachtete Maximen. 'Mein Kampf' und die Öffentlichkeit.* Stuttgart 1968. "Der **Terminus** 'Lebensraum' in Hitlers 'Mein Kampf.' " *VfZ* XIII (1965), 426–37.

Lange-Eichbaum, Wilhelm, and Wolfram Kurth. *Genie, Irrsinn und Ruhm. Genie-Mythus und Pathographie des Genies.* Munich 1967.

Laqueur, Walter. *Russia and Germany. A Century of Conflict.* London 1965.

Leach, Barry A. *German Strategy against Russia 1939–1941.* Oxford 1973.

Leridon, H. "Nouvelles données biométriques sur le post-partum." *Population,* XXVII (1972), 117–20.

Lewin, Louis. *Gifte und Giftwirkungen.* Berlin 1929.

Luckau, Alma. *The German Delegation at the Paris Peace Conference.* New York 1941.

Ludendorff, Erich. *Vom Feldherrn zum Weltrevolutionär und Wegbereiter deutscher Volksschöpfung. Meine Lebenserinnerungen von 1919 bis 1925.* Munich 1940.

Lüdecke, Kurt G. W. *I Knew Hitler.* London 1938.

Lurker, Otto. *Hitler hinter Festungsmauern. Ein Bild aus trüben Tagen.* Berlin 1933.

McKibbin, R. I. "The Myth of the Unemployed: Who Did Vote for the Nazis?" *Australian Journal of Politics and History,* XV (August 1969), 25–40.

Mann, Golo. "Hitler—for the Last Time?" *Encounter,* XLII (1974), 56–66.

Manvell, Roger, and Heinrich Fraenkel. **Hess.** *A Biography.* London 1971. **Himmler.** New York 1965.

Marshall, Francis H. A. *The Physiology of Reproduction,* Vol. I, Part I. London 1956.

Martin, Bernd. **Friedensinitiativen** und Machtpolitik im Zweiten Weltkrieg 1939–1942. Düsseldorf 1974. *Deutschland und* **Japan** *im Zweiten Weltkrieg. Vom Angriff auf Pearl Harbor bis zur deutschen Kapitulation.* Göttingen 1969.

Maser, Werner. *Hitlers* **Briefe** *und Notizen. Sein Weltbild in handschriftlichen Dokumenten.* Düsseldorf 1973. *Adolf* **Hitler.** *Legende, Mythos, Wirklichkeit.* Munich 1971. *Hitlers Mein* **Kampf.** *Entstehung, Aufbau, Stil, Änderungen, Quellen, Quellenwert, kommentierte Auszüge.* Munich 1966. *Die Frühgeschichte der* **NSDAP.** *Hitlers Weg bis 1924.* Bonn 1965.

Matthias, Erich. "Die Sozialdemokratische Partei Deutschlands." In *Das Ende der Parteien 1933,* edited by Erich Matthias and Rudolf Morsey. Düsseldorf 1960.

Matthias, Erich, and Rudolf Morsey. "Die Bildung der Regierung des Prinzen Max von Baden." In *Vom Kaiserreich zur Weimarer Republik,* edited by Eberhard Kolb. Cologne 1972.

Max von Baden. *Erinnerungen und Dokumente.* Stuttgart 1927.

Mehring, Walter. *Die verlorene Bibliothek*. Revised edition. Munich 1964.

Mend, Hans. *Adolf Hitler im Felde 1914–1918*. Munich 1931.

Merkl, Peter H. *Political Violence under the Swastika. 581 Early Nazis*. Princeton 1975.

Meyer, Hans H., and R. Gottlieb. *Die experimentelle Pharmakologie als Grundlage der Arzneibehandlung*. Second edition. Berlin 1911.

Milward, Alan. *The German Economy at War*. London 1965.

Mitchell, Allan. *Revolution in Bavaria 1918–1919. The Eisner Regime and the Soviet Republic*. Princeton 1965.

Møller, Knud O. *Pharmakologie als theoretische Grundlage einer rationellen Pharmakotherapie*. Stuttgart 1966.

Moeschlin, Sven. *Poisoning*. New York 1965.

Mohler, Armin. *Die konservative Revolution in Deutschland 1918–1932. Ein Handbuch*. Darmstadt 1972.

Moll, Albert. *Ärztliche* **Ethik**. Stuttgart 1902.

Moll, Leopold. **Säuglingssterblichkeit** in *Österreich. Ursachen und Bekämpfung*. Vienna 1914.

Moltmann, Günter. "Weltherrschaftsideen Hitlers." In *Europa und Übersee. Festschrift für Egmont Zechlin*, edited by Otto Brunner. Hamburg 1961.

Mommsen, Hans. "The Reichstag Fire and Its Political Consequences." In *Republic to Reich. The Making of the Nazi Revolution*, edited by Hajo Holborn, translated by Ralph Manheim. New York 1972.

Monaco, Paul. *Cinema and Society. France and Germany during the Twenties*. New York 1976.

Moser von Filseck, Carl. *Politik in Bayern 1919–1933. Berichte des württembergischen Gesandten Moser von Filseck*, edited by Wolfgang Benz. Stuttgart 1971.

Müller, Karl Alexander von. **Mars** *und Venus. Erinnerungen 1914–1919*. Stuttgart 1954. *Im* **Wandel** *einer Welt. Erinnerungen Band drei 1919–1932*, edited by Otto Alexander von Müller. Munich 1966.

Müllern-Schönhausen, Johannes von. *Die Lösung des Rätsel's* [sic] *Adolf Hitler. Der Versuch einer Deutung der geheimnisvollsten Erscheinung der Weltgeschichte*. Vienna n.d.

Muslin, Hyman L., and William J. Pieper. "Separation Experience and Cancer of the Breast." *Psychosomatics*, III (1962), 230–36.

Muslin, Hyman L., Kalman Gyarfas, and William J. Pieper. "Separation Experience and Cancer of the Breast." *Annals of the New York Academy of Sciences*, CXXV (1965–1966), 802–06.

Nicholls, A. J. *Weimar and the Rise of Hitler*. London 1968.

Niekisch, Ernst. *Gewagtes* **Leben.** *Erinnerungen und Begebnisse*. Cologne 1958. *Hitler—ein deutsches* **Verhängnis.** Berlin 1932.

Nolte, Ernst. *Three Faces of Fascism. Action Française, Italian Fascism, National Socialism*. Translated by Leila Vennewitz. New York 1966.

Oettingen, W. F. von. *The Halogenated Aliphatic, Olefinic, Cyclic, Aromatic, and Aliphatic-Aromatic Hydrocarbons*. Washington, D.C., 1955.

Olden, Rudolf. *Hitler*. Amsterdam 1936.

O'Lessker, Karl. "Who Voted for Hitler? A New Look at the Class Basis of Nazism." *American Journal of Sociology*, LXXIV (1968), 63–69.

O'Neill, Robert J. *The German Army and the Nazi Party 1933/39*. New York 1966.

Oplt, Miroslav. "Gespräch mit Hitlers Halbbruder." *Wiener Wochenausgabe*, IV, No. 37 (11 September 1948), 4.

Orlow, Dietrich. *The History of the Nazi Party.* 2 vols. Pittsburgh 1969, 1973.

Osol, Arthur, Robertson Pratt, and Mark D. Altschule. *The United States Dispensatory and Physicians' Pharmacology.* Twenty-sixth edition. Philadelphia 1967.

Papen, Franz von. *Der Wahrheit eine Gasse.* Munich 1952.

Pechel, Rudolf. *Deutscher Widerstand.* Erlenbach 1947.

Perez, A., P. Vela, R. Potter, and G. S. Masnick. "Timing and Sequence of Resuming Ovulation and Menstruation after Childbirth." *Population Studies,* XXV (1971), 491–503.

Phelps, Reginald H. "Hitler als **Parteiredner** im Jahre 1920." *VfZ,* XI (1963), 274–330. "Hitlers 'grundlegende' **Rede** über den Antisemitismus." *VfZ,* XVI (1968), 390–420. " 'Before Hitler Came': **Thule** Society and Germanen Orden." *Journal of Modern History,* XXXV (1963), 245–61.

Philippi, Alfred, and Ferdinand Heim. *Der Feldzug gegen Sowjetrussland 1941 bis 1945. Ein operativer Überblick.* Stuttgart 1962.

Picker, Henry, editor. *Hitlers Tischgespräche im Führerhauptquartier 1941/ 42.* Stuttgart 1965.

Pöll, Wilhelm. *Die Suggestion. Wesen und Grundformen.* Munich 1951.

Pogge-von Strandmann, Hartmut. "Staatsstreichpläne, Alldeutsche und Bethmann Hollweg." In Hartmut Pogge-von Strandmann and Imanuel Geiss. *Die Erforderlichkeit des Unmöglichen. Deutschland am Vorabend des ersten Weltkrieges.* Frankfurt/Main 1965.

Potter, Robert G., Mary L. New, John B. Wyon, and John E. Gordon. "Lactation and Its Effects upon Birth Intervals in Eleven Punjab Villages, India." *Journal of Chronic Diseases,* XVIII (1965), 1125–40.

Preiss, Heinz, editor. *Adolf Hitler in Franken. Reden aus der Kampfzeit.* Nuremberg 1939.

Pribilla, Max. *Deutsche Schicksalsfragen. Rückblick und Ausblick.* Frankfurt/ Main 1950.

Rauscher, Heinrich. "Volkskunde des Waldviertels." In *Volkskunde,* Vol. III of *Das Waldviertel,* edited by Eduard Stepan. Vienna 1926.

Rauschning, Hermann. *Gespräche mit Hitler.* Zurich 1940.

Reck-Malleczewen, Friedrich Percyval. *Bockelson. Geschichte eines Massenwahns.* Reprinted: Stuttgart 1968.

Rees, J. R., editor. *The Case of Rudolf Hess. A Problem in Diagnostic and Forensic Psychiatry.* London 1947.

Reimann, Viktor. *Dr. Joseph Goebbels.* Vienna 1971.

Reitlinger, Gerald. *Die Endlösung. Hitlers Versuch der Ausrottung der Juden Europas 1939–1945.* Berlin 1956.

Revers, W. J. *Persönlichkeit und Vermassung. Eine psychologische und kulturanthropologische Studie.* Würzburg 1947.

Ribbentrop, Joachim von. *Zwischen London und Moskau. Erinnerungen und letzte Aufzeichnungen.* Leoni 1953.

Rich, Norman. *Hitler's War Aims.* 2 vols. New York 1973, 1974.

Ringer, Fritz K. *The Decline of the German Mandarins. The German Academic Community, 1890–1933.* Cambridge, Massachusetts, 1969.

Ritter, Gerhard A. "Kontinuität und Umformung des deutschen Parteisystems 1918–1920." In *Vom Kaiserreich zur Weimarer Republik,* edited by Eberhard Kolb. Cologne 1972.

Röhm, Ernst. *Die Geschichte eines Hochverräters.* Munich 1928.

Röhrs, Hans-Dietrich. *Hitlers Krankheit. Tatsachen und Legenden. Medizinische und psychische Grundlagen seines Zusammenbruchs.* Neckargemünd 1966.

Rosenberg, Alfred. Letzte **Aufzeichnungen.** Ideale und Idole der nationalsozialistischen Revolution. Göttingen 1955. Das politische **Tagebuch** Alfred Rosenbergs 1934/35 und 1939/40, edited by Hans-Günter Seraphim. Munich 1964.

Rudin, Harry R. Armistice 1918. New Haven 1944.

Ryder, A. J. The German Revolution of 1918. A Study of German Socialism in War and Revolt. Cambridge 1967.

Sauer, Wolfgang. "Die Mobilmachung der **Gewalt.**" In Karl Dietrich Bracher, Wolfgang Sauer, and Gerhard Schulz, Die nationalsozialistische Machtergreifung. Studien zur Errichtung des totalitären Herrschaftssystems 1933/34. Cologne 1962. "Das **Scheitern** der parlamentarischen Monarchie." In Vom Kaiserreich zur Weimarer Republik, edited by Eberhard Kolb. Cologne 1972.

Schacht, Hjalmar. Abrechnung mit Hitler. Hamburg 1948.

Schaltenbrand, Georges. "War Hitler geisteskrank?" In Ein Leben aus freier Mitte. Beiträge zur Geschichtsforschung. Festschrift für Prof. Dr. Ulrich Noack. Göttingen 1961.

Schauwecker, Franz. Deutsche allein. Schnitt durch die Zeit. Berlin 1931.

Schellenberg, Walter. Memoiren. Cologne 1956.

Schieder, Theodor. Das Deutsche Kaiserreich von 1871 als Nationalstaat. Cologne 1961.

Schildt, Gerhard. Die Arbeitsgemeinschaft Nord-West. Untersuchungen zur Geschichte der NSDAP 1925/26. Dissertation: Freiburg im Breisgau 1964.

Schirach, Baldur von. Text of **Hitler** wie ihn keiner kennt. 100 Bild-Dokumente aus dem Leben des Führers, edited by Heinrich Hoffmann. Berlin [1939]. **Ich** glaubte an Hitler. Hamburg 1967.

Schlabrendorff, Fabian von. The Secret War against Hitler. Translated by John J. McCloy. New York 1965.

Schleunes, Karl A. The Twisted Road to Auschwitz. Nazi Policy toward German Jews 1933–1939. Urbana 1970.

Schmidt, Paul. Statist auf diplomatischer Bühne 1923–1945. Erlebnisse des Chefdolmetschers im Auswärtigen Amt mit den Staatsmännern Europas. Bonn 1954.

Schmolze, Gerhard, editor. Revolution und Räterepublik in München 1918/19 in Augenzeugenberichten. Düsseldorf 1969.

Schnaiberg, Allan. "A Critique of Karl O'Lessker's 'Who Voted for Hitler?'" American Journal of Sociology, LXXIV (1969), 732–35.

Schnauber, Cornelius. Wie Hitler sprach und schrieb. Zur Psychologie und Prosodik der faschistischen Rhetorik. Frankfurt/Main 1972.

Schoenbaum, David. Hitler's Social Revolution. Class and Status in Nazi Germany 1933–1939. Garden City 1967.

Schott, Georg. Das Volksbuch vom Hitler. Munich 1934 (originally 1924).

Schramm, Percy Ernst. "Adolf Hitler. **Anatomie** eines Diktators." Der Spiegel, XVIII, Nos. 5–10 (29 January–4 March 1964). Hitler als militärischer **Führer.** Frankfurt/Main 1965.

Schubert, Günter. Die Anfänge der nationalsozialistischen Aussenpolitik, 1919–1923. Berlin 1961.

Schüddekopf, Otto-Ernst. Nationalbolschwismus in Deutschland 1918–1933. Frankfurt/Main 1972.

Schulz, Gerhard. Aufstieg des Nationalsozialismus. Krise und Revolution in Deutschland. Frankfurt/Main 1975.

Schulze, Hagen. Freikorps und Republik 1918–1920. Boppard am Rhein 1969.

Schwabe, Klaus. Deutsche Revolution und Wilson-Frieden. Die amerikanische und deutsche Friedensstrategie zwischen Ideologie und Machtpolitik 1918/19. Düsseldorf 1971.

Schwarzschild, Leopold. "Die Woche." *Das neue Tage-Buch*, I (1933), 271–75.

Schwerin von Krosigk, Lutz Graf. *Es geschah in Deutschland. Menschenbilder unseres Jahrhunderts.* Tübingen 1951.

Seaton, Albert. *The Russo-German War 1941–1945.* London 1971.

Shirer, William L. *Berlin Diary. The Journal of a Foreign Correspondent 1934–1941.* New York 1941.

Shively, W. Phillips. "Party Identification, Party Choice, and Voting Stability: The Weimar Case." *American Political Science Review*, LXVI (1972), 1203–25.

Smith, Bradley F. *Heinrich Himmler. A Nazi in the Making, 1900–1926.* Stanford 1971. *Adolf Hitler. His Family, Childhood and Youth.* Stanford 1967.

Sommer, Hartmut. "Gesucht: der Arzt von Pasewalk." *Abend Zeitung* (Munich), 30 April / 1 May 1966.

Sommer, Theo. *Deutschland und Japan zwischen den Mächten 1935–1940. Vom Antikominternpakt zum Dreimächtepakt. Eine Studie zur diplomatischen Vorgeschichte des Zweiten Weltkriegs.* Tübingen 1962.

Sontheimer, Kurt. *Antidemokratisches Denken in der Weimarer Republik. Die politischen Ideen des deutschen Nationalismus zwischen 1918 und 1933.* Munich 1962.

Stein, George H., editor. *Hitler.* Englewood Cliffs, 1968.

Steinert, Marlis. *Hitlers Krieg und die Deutschen. Stimmung und Haltung der deutschen Bevölkerung im Zweiten Weltkrieg.* Düsseldorf 1970.

Thies, Jochen. *Architekt der Weltherrschaft. Die "Endziele" Hitlers.* Düsseldorf 1976.

Thimme, Anneliese. *Flucht in den Mythos. Die Deutschnationale Volkspartei und die Niederlage von 1918.* Göttingen 1969.

Todd, R. G., editor. *Extra Pharmacopoeia Martindale.* Twenty-fifth edition. London 1967.

Toynbee, Arnold J. **Acquaintances.** London 1967. **Experiences.** New York 1969.

Treue, Wilhelm. "Hitlers Denkschrift zum Vierjahresplan 1936." *VfZ*, III (1955), 184–210.

Trevor-Roper, Hugh. *The Last Days of Hitler.* New York 1962.

Troeltsch, Ernst. *Spektator-Briefe. Aufsätze über die deutsche Revolution und die Weltpolitik 1918/22.* Edited by Hans Baron. Tübingen 1924.

Tyrell, Albrecht, editor. **Führer** befiehl ... *Selbstzeugnisse aus der 'Kampfzeit' der NSDAP.* Düsseldorf 1969. "**Führergedanke** und Gauleiterwechsel. Die Teilung des Gaues Rheinland der NSDAP 1931." *VfZ*, XXIII (1975), 341–74. *Vom 'Trommler' zum 'Führer'. Der Wandel von Hitlers Selbstverständnis zwischen 1919 und 1924 und die Entwicklung der NSDAP.* Munich 1975.

Ulam, Adam B. *Stalin. The Man and His Era.* New York 1973.

Viereck, George Sylvester. "Hitler the German Explosive." *American Monthly*, XV (1923), 235–38.

Vogelsang, Thilo. "Hitlers **Brief** an Reichenau vom 4. Dezember 1932." *VfZ*, VII (1959), 429–37. "Neue **Dokumente** zur Geschichte der Reichswehr 1930–1933." *VfZ*, II (1954), 397–436.

Volkmann, Hans-Erich. *Die deutsche Baltikumpolitik zwischen Brest-Litowsk und Compiègne. Ein Beitrag zur 'Kriegszieldiskussion'.* Cologne 1970.

Vondung, Klaus. *Magie und Manipulation. Ideologischer Kult und politische Religion des Nationalsozialismus.* Göttingen 1971.

Wagner, Friedelind. *The Royal Family of Bayreuth.* London 1948.

198

Waite, Robert G. L. *Vanguard of Nazism. The Free Corps Movement in Postwar Germany 1918–1923.* New York 1952.

Walter, Hans-Albert. *Deutsche Exilliteratur,* Vol. II. Darmstadt 1972.

Warlimont, Walter. *Im Hauptquartier der deutschen Wehrmacht 1939–1945. Grundlagen, Formen, Gestalten.* Frankfurt/Main 1964.

Weber, Alfred. *Abschied von der bisherigen Geschichte. Überwindung des Nihilismus?* Hamburg 1946.

Weinberg, Gerhard L. *The Foreign Policy of Hitler's Germany. Diplomatic Revolution in Europe 1933–36.* Chicago 1970.

Weiss, Ernst. *Der Augenzeuge.* Munich 1963.

Wheaton, Eliot Barculo. *The Nazi Revolution 1933–1935: Prelude to Calamity.* Garden City 1969.

Wiedemann, Fritz. *Der Mann, der Feldherr werden wollte. Erlebnisse und Erfahrungen des Vorgesetzten Hitlers im 1. Weltkrieg und seines späteren Persönlichen Adjutanten.* Velbert 1964.

Wiegand, Karl H. von. "Hitler Foresees His End." *Cosmopolitan,* April 1939, 28–29, 152–55.

Woerden, A. V. N. van. "Een slordige improvisatie over een slecht boek. Werner Maser, Hitlers Mein Kampf." *Tijdschrift voor Geschiedenis,* LXXX (1967), 113–16.

Wörtz, Ulrich. *Programmatik und Führerprinzip. Das Problem des Strasser-Kreises in der NSDAP. Eine historisch-politische Studie zum Verhältnis von sachlichem Programm und persönlicher Führung in einer totalitären Bewegung.* Dissertation: Erlangen-Nürnberg 1966.

Wollheim, Mona. *Begegnung mit Ernst Weiss. Paris 1936–1940.* Munich 1970.

Wollstein, Günter. *Vom Weimarer Revisionismus zu Hitler. Das deutsche Reich und die Grossmächte in der Anfangsphase der nationalsozialistischen Herrschaft in Deutschland.* Bonn 1973.

Wright, Gordon. *The Ordeal of Total War 1939–1945.* New York 1968.

Zechlin, Egmont. "Bethmann Hollweg, Kriegsrisiko und SPD **1914**." In *Erster Weltkrieg. Ursachen, Entstehung und Kriegsziele,* edited by Wolfgang Schieder. Cologne 1969. "Ludendorff im Jahre **1915**. Unveröffentlichte Briefe." *Historische Zeitschrift,* CCXI (1970), 316–53.

Zimmermann, Aloys. *Über* **Psychosen** *in Folge von Jodoformgebrauch.* Bonn 1893.

Zimmermann, Werner Gabriel. **Bayern** *und das Reich 1918–1923. Der bayerische Föderalismus zwischen Revolution und Reaktion.* Munich 1953.

Zipfel, Friedrich. "Krieg und Zusammenbruch." In *Das Dritte Reich,* edited by Eberhard Aleff. Hannover 1963.

INDEX

[*Implicit references are bracketed.*]

Knodel, John, 143–45, 182
Koch, Erich, 98
Koerber, Adolf-Viktor von, 137–38
Krause, Karl Wilhelm, [18]
Krebs, Albert, 22
Krohn, Friedrich, [1], 148, 178
Kubizek, August, 2, 14–17, 20, 22, 54, 55, 123, 139, 143, 144, 181

La Montagne, 5
Landsberg, 40, 68, 87, 112, 175
Ledebour, Georg, 46
Leipzig, 4, 25, 113, 175
Lenin, Nikolai, 45, 84; Leninism, 82
Leningrad, 46
Levien, Max, 40
Lille, 108, 174
Linz, 2, 14–19, 22, 34, 123, 139–41, 151
Lisbon, 15
List Regiment, see under Hitler, Adolf
Lithuania, 62
Locarno treaty, 84
Lossow, Otto von, [111]
Low Countries, 44. See also Belgium; Flanders
Ludendorff, Erich: in World War I, xi, 37, 43, 45–46, 61–62, 78, 80, 82, 106–07, 109, 128; in Weimar politics, 80, 169; contacts with Hitler, 62, 111, 114; influence on Hitler, 62; superseded by Hitler, 78, 114–18
Lüdecke, Kurt, 121, 124–25
Lugauer, Heinrich, [2]
Luxemburg, Rosa, 29

Mann, Golo, 44
Marne river, 108
Marxism, Hitler on, see under Hitler, Adolf: anti-Semitism
Matzelsberger, Franziska, see Hitler, Franziska
Mayr, Karl, [3]
Mehring, Walter, 8, 11
Mein Kampf, see under Hitler, Adolf
Mellenthin, Horst von, 171
Memmingen, 156
Mend, Hans, [3]
Messines, 174
Moeller van den Bruck, Arthur, 181

Molotov, Vyacheslav, 69
Morell, Theo, 22–23
Moscow, 34, 46, 62, 87, 132, 175
Müller, Karl Alexander von, [1]
Munich, ix, 1, 3, 4, 8, 20, 22, 60, 66, 111–12, 123, 124, 125, 132, 137, 138, 177
Mussolini, Benito, 93
Mustard gas, 5–6, 130–31, 153. See also under Hitler, Adolf

Napoleon, 47
Nazi Archive, 2, 18, 139, 142
Nazi (National Socialist German Workers) Party, ix, 1, 47, 59, 66, 67–68, 89–90, 111, 119, 125, 148
New York, 15
Nissen, Rudolf, [9]
Nonnenhorn, 8
Normandy, 102, 105
Nuremberg, 4, 32, 33, 121, 122, 125, 126, 127, 133

Odeonsplatz (Munich), 40, 111–12
Oedipus, 132
Office of Strategic Services, 15, 137
Olden, Rudolf, 138
Oudenaarde, 5

Papen, Franz von, 122
Paris, 8–12, 114
Pasewalk, 3, 5–8, 10, 21–23, 28, 33, 44, 57, 77, 85, 123, 127, 129–30, 136–38, 149, 150, 153. See also under Hitler, Adolf
Pentheus, 119–20, 134
Pfeffer, Franz von, [126]
Pirow, Oswald, [30, 115]
Playne, Caroline E., xiii
Pölzl, Johann, [55], 146, [162]
Pölzl, Johanna, 14
Pölzl, Johanna (born Hüttler), 53, [55], 145–46
Pölzl, Klara, see Hitler, Klara
Poland, 33, 42, 44, 52, 94, 99, 101, 106, 116, 117
Politische Wochenschrift, 181
"Politischer Wochenbrief," 136
Pomerania, 5, 137. See also Pasewalk

Quisling, Vidkun, 122, 124

205

Weimar, 125
Weimar Republic, *see under* Germany
Weiss, Ernst, 8, 11–13, 150; *Der*
 Augenzeuge, 11–13, [130], 150
Westenkirchner, Ignaz, 2, 4, 13, 148
Wiedemann, Fritz, 2, 4, 108–09
Wiegand, Karl von, 136
Wilhelm II, 3, [38, 128], 156;
 Wilhelmian, *see* Germany: Second
 Empire

Wilson, Woodrow, 37–39, 51, 104–05;
 Wilson legend, *see under* Germany;
 Wilsonism, 82
Wirth, Christian, [32]
World Jewish Congress, 99

Zádor, Julius, 8
Zeitzler, Kurt, 109
Zutt, Jürg, [7]

20 April 1889 Hitler born   3 January 1903 father dies   14–16 January 1907 mother's cancer diagnosed   4 November 1907 mother's iodoform treatment begins   21 December 1907 mother dies   mid-February 1908 Hitler moves to Vienna   24–26 June 1913 Hitler moves to Munich   1–3 August 1914 European war begins   16 August 1914 Hitler inducted into Bavarian army   5 October 1916 Hitler wounded by shrapnel, hospitalized   4 August 1918 Hitler receives Iron Cross First Class   29 September 1918 Ludendorff calls for a coalition government to negotiate an armistice   15 October 1918 Hitler gassed, hospitalized   8–11 November 1918 revolution sweeps Germany while armistice concluded; Hitler's relapse and hallucination in Pasewalk infirmary   1 May 1919 Allies notify Germany of peace terms   5–12 June 1919 Hitler trained as Reichswehr political lecturer   28 June 1919 peace treaty signed in Versailles   31 July 1919 Weimar constitution adopted   12 September 1919 Hitler attends German Workers Party meeting   16 September 1919 Hitler's first political document (letter on removing the Jews "altogether")   late-February 1920 German Workers Party renamed National Socialist German Workers Party   31 May 1921 Hitler's "land and soil" speech   July 1921 Hitler takes over Party   late-December 1922 Hitler confidentially states eastern aim   8–9 November 1923 unsuccessful Hitler-Ludendorff Putsch in Munich   11 November 1923 Hitler arrested   26 February 1924 Hitler trial begins   1 April 1924 Hitler sentenced   7 July 1924 Hitler resigns as Party leader   20 December 1924 Hitler released   26 February 1925 Hitler refounds Party: bans on his public speaking follow in most German states   1925–1926 Mein Kampf published   1927–1928 bans on Hitler's public speaking lifted   12 May and 8 December 1929 Nazi gains in state elections   14 September 1930 Nazis score 18.2 percent in Reichstag elections   March–April 1932 Hitler runs for President of Germany; Hindenburg reelected on second ballot   31 July 1932 Nazis score 37.3 percent in Reichstag elections   6 November 1932 Nazi vote falls to 33.1 percent in new Reichstag elections   15 January 1933